PR3588.   67-9679
T56   Thorpe
Mi   Milton criticism
1966   M

Date Due

JUL   2000

DEC 27 '68		JUN	2004
MAR 7 '69			
AUG 8 '89			
		JUN 09	
		JUL X X 2015	

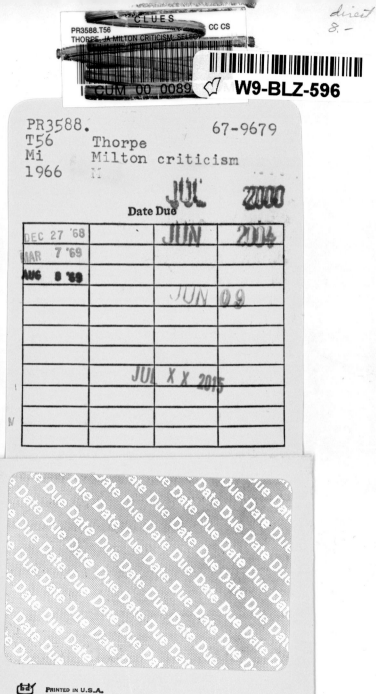

MILTON CRITICISM

MILTON CRITICISM

Selections from Four Centuries

EDITED BY

JAMES THORPE

1966

OCTAGON BOOKS, INC.

New York

Copyright 1950 by James Thorpe

Reprinted 1966
by special arrangement with Holt, Rinehart and Winston, Inc.

OCTAGON BOOKS, INC.
175 FIFTH AVENUE
NEW YORK, N. Y. 10010

LIBRARY OF CONGRESS CATALOG CARD NUMBER: 66-19730

Printed in U.S.A. by
NOBLE OFFSET PRINTERS, INC.
NEW YORK 3, N. Y.

PREFACE

This book is an invitation to the reading of Milton. It was compiled primarily to provide a convenient collection of criticisms that can, by their intrinsic merits, lead to a more complete understanding of the achievement of Milton and send the reader back to the text of Milton. The major portion of the volume consists of sixteen extended essays and studies from the eighteenth, nineteenth, and twentieth centuries. In most cases the material is printed in its complete form; in a few instances it was necessary to make certain omissions in order to prevent undue repetition of biographical data and to maintain the limits imposed by a single volume. A brief concluding section comprises excerpts and brief statements, ranging from 1674 to 1888, from the works of sixteen critics whose remarks (though not admitting of extended presentation) are of importance and have been of notable influence. In order to assuage the pain of the individual reader who discovers that some personal favorite is not here included, I had originally intended to justify the ways of the editor to the reader. The mass of Milton criticism is so great, however, that I can do no more than plead that this book, growing out of a re-examination of all that criticism, is an attempt at a balanced selection of what seems to me to have permanent significance.

The book has a secondary aim, which is indicated in Emerson's dictum that "the fame of a great man is not rigid and stony like his bust. . . . [It] characterizes those who give it, as much as him who receives it." These selections, by displaying the diversity of opinions on Milton held by outstanding critics and poets and scholars of four centuries, elucidate important aspects of the history of literary criticism. They suggest that one guaranteed method of comprehending the nature of general critical theory in its constant change is to analyze the practical criticism of several periods at work on the same body of material.

The introduction to this volume presents a very brief outline of the history of Milton criticism. Its purpose is not to offer a direct commentary on the essays and studies which make up the body of the book, but rather to aid in understanding their aims and significance by suggesting the general trends and developments in Milton criticism.

JAMES THORPE

Princeton, New Jersey,
January, 1950

CONTENTS

Preface   v

Introduction: A Brief History of Milton Criticism   3

PART ONE: ESSAYS AND STUDIES

Joseph Addison, SIX *Spectator* PAPERS ON *Paradise Lost* (1712)   23

Jonathan Richardson, EXPLANATORY NOTES AND REMARKS ON MILTON'S *Paradise Lost* (1734)   54

Samuel Johnson, MILTON (1779)   65

Samuel Taylor Coleridge, MILTON (1818)   89

William Hazlitt, ON SHAKESPEARE AND MILTON (1818)   98

Sir Walter Alexander Raleigh, THE STYLE OF MILTON (1900)   114

James Holly Hanford, MILTON AND THE RETURN TO HUMANISM (1919)   143

Denis Saurat, FAITH, PHILOSOPHY, AND POETRY IN MILTON'S WORK (1925)   169

E. M. W. Tillyard, Paradise Lost: CONSCIOUS AND UNCONSCIOUS MEANINGS (1930)   178

Elmer Edgar Stoll, FROM THE SUPERHUMAN TO THE HUMAN IN *Paradise Lost* (1933)   211

John Crowe Ransom, A POEM NEARLY ANONYMOUS [*Lycidas*] (1933)   225

Sir Herbert J. C. Grierson, Paradise Regained AND *Samson Agonistes* (1937)   239

Charles Williams, AN INTRODUCTION TO MILTON'S POEMS (1940)   252

C. S. Lewis, THE STYLE OF SECONDARY EPIC AND DEFENCE OF THIS STYLE (1942)   267

Douglas Bush, MILTON (1945)   289
T. S. Eliot, MILTON (1947)   310

PART TWO: EXCERPTS AND
BRIEF COMMENT

Andrew Marvell, ON *Paradise Lost* (1674)   335
John Dryden, EPIGRAM ON MILTON (1688) and ESSAY ON
   SATIRE (1693)   337
John Toland, THE LIFE OF JOHN MILTON (1698)   339
John Dennis, THE PASSION OF BYBLIS (1692), THE GROUNDS
   OF CRITICISM IN POETRY (1704), LETTERS ON MILTON &
   WYCHERLEY (1721-1722)   344
Alexander Pope, POSTSCRIPT TO THE ODYSSEY (1723)   349
Thomas Warton, PREFACE TO MILTON'S POEMS UPON SEV-
   ERAL OCCASIONS (1785)   350
—*William Blake,* THE MARRIAGE OF HEAVEN AND HELL (1793)   352
William Wordsworth, LONDON (1802)   354
John Keats, LETTERS (1818-1819)   355
—*Percy Bysshe Shelley,* A DEFENCE OF POETRY (1821)   358
Thomas Babington Macaulay, ESSAY ON MILTON (1825)   360
Ralph Waldo Emerson, MILTON (1838)   364
Walter Savage Landor, SOUTHEY AND LANDOR (1846)   368
Alfred Lord Tennyson, MILTON (ALCAICS) (1863)   370
Gerard Manley Hopkins, LETTERS (1877-1879)   371
Matthew Arnold, MILTON (1888)   373

MILTON CRITICISM

INTRODUCTION

A BRIEF HISTORY OF MILTON CRITICISM

I

(To 1674)

Iᴛ ɪꜱ a shock to most of us when we first realize that Milton cut a relatively small figure during his own lifetime. He who liked to think of himself as a regular subject for the trumpetings of Fame actually was signalized by only a few shrill notes that most of his contemporaries considered out of tune. The divorce pamphlets (1643-1645) did little more than attach a certain odium to his name. *The Tenure of Kings and Magistrates* (1649), *Eikonoklastes* (1649), and (most of all) *Defensio Prima* (1651) attracted a good deal of attention at the times of their publication, but even these contributions did not make Milton particularly prominent among that rugged race, the seventeenth-century pamphleteers. The remainder of his prose received minimal recognition; even such essays as *Areopagitica* and *Of Education,* which aftertimes would not willingly let die, went virtually unnoticed.

Our interest in Milton as a controversialist, however, is secondary to our interest in him as a poet. Here again he lacked the prominence that later readers have felt he ought to have had. His minor poems were generally unknown during his lifetime. As a representative example of various possible tests, there is apparently no contemporary printed reference to "L'Allegro" or to "Lycidas." The publication of *Paradise Lost* (in 1667) and of *Paradise Regained* and *Samson Agonistes* (in 1671) created no sensation. In short, Milton lived and died as a relatively obscure poet.

II

(1674-1700)

It was not until about the time of Milton's death, in 1674, that he began to enjoy a general reputation as a poet. During the last quarter of the seventeenth century, however, his poetry rapidly achieved considerable fame. Attention was centered on *Paradise Lost,* but there is enough scattered evidence to prove that his other poems were not unknown and not disliked.

The fact that a Miltonic tradition was established in the last quarter of the seventeenth century has sometimes been obscured by the notion that Addison's *Spectator* papers on *Paradise Lost* in 1712 "introduced" Milton. The fact is that for more than twenty-five years before that time Milton had been receiving very high praise in critical asides of leading writers of the time; Dryden, Roscommon, Buckingham, Burnet, Dennis, and Gildon are representative of levels of opinion which, though varied, generally ranked Milton as at least the equal of any other English poet. It is true that this criticism usually lacked definition and viewed Milton somewhat narrowly as the chief representative of the English heroic tradition. But it is also true that this criticism unequivocally identified Milton as a supremely great poet. In 1678 Thomas Rymer was representative of only a minority of the critics in his manner of referring to the *"Paradise Lost* of Milton's which some are pleased to call a poem."

III

(1700-1800)

Addison's study was the most prominent of several that served to crystallize and elaborate a prevalent opinion of the early eighteenth century by providing the basis of a detailed examination. The tremendous influence of Addison's critique (which consisted of six general essays on *Paradise Lost* and one essay on each of the twelve books) is inadequately illustrated even by the fact that it appeared in English at least thirty times within the century.

Milton's reputation was progressively extended during the eighteenth century, but a Miltonic tradition had been established by about 1730 that persisted in a general way throughout the remainder of the century. This tradition consisted of a compound of three complex, interdependent, and yet distinguishable conceptions: that of the man, that of the philosopher, and that of the artist.

Most of the early opinions on Milton the man seem to have been motivated by political considerations. In the seventeenth century, for instance, he was frequently reviled by the Royalists, who did not readily forget his part in the rebellion. William Winstanley observed in 1687 that *"John Milton* was one, whose natural parts might deservedly give him a place amongst the principal of our English Poets, having written two Heroic Poems and a Tragedy. . . . But his Fame is gone out like a Candle in a Snuff, and his Memory will always stink, which might have ever lived in honourable Repute, had not he been a notorious Traytor, and most impiously and villanously bely'd that blessed Martyr *King Charles* the First." Though political objections came to be expressed with less and less fervor, eighteenth-century Tories often tempered their admiration on that account. Dr. Johnson, a staunch Tory and Anglican, illustrates this tendency; he peevishly presented Milton's character as obliquely informed by spiteful republicanism and displeasing personal qualities. On the other hand, the Whigs were disposed to eulogize Milton as a great liberator of mankind.

The greatest emphasis of the eighteenth-century critics of Milton was on his philosophy, or (more accurately) on his religious teaching. Criticism centered on *Paradise Lost,* which was venerated as a principal support of the orthodox creed. The epithets "sacred" and "divine" were scattered with a lavish hand. The heterodox elements were not noticed, and the poem appealed equally to Anglicans, Dissenters, Roman Catholics, and Deists. In 1792 it was maintained that *Paradise Lost* had "contributed more to support the orthodox creed than all the books of divinity that were ever written."

Allied to the conceptions both of the philosopher and of the artist was the characteristic of Milton most universally admired, his "sublimity"—the capacity of his poetry to enlarge the imagination of the reader. "Sublime" was the stock epithet; and when one of his poems (usually *Paradise Lost,* of course) was examined in any detail, it was generally for the purpose of noticing this quality in an extended passage. No doubt the unusual esteem for Longinus provided a basis for this concept and for the terminology. The critics made little effort at isolating the artistry from the message which they admired; they were content with a fusion of thought and expression in which (they felt) the expression felicitously and unobtrusively elevated the subject matter. In this important respect, the eighteenth-century critics had, despite their somewhat indistinct discernment of the methods utilized in achieving the total effects, perhaps a more valid approach to *Paradise Lost*—following the classical and English tradition of the intent of epic poetry —than many later critics have had.

Whenever Milton's artistry was considered separately, it was eyed suspiciously. Milton was acknowledged as a great though irregular genius—a writer whose diction often lacked common sense and whose verses were excessively rough, but nevertheless a poet who achieved remarkable results without holding strictly to the rules which he should have obeyed. For example, John Dennis—who was a great admirer of Milton—characterized *Paradise Lost* as "the most lofty, but most irregular Poem, that has been produc'd by the Mind of Man." It was not until the times of Gray, and the Wartons, and Cowper that attention turned to subtle matters of style; and even at the end of the century Milton's artistic purpose in studied variations from the basic pattern of his verse had hardly been examined.

The eighteenth-century chorus in praise of Milton was, for the most part, a harmonious one. However, three instances of discord should be identified. Richard Bentley edited *Paradise Lost* in 1732 and slashed or emended any passages that offended his sensitive classical taste; in 1747 and 1749 William Lauder charged Milton with plagiarism and produced a Latin "source" (into which he had interpolated passages from a Latin translation of *Paradise Lost*) to prove his imputation; and Dr. Johnson stirred a good deal of adverse criticism into his praise of Milton in a series of *Rambler* papers in 1751 and in his *Life of Milton* in 1779. Bentley and Lauder were buried under a heap of execrations, but Dr. Johnson's unfavorable remarks weathered a storm of contemporary protest and have since been increasingly influential. Although he ranked *Paradise Lost* in the first place with respect to design and in the second place with respect to performance *among all productions of the human mind,* and although he praised some of Milton's other poems highly, the various exceptions and objections made his *Life of Milton* notorious and unsettled his own contemporary reputation as a critic. For example, he characterized *Comus* as "a drama in the epick style; inelegantly splendid, and tediously instructive." Milton's sonnets, he said, "deserve not any particular criticism; for of the best it can only be said, that they are not bad." As a final example, Dr. Johnson's evaluation of "Lycidas" may be typified by these remarks: "the diction is harsh, the rhymes uncertain, and the numbers unpleasing. Its form is that of a pastoral, easy, vulgar, and therefore disgusting. Surely no man could have fancied that he read *Lycidas* with pleasure, had he not known its author." The inordinate adulation of Milton by Dr. Johnson's contemporaries no doubt intensified his strictures. However, his depreciatory views were neither popular in nor representative of the eighteenth century. On the other hand, Dr. Johnson has in later times been the most influential of all critics of Milton. His remarks—especially his disparaging remarks—have stimulated criticism and served as constant points of departure for critics whose purpose has been to assess Milton, including those who would belittle as well as those who would magnify Milton's achievement.

The idolatry of Milton in the eighteenth century certainly had its faddish and unnatural elements, but that age felt uneasy in questioning what appeared to be a poetic redaction of the received religious beliefs. In any event, there were over a hundred editions of *Paradise Lost* during the century—more than twice as many as of Shakespeare's plays, fifteen times as many as of the *Faerie Queene*. Milton was the most popular subject in the periodicals; he was talked about (and even read) by all classes of people; and perhaps a majority of eighteenth-century verse can be said to have been either modelled on, imitative of, or influenced by Milton. It would be difficult to imagine a more exalted poetic reputation, and the attitude of the eighteenth century toward Milton will probably never be duplicated in favor of any writer.

There was remarkable consistency in the main currents of Milton criticism in the eighteenth century. The three concepts of Milton were constantly undergoing some change, of course, but the relative uniformity of the critical attitudes within the century makes it possible to render each of those concepts in the summary form in which it has been stated. During the nineteenth and twentieth centuries, however, the changes in attitude were so accelerated that certain patterns in the evolution of the Milton criticism of the last hundred and fifty years are clearly apparent. In order to trace those patterns it is necessary to resort to a chronological division of the criticism into several arbitrary periods that have no real significance or validity for the present purpose other than as denominators for phases in the development of Milton criticism.

IV

(1800-1825)

During the first quarter of the nineteenth century Milton began to gain attention as a conscious literary artist. The men who were contemporaneously considered the leading critics—Jeffrey, Gifford, Croker, and Lockhart—had little to say about

Milton; but the technical excellence and highly sophisticated nature of Milton's verse were pointed out and emphasized by Coleridge, Hazlitt, Keats, and many of the others who are today regarded as the most outstanding critics of that age. Although their opinions were favorable, they were variously expressed: Shelley, Wordsworth, Byron, and Lamb recognized skilful artistry in Milton, but they praised it in vague terms somewhat reminiscent of eighteenth-century criticism; Keats inserted a note of condemnation into his sincere approbation of Milton's technique; Coleridge placed high on the credit side of the Milton ledger artificial and musical qualities (which have lately been charged against Milton in red ink) ; and Hazlitt observed laboriously successful stylistic effects. Collectively these critics were moving in a new direction of closer attention to style, however, and their praise was more complete than may be immediately apparent to us.

At the same time, Milton began to lose the force of religious authority. Practically no one had yet attempted anything more than a theological interpretation of Milton's thought, and the diminishing respect for theology undercut one traditional reason for the exaltation of Milton as a divine poet. Blake and Shelley contradicted Milton's theological system, but Milton's ideas were otherwise largely ignored. The cult of Satan, which flourished for a century and still has to be combatted, began about this time. Satan had been called the hero of *Paradise Lost* by as early a critic as Dryden (and by various people in between) ; but the nineteenth-century interest, beginning with Blake and Shelley, tended more toward crystallizing in Satan's character the impact of the poem or even toward commending the moral and ethical codes that he represented. The force of the Satanists' beliefs (as they developed during the later nineteenth century) is really an attack (sometimes unconscious) on the underlying ideas of *Paradise Lost*—an attack that obliquely condemns the poem for enshrining false and pernicious theological, moral, and ethical notions. In the first quarter of the nineteenth century, however, there were only intimations of the outspoken dissatisfaction that was later expressed about Milton's thought.

The controversy over Milton as a man, which had previously consisted largely of partisan reactions to Milton's political activities, began to subside. In the early nineteenth century Milton was frequently lauded for his unswerving devotion to the political cause he had espoused. However, there was very little interest in Milton as an individual, and the details of his private life were largely ignored. The concept of Milton as a man had relatively little influence on his reputation as a writer.

V

(1825-1860)

During the first quarter of the nineteenth century there was a tendency to admire Milton's poetic technique and to ignore his thought. This attitude foreshadowed an important develop- ment in Milton criticism. Between 1825 and 1860 the critics began to dichotomize Milton's poetry into "expression" and "thought" and to assign a separate and insulated compartment to each of those two divisions; by the end of the century this fission became virtually complete. But in the second quarter of the century the disjunction proceeded only to an open avowal of dissatisfaction with Milton's ideas and to a general belief that technique was the most important aspect of Milton's work.

The publication in 1825 of Milton's "lost" study of Chris- tian doctrine, the *De Doctrina Christiana,* gave unmistakable evidence that he held heterodox religious beliefs. This study presents a reasoned theological basis for Milton's liberal Chris- tianity and serves as a precise and intellectual commentary on the doctrine underlying his poetry; the reaction to such a docu- ment upon its first publication should indicate something about how seriously the ideas in Milton's poetry were being taken. It may be supposed that the *De Doctrina Christiana* would have been hostilely received by the leading critics of Milton in the eighteenth century. Some would have branded it as a forgery, others would have dissociated the ideas of *Paradise Lost* from it, and many would have been discomfited and embarrassed by it. Its appearance in 1825 was greeted by a flurry of critical reviews, the most celebrated of which was Macaulay's essay on Milton (which, despite its popularity, is for the most part little more than a monument in rhetoric to Macaulay's prejudice and juvenility) . But the publication of the *De Doctrina Christiana* had little effect that can be recorded in the history of Milton criticism. It might be presumed that the attitudes of the critics toward Milton as a man and a thinker would have been altered by the discovery of a work which marked him as something of a religious radical. But there was in fact no perceptible change in Milton's reputation on this account. The indifferent reception of the *De Doctrina Christiana* is an indication that the weight of religious authority was no longer a significant support of the Miltonic tradition.

Several critical opinions of Milton's thought were frequently expressed, however, and all of them indicated either indifference or distaste. The overwhelming majority of critics considered Milton's thought to be primarily theology. Of these critics, some (such as Macaulay and Emerson) ignored it; others (such as Landor, and to a lesser exent Hunt, De Quincey, Ruskin, and Henry Hallam) expressed an active dislike for it; the few (such as John Wilson) who tried to make a nontheological interpretation concluded with grave doubts as to the validity of Milton's thought.

All of these critics agreed, however, that Milton's craftsmanship fully justified his eminence. Most of them (such as Macaulay, Channing, Emerson, and Tennyson) had unqualified praise for his poetic technique. Some (such as De Quincey, Hunt, Landor, Henry Hallam, and Ruskin) made certain limited reservations to their approbation of the artistry. Milton, they said, introduced a great many foreign idioms (mostly of Latin origin) into his poetry and used native English idioms sparingly. He also employed unusual rhythms and was unduly prepossessed with the creation of sound-effects. In short, his style was eminently artificial. These characteristics were not generally regarded as stylistic faults, however, but as essential elements of Milton's personal and unique poetry. The belief that his poetry was unique actually increased the admiration of these critics, but such a doctrine was a narrow and unsteady basis for continuing fame.

Toward the middle of the century Milton the man was praised more for his private nobility and exemplary life than for his public virtue. At the same time, there were one or two uneasy suggestions that Milton had possessed a rather peculiar character. It was further observed by a few critics (such as Macaulay, De Quincey, Landor, Tennyson, and Ruskin) that Milton had been a Puritan. Though the connection was not made pejoratively, associations detrimental to the reputation of a poet lurked behind that name in the middle of the nineteenth century. One more of the traditional supports to Milton's fame was in danger of being lost.

VI

(1860-1915)

The critical tendencies operating in the first half of the nineteenth century assumed a definite form in the latter Victorian period, from about 1860 to about 1915. To put it briefly, Milton the man and Milton the thinker were dismissed for the sake of Milton the artist.

Largely on the basis of David Masson's half-century of labors, from the 1840's to the 1890's, Milton the man was typified almost universally as solemn, austere, proud, intolerant, and scornful. Masson's greatest contribution was his six-volume *Life of John Milton: Narrated in Connexion with the Political, Ecclesiastical, and Literary History of His Time.* This work was accepted as establishing Milton on the one hand as a disagreeable man and on the other hand as a Puritan. Most of the critics who directly succeeded Masson used his conclusions as a two-handed engine against Milton and employed the term Puritan as a ready and easy way of asserting that Milton had been a disagreeable man. There were, however, two variations on this theme by Masson. One (exemplified by Taine, Scherer, Pattison, Brooke, and Moody) held that until about 1640 Milton was a child of both the Renaissance and Puritanism, and a moderately normal young man; thereafter he became a Puritan in a disagreeable sense. The other (expressed by Lowell, Garnett, Trent, Raleigh, and Saintsbury) maintained that the term Puritanism was unnecessary in characterizing Milton, that he was grimly austere without benefit of party. These several views harmonized in rendering respect and reverence to Milton the man because he seemed to command them. But he could not beget admiration from any quarter: he was a stern, unpleasant old man.

At the same time, if Milton was even considered as a philosopher, he was thought of only as a strict theologian who set down in poetry severe Puritan dogmas which were disagreeable to the philosophic conceptions of most of the critics. For the most part, his ideas were therefore ignored. Other opinions reflected no more credit on Milton as a thinker: Lowell and Stephen found his philosophy worthless, Birrell could discover nothing but a story, and Saintsbury avowed that Milton's ideas did not merit discussion. Even the most favorable attitude is reducible to a simple syllogism: Milton's theology (reality to him) is worthless; Milton's stock of ideas is only theology; Milton's ideas are worthless. Satan figured prominently in discussions of the subject and ideas of *Paradise Lost*. Many critics rated his importance above that of the poem in which he occurred: he was thought to be the central figure about which the whole poem was built; he was considered the most interesting and successful character; and all other personages were counted subordinate to him. When the critics noted a profound defect in the scheme of the poem on the basis of this imbalance of Satan, they were simply rephrasing their general conclusion that Milton's philosophy was only a repellent theological system.

If one holds that thought and expression are two aspects of writing which cannot be isolated one from the other except in an admittedly artificial manner for the purpose of inspection, one might expect that Milton's poetry would have been pretty thoroughly discredited by these critics, who had so little regard for his thought. But thought and expression occupied separate mansions. If the mansion of Milton's thought was considered a dilapidated house frequented only by ghosts, the mansion of his expression was a furbished shrine for critical pilgrims. Milton was praised more highly for his artistry than he ever had been before or ever has been since. There was a gradual and perceptible increase in esteem from the qualified or inexplicit admiration of Masson, Taine, and Pattison through the more open praise of Bagehot, Arnold, and Hopkins to the judgment of Bridges, Raleigh, Saintsbury, and Mackail that Milton was *the* master stylist and *the* great, conscious, technical artist. There was a continually increasing admiration of art for art's sake, and art was practically the only thing that these critics could see in Milton. That was the quality which for them made his poetry truly great. Milton's artistry was really praised in such a way that his poetry appeared distinctly unlike that of any other poet, exotic, a unique performance, an inimitable marvel. When Coleridge had characterized Milton's verse as artificial, he had merely been urging the skillfulness of the technique; when such critics as Taine, Lowell, and Saintsbury applied the same term to Milton, they clearly implied that factitiousness was a constituent element of his art. Closely allied to the new application of artificiality was the emphasis (by Trent, Raleigh, Stephen, and Gosse, for example) on the uniqueness of Milton's artistry. When these four critics remarked on Milton's influence, only Trent did not insist that it had been baneful; but none of them condemned Milton because of his influence, not even Raleigh, who felt that Milton's example had for two hundred years strangled all poets who had attempted to write blank verse. It seems to have been commonly agreed that a poet should be judged on his own performance. It is interesting to notice the stress that was put on the musical qualities of Milton's verse. Most of the critics insisted that its sonorous music was one of its most pleasing characteristics, and some (such as Lowell and Saintsbury) openly avowed that the meaning of *Paradise Lost* was entirely irrelevant and unessential when its music was so enchanting. It should be added that Milton was not, of course, alone in being examined through a stereoscope by critics who opened only one eye; those were the same times, for instance, when Magnificats were chanted in praise of seventeenth-century prose writers for their style without attention to their substance. This is, according to Bacon, the first distemper of learning, when men study words and not matter.

VII

(1915 to the present)

Criticism of Milton before 1915 had placed him in a very high and in a very precarious position. The criticism since that time, though increasingly complex, forms a historical continuity with the Victorian tradition. The controversies about Milton that have raged chronically in the last thirty years were, when viewed historically, almost inescapable. Far from being an isolated phenomenon of critical aberration, the recent denunciations of Milton's verse represent a development, on later critical principles, of the conceptions of Milton held in the later Victorian period. These modern controversies have, for the most part, been healthy, and they seem to constitute a natural preface to a consolidation of positions on more tenable critical and scholarly grounds.

To simplify a good deal, it might be said that recent critics of Milton fall into two broad groups that are not mutually exclusive: those who have provided revaluations of the concepts of Milton as a man and as a thinker, and those who have reanalyzed the concepts of Milton as an artist.

The first group set themselves to rescue Milton's thought

from the trough of sectarian theology and the man from the pillory of anti-Puritan prejudice. These efforts might be called a positive reaction against the earlier attitudes: a reaction in that the efforts obviously stemmed out of a disbelief in the validity of those earlier concepts, and positive in that further researches and reassessments produced more acceptable substitutes. Such American scholars as Greenlaw and Hanford tried to establish Milton as a Renaissance thinker by restudying his thought from a non-theological point of view and by connecting it with that of the Renaissance in general and of such English representatives as Spenser in particular. They found the connections so close that they felt justified in calling Milton a humanist; as a corollary, the man was made to appear attractive along the broad, humane lines associated with the Renaissance. The beliefs of these scholars were perhaps unreasonably extended when they tried to strip Milton of all elements of Puritanism and represent him as all of a part out of the Renaissance.

At the same time, continental scholars such as Saurat and Liljegren reassessed the man by emphasizing his faults to show that he was not a pillar of righteousness and an inexplicable genius but a person of normal frailty and therefore an understandable mortal. Their apparently perverse interest in groundless charges (Milton was an unscrupulous liar, he had hereditary syphilis, he was an albino, and so forth) discountenanced their efforts at setting up a psychology that would explain Milton's mind and personality and depict an urbane gentleman. More important was their pioneering into Milton's thought; their emphasis on its systematic character and universal validity made Milton appear a daring and original thinker. Although this organizing of his thought into something of much broader intent and of more contemporary relevance than sectarian theology was a considerable contribution, the conclusions were carried further than the evidence seemed to warrant when their offices made Milton look like a rationalistic anti-theologian.

In the thirties and forties the work of such men as Tillyard,
Woodhouse, and Bush made a historical balance. These scholars pointed out the fusion of Protestant and Renaissance elements in Milton's thought and maintained that, although Milton was perhaps not a profound and original philosopher, at
least he was a thinker, and a thinker not circumscribed by
theology. Recently the moral and ethical usefulness of Milton's
poetry to a world groping for standards has been emphasized
by many writers, such as Tillyard, Grierson, Bush, Williams,
and Lewis. The attempt to humanize Milton by making a
lawless criminal or a physical freak of him was also rejected;
he has come to be viewed as a human—though none the less
great—person along the lines of the portrayal by his early
biographers as a pleasant, sociable, and agreeable man. The
attempt is no longer being made to characterize him by either
Renaissance or Puritan traits exclusively. It has been demon-
strated that many of the chief characteristics of Puritan thought
were also characteristic of the Renaissance in general. On such
a basis is Milton termed a Christian humanist, or "the last
exponent of Christian humanism in its historical continuity."
These revaluations of Milton as a man and as a thinker are
gradually gaining wider currency. It is significant to notice that
the scholars and critics who oppose these ideas ally themselves
with the older belief that Milton's "art"—for better or for
worse—is the consideration of transcending importance.

At the same time that scholars were treating the concepts of
Milton as a man and as a thinker, a powerful group of critics
was conducting a vociferous and somewhat self-conscious revaluation of Milton's artistry. They generally accepted without
question the Victorian estimate of Milton as a man and as a
thinker. Their attack might be called a negative inversion of
the Victorian adulation of Milton's artistry: an inversion in
that the commonplaces of previous laudatory criticisms were
repeated but turned into condemnation by the operation of
newer critical theory; and negative in that no substitute conception was proposed for acceptance.

These critics (such as Pound, Eliot, Murry, Read, and Leavis) leveled two distinct classes of attacks. The first was a complaint against the intrinsic deficiencies of Milton's style, and the second against the extrinsic influence of Milton's verse. The staple of the strictures on Milton's style are familiar to those acquainted with the earlier criticism of Milton, in which similar remarks constituted praise, or characterization, or limited qualification. Artificiality, in the language of the earlier critics, was used as a characteristic; now, having become a sin, it was the basis for the condemnation of the style. The sin consisted of the employment of inflated and Latinized diction, idiom, and syntactical structure, the fabrication of heavy, inflexible, and unnatural formalism of speech and rhythm, the reliance on pompous, magniloquent, and meaningless sound. The second charge was premised on the belief that Milton's influence on English poetry has been baneful. This idea had been frequently voiced before, but Milton had not previously been censured for his influence. Now Milton was condemned for having destroyed the indigenous metaphysical tradition and the unified sensibility of that tradition by dissociating thought and emotion, for having ruined blank verse as a subtle medium of expression, for having had a disastrous effect on both good and bad poets of all later times. These two charges are connected, of course; the second follows the first on the pragmatic theory of judging a poet by his modern relevance and his usefulness to the practising poet. After these adverse criticisms were recorded, however, there still remained the unanswered (and for these critics, unanswerable) question as to what, then, Milton's place really *is*. Though they denied him the position that he has been permitted for more than two hundred years, they nevertheless admitted that he has a certain greatness that is not assessable. While holding fast to the Victorian conceptions of Milton as a man and as a thinker, they have either ignored or denounced the work of recent scholars in developing different ideas. Another group of scholars and critics (primarily those earlier mentioned for their work in modifying the concepts of Milton as a man and as a thinker) has, in turn, responded to the attacks leveled at Milton's artistry as a call to arms and has attempted to repel each individual charge. The field has not been cleared, however, for the general critical theories of the two groups are still at odds. There is recent evidence (from Eliot, for example) that the condemnation of Milton for his influence is being mitigated, together with that larger theory. Although the adverse view has recently lost most of its attractive power, this controversy on the verse had an undeniable effect on the course of Milton criticism. A good deal has been done toward discrediting clichés as current criticism (such as the organ music, planetary circlings, the grand style, and so forth) ; and the effects of the verse can now be more readily examined in all their variety. Milton's verse will not hereafter be regarded with blind idolatry.

Although an account of this modern controversy on Milton's artistry—a unique phenomenon in the history of literary criticism—does not tell the whole story of the contemporary criticism of Milton, relatively few people have, like Ransom and Brooks, been writing significantly about Milton's poetry without becoming involved in or directly affected by the controversy. Those few have usually addressed themselves to Milton's poems for the purpose of treating—amid alien corn—the consuming modern problem of "communication." The controversy has now, it seems, run its full course, and the end of an age in the history of Milton criticism has apparently been reached. Although these matters are the concern of the immediate past rather than of the future, the ultimate effect of the seminal controversies and explanations about Milton as a man, a thinker, and an artist has not yet been produced. We may properly expect that the next years will produce a greater body of significant and synthesized evaluations based more thoroughly on the results of the best scholarly and critical studies and capable of exemplifying the genuine foundations of Milton's achievement.

PART ONE

ESSAYS AND STUDIES

JOSEPH ADDISON

ᵹᵽᴧ∩ᴿᴿᴜ

SIX SPECTATOR PAPERS ON PARADISE LOST
(1712)*

No. 267. Saturday, January 5.

CEDITE ROMANI SCRIPTORES, CEDITE GRAII • PROPERTIUS

THERE is nothing in nature more irksome than general dis-
courses, especially when they turn chiefly upon words. For
this reason I shall waive the discussion of that point which was
started some years since, Whether Milton's *Paradise Lost* may
be called an heroic poem? Those who will not give it that title,
may call it (if they please) a divine poem. It will be sufficient
to its perfection, if it has in it all the beauties of the highest
kind of poetry; and as for those who allege it is not an heroic
poem, they advance no more to the diminution of it, than if
they should say Adam is not Aeneas, nor Eve, Helen.

I shall therefore examine it by the rules of epic poetry, and
see whether it falls short of the *Iliad* or *Aeneid,* in the beauties
which are essential to that kind of writing. The first thing
to be considered in an epic poem is the fable, which is perfect
or imperfect, according as the action which it relates is more
or less so. This action should have three qualifications in it.
First, it should be but one action. Secondly, it should be an

---

* These six essays from *The Spectator,* issued on consecutive Saturdays,
deal with *Paradise Lost* as a whole. They were followed by twelve more
essays, also issued on consecutive Saturdays; each of those papers treats one
book of *Paradise Lost.* ·

entire action. And thirdly, it should be a great action. To consider the action of the *Iliad, Aeneid,* and *Paradise Lost,* in these three several lights. Homer, to preserve the unity of his action, hastens into the midst of things, as Horace has observed: had he gone up to Leda's egg, or begun much later, even at the rape of Helen, or the investing of Troy, it is manifest that the story of the poem would have been a series of several actions. He therefore opens his poem with the discord of his princes, and artfully interweaves, in the several succeeding parts of it, an account of everything material which relates to them, and had passed before this fatal dissension. After the same manner Aeneas makes his first appearance in the Tyrrhene seas, and within sight of Italy, because the action proposed to be celebrated was that of his settling himself in Latium. But because it was necessary for the reader to know what had happened to him in the taking of Troy, and in the preceding parts of his voyage, Virgil makes his hero relate it by way of episode in the second and third books of the *Aeneid.* The contents of both which books come before those of the first book in the thread of the story, though, for preserving of this unity of action, they follow it in the disposition of the poem. Milton, in imitation of these two great poets, opens his *Paradise Lost* with an infernal council plotting the fall of man, which is the action he proposed to celebrate; and as for those great actions, the battle of the angels, and the creation of the world, (which preceded in point of time, and which, in my opinion, would have entirely destroyed the unity of his principal action, had he related them in the same order that they happened,) he cast them into the fifth, sixth, and seventh books, by way of episode to this noble poem.

Aristotle himself allows, that Homer has nothing to boast of as to the unity of his fable, though at the same time, that great critic and philosopher endeavours to palliate this imperfection in the Greek poet, by imputing it in some measure to the very nature of an epic poem. Some have been of opinion, that the *Aeneid* also labours in this particular, and has episodes which may be looked upon as excrescences rather than as parts of the action. On the contrary, the poem which we have now under our consideration, hath no other episodes than such as naturally arise from the subject, and yet is filled with such a multitude of astonishing incidents, that it gives us at the same time a pleasure of the greatest variety, and of the greatest simplicity; uniform in its nature, though diversified in the execution.

I must observe, also, that as Virgil, in the poem which was designed to celebrate the original of the Roman empire, has described the birth of its great rival, the Carthaginian commonwealth; Milton, with the like art, in his poem on the Fall of Man, has related the fall of those angels who are his professed enemies. Beside the many other beauties in such an episode, its running parallel with the great action of the poem hinders it from breaking the unity so much as another episode would have done, that had not so great an affinity with the principal subject. In short, this is the same kind of beauty which the critics admire in the *Spanish Friar, or the Double Discovery*, where the two different plots look like counterparts and copies of one another.

The second qualification required in the action of an epic poem is, that it should be an entire action: an action is entire when it is complete in all its parts; or, as Aristotle describes it, when it consists of a beginning, a middle, and an end. Nothing should go before it, be intermixed with it, or follow after it, that is not related to it; as, on the contrary, no single step should be omitted in that just and regular process which it must be supposed to take from its original to its consummation. Thus we see the anger of Achilles in its birth, its continuance, and effects; and Aeneas's settlement in Italy, carried on through all the oppositions in his way to it both by sea and land. The action in Milton excels (I think) both the former in this particular; we see it contrived in hell, executed upon earth, and punished by heaven. The parts of it are told in the most distinct manner, and grow out of one another in the most natural order.

The third qualification of an epic poem is its greatness. The anger of Achilles was of such consequence, that it embroiled the kings of Greece, destroyed the heroes of Asia, and engaged all the gods in factions. The settlement of Aeneas in Italy produced the Caesars, and gave birth to the Roman empire. Milton's subject was still greater than either of the former; it does not determine the fate of single persons or nations, but of a whole species. The united powers of hell are joined together for the destruction of mankind, which they effected in part, and would have completed, had not Omnipotence itself interposed. The principal actors are, man in his greatest perfection, and woman in her highest beauty. Their enemies are the fallen angels: the Messiah their friend, and the Almighty their protector. In short, everything that is great in the whole circle of being, whether within the verge of nature or out of it, has a proper part assigned it in this admirable poem.

In poetry, as in architecture, not only the whole, but the principal members, and every part of them, should be great. I will not presume to say, that the book of Games in the *Aeneid,* or that in the *Iliad,* are not of this nature; nor to reprehend Virgil's simile of a top and many other of the same kind in the *Iliad,* as liable to any censure in this particular; but I think we may say, without derogating from those wonderful performances, that there is an indisputable and unquestioned magnificence in every part of *Paradise Lost,* and, indeed, a much greater than could have been formed upon any Pagan system.

But Aristotle, by the greatness of the action, does not only mean that it should be great in its nature, but also in its duration; or, in other words, that it should have a due length in it, as well as what we properly call greatness. The just measure of this kind of magnitude, he explains by the following similitude. An animal, no bigger than a mite, cannot appear perfect to the eye, because the sight takes it in at once, and has only a confused idea of the whole, and not a distinct idea of all its parts; if, on the contrary, you should suppose an animal of ten thousand furlongs in length, the eye would be so filled with a single part of it, that it could not give the mind an idea of the whole. What these animals are to the eye, a very short or a very long action would be to the memory. The first would be, as it were, lost and swallowed up by it, and the other difficult to be contained in it. Homer and Virgil have shown their principal art in this particular; the action of the *Iliad,* and that of the *Aeneid,* were in themselves exceeding short; but are so beautifully extended and diversified by the invention of episodes, and the machinery of gods, with the like poetical ornaments, that they make up an agreeable story sufficient to employ the memory without overcharging it. Milton's action is enriched with such variety of circumstances, that I have taken as much pleasure in reading the contents of his books, as in the best invented story I ever met with. It is possible, that the traditions on which the *Iliad* and *Aeneid* were built, had more circumstances in them than the history of the Fall of Man, as it is related in Scripture. Besides, it was easier for Homer and Virgil to dash the truth with fiction, as they were in no danger of offending the religion of their country by it. But as for Milton, he had not only a very few circumstances upon which to raise his poem, but was also obliged to proceed with the greatest caution in everything that he added out of his own invention. And, indeed, notwithstanding all the restraints he was under, he has filled his story with so many surprising incidents, which bear so close an analogy with what is delivered in holy writ, that it is capable of pleasing the most delicate reader, without giving offence to the most scrupulous.

The modern critics have collected, from several hints in the *Iliad* and *Aeneid,* the space of time which is taken up by the action of each of those poems; but as a great part of Milton's story was transacted in regions that lie out of the reach of the sun and the sphere of day, it is impossible to gratify the reader with such a calculation, which, indeed, would be more curious than instructive; none of the critics, either ancient or modern, having laid down rules to circumscribe the action of an epic poem with any determined number of years, days, or hours.

But of this more particularly hereafter.

No. 273. Saturday, January 12.

—NOTANDI SUNT TIBI MORES · HORACE

Having examined the action of *Paradise Lost,* let us in the next place consider the actors. This is Aristotle's method of considering, first the fable, and secondly the manners; or, as we generally call them in English, the fable and the characters.

Homer has excelled all the heroic poets that ever wrote, in the multitude and variety of his characters. Every god that is admitted into his poem, acts a part which would have been suitable to no other deity. His princes are as much distinguished by their manners as by their dominions; and even those among them, whose characters seem wholly made up of courage, differ from one another as to the particular kinds of courage in which they excel. In short, there is scarce a speech or action in the *Iliad,* which the reader may not ascribe to the person that speaks or acts, without seeing his name at the head of it.

Homer does not only outshine all other poets in the variety, but also in the novelty of his characters. He hath introduced among his Grecian princes a person who had lived thrice the age of man, and conversed with Theseus, Hercules, Polyphemus, and the first race of heroes. His principal actor is the son of a goddess, not to mention the offspring of other deities, who have likewise a place in his poem, and the venerable Trojan prince, who was the father of so many kings and heroes. There is in these several characters of Homer, a certain dignity as well as novelty, which adapts them in a more peculiar manner to the nature of an heroic poem. Though at the same time, to give them the greater variety, he has described a Vulcan, that is, a buffoon among his gods, and a Thersites among his mortals.

Virgil falls infinitely short of Homer in the characters of his poem, both as to their variety and novelty. Aeneas is, indeed, a perfect character; but as for Achates, though he is styled the hero's friend, he does nothing in the whole poem which may deserve that title. Gyas, Mnestheus, Sergestus, and Cloanthus, are all of them men of the same stamp and character.

—FORTEMQUE GYAN, FORTEMQUE CLOANTHUM · VIRGIL

There are, indeed, several natural incidents in the part of Ascanius: as that of Dido cannot be sufficiently admired. I do not see anything new or particular in Turnus. Pallas and Evander are remote copies of Hector and Priam, as Lausus and Mezentius are almost parallels to Pallas and Evander. The characters of Nisus and Euryalus are beautiful, but common. We must not forget the parts of Sinon, Camilla, and some few others, which are fine improvements on the Greek poet. In short, there is neither that variety nor novelty in the persons of the *Aeneid,* which we meet with in those of the *Iliad.*

If we look into the characters of Milton, we shall find that he has introduced all the variety his fable was capable of receiving. The whole species of mankind was in two persons at the time to which the subject of his poem is confined. We have, however, four distinct characters in these two persons. We see man and woman in the highest innocence and perfection, and in the most abject state of guilt and infirmity. The two last characters are, indeed, very common and obvious; but the two first are not only more magnificent, but more new, than any characters either in Virgil or Homer, or indeed in the whole circle of nature.

Milton was so sensible of this defect in the subject of his poem, and of the few characters it would afford him, that he has brought into it two actors of a shadowy fictitious nature, in the persons of Sin and Death, by which means he has wrought into the body of his fable a very beautiful and well-invented allegory. But, notwithstanding the fineness of this allegory may atone for it in some measure, I cannot think that persons of such a chimerical existence are proper actors in an epic poem; because there is not that measure of probability annexed to them, which is requisite in writings of this kind, as I shall show more at large hereafter.

Virgil has, indeed, admitted Fame as an actress in the *Aeneid,* but the part she acts is very short, and none of the most admired circumstances in that divine work. We find in mock-heroic poems, particularly in the *Dispensary* and the *Lutrin,* several allegorical persons of this nature, which are very beautiful in those compositions, and may, perhaps, be used as an argument, that the authors of them were of opinion, such characters might have a place in an epic work. For my own part, I should be glad the reader would think so, for the sake of the poem I am now examining; and must further add, that if such empty, unsubstantial beings may be ever made use of on this occasion, never were any more nicely imagined, and employed in more proper actions, than those of which I am now speaking.

Another principal actor in this poem is the great enemy of mankind. The part of Ulysses in Homer's *Odyssey* is very much admired by Aristotle, as perplexing that fable with very agreeable plots and intricacies, not only by the many adventures in his voyage, and the subtilty of his behaviour, but by the various concealments and discoveries of his person in several parts of that poem. But the crafty being I have now mentioned makes a much longer voyage than Ulysses, puts in practice many more wiles and stratagems, and hides himself under a greater variety of shapes and appearances, all of which are severally detected, to the great delight and surprise of the reader.

We may likewise observe with how much art the poet has varied several characters of the persons that speak in his infernal assembly. On the contrary, how has he represented the whole Godhead exerting itself towards man in its full benevolence, under the three-fold distinction of a Creator, a Redeemer, and a Comforter!

Nor must we omit the person of Raphael, who, amidst his tenderness and friendship for man, shows such a dignity and condescension in all his speech and behaviour, as are suitable to a superior nature. The angels are, indeed, as much diversified in Milton, and distinguished by their proper parts, as the gods are in Homer or Virgil. The reader will find nothing ascribed to Uriel, Gabriel, Michael, or Raphael, which is not in a particular manner suitable to their respective characters.

There is another circumstance in the principal actors of the *Iliad* and *Aeneid,* which gives a peculiar beauty to those two poems, and was therefore contrived with very great judgment. I mean the authors having chosen for their heroes, persons who were so nearly related to the people for whom they wrote. Achilles was a Greek, and Aeneas the remote founder of Rome. By this means their countrymen (whom they principally proposed to themselves for their readers) were particularly attentive to all the parts of their story, and sympathized with their heroes in all their adventures. A Roman could not but rejoice in the escapes, successes, and victories of Aeneas, and be grieved at any defeats, misfortunes, or disappointments that befell him; as a Greek must have had the same regard for Achilles. And it is plain, that each of those poems have lost this great advantage, among those readers to whom their heroes are as strangers, or indifferent persons.

Milton's poem is admirable in this respect, since it is impossible for any of its readers, whatever nation, country, or people he may belong to, not to be related to the persons who are the principal actors in it; but what is still infinitely more to its advantage, the principal actors in this poem are not only our progenitors, but our representatives. We have an actual interest in everything they do, and no less than our utmost happiness is concerned and lies at stake in their behaviour.

I shall subjoin, as a corollary to the foregoing remark, an admirable observation out of Aristotle, which hath been very much misrepresented in the quotations of some modern critics. "If a man of perfect and consummate virtue falls into a misfortune, it raises our pity, but not our terror, because we do not fear that it may be our own case, who do not resemble the suffering person. But (as that great philosopher adds) if we see a man of virtue, mixt with infirmities, fall into any misfortune, it does not only raise our pity, but our terror; because we are afraid that the like misfortune may happen to ourselves, who resemble the character of the suffering person."

I shall only remark in this place, that the foregoing observation of Aristotle, though it may be true in other occasions, does not hold in this; because in the present case, though the persons who fall into misfortune are of the most perfect and consummate virtue, it is not to be considered as what may possibly be, but what actually is our own case; since we are embarked with them on the same bottom, and must be partakers of their happiness or misery.

In this, and some other very few instances, Aristotle's rules for epic poetry (which he had drawn from his reflections upon Homer) cannot be supposed to square exactly with the heroic poems which have been made since his time; since it is evident to every impartial judge, his rules would still have been more perfect, could he have perused the *Aeneid,* which was made some hundred years after his death.

In my next I shall go through other parts of Milton's poem; and hope that what I shall there advance, as well as what I have already written, will not only serve as a comment upon Milton, but upon Aristotle.

No. 279. Saturday, January 19.

REDDERE PERSONAE SCIT CONVENIENTIA CUIQUE · HORACE

W<small>E HAVE</small> already taken a general survey of the fable and characters in Milton's *Paradise Lost:* the parts which remain to be considered, according to Aristotle's method, are the sentiments and the language. Before I enter upon the first of these, I must advertise my reader, that it is my design, as soon as I have finished my general reflections on these four several heads, to give particular instances out of the poem now before us, of beauties and imperfections which may be observed under each of them, as also of such other particulars as may not properly fall under any of them. This I thought fit to premise, that the reader may not judge too hastily of this piece of criticism, or look upon it as imperfect, before he has seen the whole extent of it.

The sentiments in an epic poem are the thoughts and behaviour which the author ascribes to the persons whom he introduces, and are just when they are conformable to the characters of the several persons. The sentiments have likewise a relation to things as well as persons, and are then perfect when they are such as are adapted to the subject. If in either of these cases the poet endeavours to argue or explain, magnify or diminish, to raise love or hatred, pity or terror, or any other passion, we ought to consider whether the sentiments he makes use of are proper for those ends. Homer is censured by the critics for his defect as to this particular in several parts of the *Iliad* and *Odyssey;* though at the same time, those who have treated this great poet with candour, have attributed this defect to the times in which he lived. It was the fault of the age, and not of Homer, if there wants that delicacy in some of his sentiments, which now appears in the works of men of a much inferior genius. Besides, if there are blemishes in any particular thoughts, there is an infinite beauty in the greatest part of them. In short, if there are many poets who would not have fallen into the meanness of some of his sentiments, there are none who could have risen up to the greatness of others. Virgil has excelled all others in the propriety of his sentiments. Milton shines likewise very much in this particular: nor must we omit one consideration which adds to his honour and reputation. Homer and Virgil introduced persons whose characters are commonly known among men, and such as are to be met with either in history, or in ordinary conversation. Milton's characters, most of them, lie out of nature, and were to be formed purely by his own invention. It shows a greater genius in Shakspeare to have drawn his Caliban, than his Hotspur or Julius Caesar: the one was to be supplied out of his own imagination, whereas the other might have been formed upon tradition, history, and observation. It was much easier, therefore, for Homer to find proper sentiments for an assembly of Grecian generals, than for Milton to diversify his infernal council with proper characters, and inspire them with a variety of sentiments. The loves of Dido and Aeneas are only copies of what has passed between other persons. Adam and Eve, before the fall, are a different species from that of mankind who are descended from them; and none but a poet of the most unbounded invention, and the most exquisite judgment, could have filled their conversation and behaviour with so many circumstances during their state of innocence.

Nor is it sufficient for an epic poem to be filled with such thoughts as are natural, unless it abound also with such as are sublime. Virgil in this particular falls short of Homer. He has not, indeed, so many thoughts that are low and vulgar; but at the same time has not so many thoughts that are sublime and noble. The truth of it is, Virgil seldom rises into very astonishing sentiments, where he is not fired by the *Iliad*. He every-where charms and pleases us by the force of his own genius; but seldom elevates and transports us where he does not fetch his hints from Homer.

Milton's chief talent, and, indeed, his distinguishing excel-lence, lies in the sublimity of his thoughts. There are others of the moderns who rival him in every other part of poetry; but in the greatness of his sentiments he triumphs over all the poets both modern and ancient, Homer only excepted. It is impossible for the imagination of man to distend itself with greater ideas, than those which he has laid together in his first, second, and sixth books. The seventh, which describes the creation of the world, is likewise wonderfully sublime, though not so apt to stir up emotion in the mind of the reader, nor consequently so perfect in the epic way of writing, because it is filled with less action. Let the judicious reader compare what Longinus has observed on several passages in Homer, and he will find parallels for most of them in the *Paradise Lost*.

From what has been said we may infer, that as there are two kinds of sentiments, the natural and the sublime, which are always to be pursued in an heroic poem, there are also two kinds of thoughts which are carefully to be avoided. The first are such as are affected and unnatural; the second, such as are mean and vulgar. As for the first kind of thoughts, we meet with little or nothing that is like them in Virgil; he has none of those trifling points and puerilities that are so often to be met with in Ovid, none of the epigrammatic turns of Lucan, none of those swelling sentiments which are so fre-quently in Statius and Claudian, none of those mixed embel-lishments of Tasso. Everything is just and natural. His senti-ments show that he had a perfect insight into human nature, and that he knew everything which was the most proper to affect it.

Mr. Dryden has in some places, which I may hereafter take notice of, misrepresented Virgil's way of thinking as to this particular, in the translation he has given us of the *Aeneid*.

I do not remember that Homer anywhere falls into the faults above-mentioned, which were, indeed, the false refinements of later ages. Milton, it must be confest, has sometimes erred in this respect, as I shall show more at large in another paper; though, considering all the poets of the age in which he writ were infected with this wrong way of thinking, he is rather to be admired that he did not give more into it, than that he did sometimes comply with the vicious taste which still prevails so much among modern writers.

But since several thoughts may be natural which are low and grovelling, an epic poet should not only avoid such sentiments as are unnatural or affected, but also such as are mean and vulgar. Homer has opened a great field of raillery to men of more delicacy than greatness of genius, by the homeliness of some of his sentiments. But, as I have before said, these are rather to be imputed to the simplicity of the age in which he lived, to which I may also add, of that which he described, than to any imperfection in that divine poet. Zöilus among the ancients, and Monsieur Perrault among the moderns, pushed their ridicule very far upon him, on account of some such sentiments. There is no blemish to be observed in Virgil under this head, and but a very few in Milton.

I shall give but one instance of this impropriety of thought in Homer, and at the same time compare it with an instance of the same nature, both in Virgil and Milton. Sentiments which raise laughter can very seldom be admitted with any decency into an heroic poem, whose business is to excite passions of a much nobler nature. Homer, however, in his characters of Vulcan and Thersites, in his story of Mars and Venus, in his behaviour of Irus, and in other passages, has been observed to have lapsed into the burlesque character, and to have departed from that serious air which seems essential to the magnificence of an epic poem. I remember but one laugh in the whole *Aeneid*, which rises in the fifth book, upon Monoetes, where he is represented as thrown overboard, and drying himself upon a rock. But this piece of mirth is so well timed, that the severest critic can have nothing to say against it, for it is in the book of games and diversions, where the reader's mind may be supposed to be sufficiently relaxed for such an entertainment. The only piece of pleasantry in *Paradise Lost,* is where the evil spirits are described as rallying the angels upon the success of their newly invented artillery. This passage I look upon to be the most exceptionable in the whole poem, as being nothing else but a string of puns, and those too very indifferent.

> —Satan beheld their plight,
> And to his mates thus in derision called.
>
> O friends, why come not on these victors proud!
> Ere while they fierce were coming, and when we,
> To entertain them fair with open front
> And breast, (what could we more?) propounded terms
> Of composition, straight they changed their minds,
> Flew off, and into strange vagaries fell,
> As they would dance; yet for a dance they seemed
> Somewhat extravagant and wild, perhaps
> For joy of offered peace; but I suppose
> If our proposals once again were heard,
> We should compel them to a quick result.
>
> To whom thus Belial, in like gamesome mood.
> Leader, the terms we sent were terms of weight,
> Of hard contents, and full of force urged home,
> Such as we might perceive amused them all,
> And stumbled many; who receives them right
> Had need, from head to foot, well understand;
> Not understood, this gift they have besides,
> They show us when our foes walk not upright.
>
> Thus they among themselves in pleasant vein
> Stood scoffing—

No. 285. Saturday, January 26.

NE QUICUNQUE DEUS, QUICUNQUE ADHIBEBITUR HEROS,
REGALI CONSPECTUS IN AURO NUPER ET OSTRO,
MIGRET IN OBSCURAS HUMILI SERMONE TABERNAS:
AUT DUM VITAT HUMUM, NUBES ET INANIA CAPTET · HORACE

Having already treated of the fable, the characters, and sentiments in the *Paradise Lost,* we are in the last place to consider the language; and as the learned world is very much divided upon Milton as to this point, I hope they will excuse me if I appear particular in any of my opinions, and incline to those who judge the most advantageously of the author.

It is requisite that the language of an heroic poem should be both perspicuous and sublime. In proportion as either of these two qualities are wanting, the language is imperfect. Perspicuity is the first and most necessary qualification; insomuch, that a good-natured reader sometimes overlooks a little slip even in the grammar or syntax, where it is impossible for him to mistake the poet's sense. Of this kind is that passage in Milton, wherein he speaks of Satan:

> —God and his Son except,
> Created thing nought valued he nor shunn'd.

And that in which he describes Adam and Eve:

> Adam the goodliest man of men since born
> His sons, the fairest of her daughters Eve.

It is plain, that in the former of these passages, according to the natural syntax, the divine persons mentioned in the first line are represented as created beings; and that in the other, Adam and Eve are confounded with their sons and daughters. Such little blemishes as these, when the thought is great and natural, we should, with Horace, impute to a pardonable inadvertency, or to the weakness of human nature, which cannot attend to each minute particular, and give the last finishing to every circumstance in so long a work. The ancient critics, therefore, who were acted by a spirit of candour, rather than that of cavilling, invented certain figures of speech, on purpose to palliate little errors of this nature in the writings of those authors who had so many greater beauties to atone for them.

If clearness and perspicuity were only to be consulted, the poet would have nothing else to do but to clothe his thoughts in the most plain and natural expressions. But since it often happens, that the most obvious phrases, and those which are used in ordinary conversation, become too familiar to the ear, and contract a kind of meanness by passing through the mouths of the vulgar, a poet should take particular care to guard himself against idiomatic ways of speaking. Ovid and Lucan have many poornesses of expression upon this account, as taking up with the first phrases that offered, without putting themselves to the trouble of looking after such as would not only be natural, but also elevated and sublime. Milton has but a few failings in this kind, of which, however, you may meet with some instances, as in the following passages.

> Embryos and Idiots, Eremites and Friars,
> White, black, and grey, with all their trumpery,
> Here pilgrims roam—

> —Awhile discourse they hold,
> No fear lest dinner cool; when thus began
> Our author—

> Who of all ages to succeed, but feeling
> The evil on him brought by me, will curse
> My head, ill fare our ancestor impure,
> For this we may thank Adam—

The great masters in composition know very well that many an elegant phrase becomes improper for a poet or an orator, when it has been debased by common use. For this reason the works of ancient authors, which are written in dead languages, have a great advantage over those which are written in languages that are now spoken. Were there any mean phrases or idioms in Virgil and Homer, they would not shock the ear of the most delicate modern reader so much as they would have done that of an old Greek or Roman, because we never hear them pronounced in our streets, or in ordinary conversation.

It is not, therefore, sufficient, that the language of a epic poem be perspicuous, unless it be also sublime. To this end it ought to deviate from the common forms and ordinary phrases of speech. The judgment of a poet very much discovers itself in shunning the common roads of expression, without falling into such ways of speech as may seem stiff and unnatural; he must not swell into a false sublime, by endeavoring to avoid the other extreme. Among the Greeks, Aeschylus, and sometimes Sophocles, were guilty of this fault; among the Latins, Claudian and Statius; and among our own countrymen, Shakspeare and Lee. In these authors the affectation of greatness often hurts the perspicuity of the style, as in many others the endeavour after perspicuity prejudices its greatness.

Aristotle has observed, that the idiomatic style may be avoided, and the sublime formed, by the following methods. First, by the use of metaphors: such are those in Milton.

> Imparadised in one another's arms.

> —And in his hand a reed
> Stood waving, tipt with fire.—

> The grassy clods now calved.—

> Spangled with eyes—

In these, and innumerable other instances, the metaphors are very bold, but just; I must, however, observe, that the metaphors are not thick-sown in Milton, which always savours too much of wit; that they never clash with one another, which, as Aristotle observes, turns a sentence into a kind of an enigma or riddle; and that he seldom has recourse to them where the proper and natural words will do as well.

Another way of raising the language, and giving it a poetical turn, is to make use of the idioms of other tongues. Virgil is full of the Greek forms of speech, which the critics call Hellenisms, as Horace in his Odes abounds with them, much more than Virgil. I need not mention the several dialects which Homer has made use of for this end. Milton, in conformity with the practice of the ancient poets, and with Aristotle's rule, has infused a great many Latinisms, as well as Graecisms, and sometimes Hebraisms, into the language of his poem; as towards the beginning of it,

> Nor did they not perceive the evil plight
> In which they were, or the fierce pains not feel,
> Yet to their general's voice they soon obeyed.

> —Who shall tempt with wandering feet
> The dark, unbottomed, infinite abyss,
> And through the palpable obscure find out
> His uncouth way, or spread his airy flight,
> Upborne with indefatigable wings
> Over the vast abrupt!

> —So both ascend
> In the visions of God—

> B. ii.

Under this head may be reckoned the placing the adjective after the substantive, the transposition of words, the turning the adjective into a substantive, with several other foreign modes of speech, which this poet has naturalized to give his verse the greater sound, and throw it out of prose.

The third method mentioned by Aristotle, is what agrees with the genius of the Greek language more than with that of any other tongue, and is therefore more used by Homer than by any other poet. I mean the lengthening of a phrase by the addition of words, which may either be inserted or omitted, as also by the extending or contracting of particular words by the insertion or omission of certain syllables. Milton has put in practice this method of raising his language, as far as the nature of our tongue will permit, as in the passage above-mentioned, *eremite* for what is *hermite* in common discourse. If you observe the measure of his verse, he has with great judgment suppressed a syllable in several words, and shortened those of two syllables into one, by which method, besides the above-mentioned advantage, he has given a greater variety to his numbers. But this practice is more particularly remarkable in the names of persons and of countries, Beëlzebub, Hessebon, and in many other particulars, wherein he has either changed the name, or made use of that which is not the most commonly known, that he might the better depart from the language of the vulgar.

The same reason recommended to him several old words, which also makes his poem appear the more venerable, and gives it a greater air of antiquity.

I must likewise take notice, that there are in Milton several words of his own coining, as *Cerberean, miscreated, hell-doom'd, embryon* atoms, and many others. If the reader is offended at this liberty in our English poet, I would recommend him to a discourse in Plutarch, which shows us how frequently Homer has made use of the same liberty.

Milton, by the above-mentioned helps, and by the choice of the noblest words and phrases which our tongue would afford him, has carried our language to a greater height than any of the English poets have ever done before or after him, and made the sublimity of his style equal to that of his sentiments.

I have been the more particular in these observations on Milton's style, because it is that part of him in which he appears the most singular. The remarks I have here made upon the practice of other poets, with my observations out of Aristotle, will perhaps alleviate the prejudice which some have taken to his poem upon this account; though, after all, I must confess, that I think his style, though admirable in general, is in some places too much stiffened and obscured by the frequent use of those methods, which Aristotle has prescribed for the raising of it.

This redundancy of those several ways of speech which Aristotle calls foreign language, and with which Milton has so very much enriched, and in some places darkened, the language of his poem, was the more proper for his use, because his poem is written in blank verse. Rhyme, without any other assistance, throws the language off from prose, and very often makes an indifferent phrase pass unregarded; but where the verse is not built upon rhymes, there pomp of sound, and energy of expression, are indispensably necessary to support the style, and keep it from falling into the flatness of prose.

Those who have not a taste for this elevation of style, and are apt to ridicule a poet when he goes out of the common forms of expression, would do well to see how Aristotle has treated an ancient author, called Euclid, for his insipid mirth upon this occasion. Mr. Dryden used to call this sort of men his prose-critics.

I should, under this head of the language, consider Milton's numbers, in which he has made use of several elisions, that are not customary among other English poets, as may be particularly observed in his cutting off the letter Y, when it precedes a vowel. This, and some other innovations in the measure of his verse, has varied his numbers, in such a manner, as makes them incapable of satiating the ear and cloying the reader, which the same uniform measure would certainly have done, and which the perpetual returns of rhyme never fail to do in long narrative poems. I shall close these reflections upon the language of *Paradise Lost,* with observing that Milton has copied after Homer, rather than Virgil, in the length of his periods, the copiousness of his phrases, and the running of his verses into one another.

No. 291. Saturday, February 2.

—UBI PLURA NITENT IN CARMINE, NON EGO PAUCIS
OFFENDAR MACULIS, QUAS AUT INCURIA FUDIT,
AUT HUMANA PARUM CAVIT NATURA— • HORACE

I HAVE now considered Milton's *Paradise Lost* under those four great heads of the fable, the characters, the sentiments, and the language; and have shown that he excels, in general, under each of these heads. I hope that I have made several discoveries which may appear new, even to those who are versed in critical learning. Were I indeed to choose my readers, by whose judgment I would stand or fall, they should not be such as are acquainted only with the French and Italian critics, but also with the ancient and modern who have written in either of the learned languages. Above all, I would have them well versed in the Greek and Latin poets, without which a man very often fancies that he understands a critic, when in reality he does not comprehend his meaning.

It is in criticism, as in all other sciences and speculations; one who brings with him any implicit notions and observations which he has made in his reading of the poets, will find his own reflections methodized and explained, and perhaps several little hints that had passed in his mind perfected and improved in the works of a good critic; whereas one who has not these previous lights, is very often an utter stranger to what he reads, and apt to put a wrong interpretation upon it.

Nor is it sufficient, that a man who sets up for a judge in criticism, should have perused the authors above-mentioned, unless he has also a clear and logical head. Without this talent, he is perpetually puzzled and perplexed amidst his own blunders, mistakes the sense of those he would confute, or if he chances to think right, does not know how to convey his thoughts to another with clearness and perspicuity. Aristotle, who was the best critic, was also one of the best logicians that ever appeared in the world.

Mr. Locke's *Essay on Human Understanding* would be thought a very odd book for a man to make himself master of, who would get a reputation by critical writings; though at the same time it is very certain, that an author who has not learned the art of distinguishing between words and things, and of ranging his thoughts, and setting them in proper lights, whatever notions he may have, will lose himself in confusion and obscurity. I might further observe, that there is not a Greek or a Latin critic who has not shown, even in the style of his criticisms, that he was a master of all the elegance and delicacy of his native tongue.

The truth of it is, there is nothing more absurd than for a man to set up for a critic, without a good insight into all the parts of learning; whereas many of those who have endeavoured to signalize themselves by works of this nature among our English writers, are not only defective in the above-mentioned particulars, but plainly discover by the phrases they make use of, and by their confused way of thinking, that they are not acquainted with the most common and ordinary systems of arts and sciences. A few general rules extracted out of the French authors, with a certain cant of words, has sometimes set up an illiterate, heavy writer for a most judicious and formidable critic.

One great mark, by which you may discover a critic who has neither taste nor learning, is this, that he seldom ventures to praise any passage in an author which has not been before received and applauded by the public, and that his criticism turns wholly upon little faults and errors. This part of a critic is so very easy to succeed in, that we find every ordinary reader, upon the publishing of a new poem, has wit and ill-nature enough to turn several passages of it into ridicule, and very often in the right place. This Mr. Dryden has very agreeably remarked in those two celebrated lines,

> Errors, like straws, upon the surface flow;
> He who would search for pearls, must dive below.

A true critic ought to dwell rather upon excellencies than imperfections, to discover the concealed beauties of a writer, and communicate to the world such things as are worth their observation. The most exquisite words and finest strokes of an author are those which very often appear the most doubtful and exceptionable, to a man who wants a relish for polite learning; and they are these, which a sour, undistinguishing critic generally attacks with the greatest violence. Tully observes, that it is very easy to brand or fix a mark upon what he calls *verbum ardens,* or, as it may be rendered into English, "a glowing, bold expression," and to turn it into ridicule by a cold, ill-natured criticism. A little wit is equally capable of exposing a beauty, and of aggravating a fault; and though such a treatment of an author naturally produces indignation in the mind of an understanding reader, it has however its effect among the generality of those whose hands it falls into; the rabble of mankind being very apt to think that everything which is laughed at with any mixture of wit, is ridiculous in itself.

Such a mirth as this is always unseasonable in a critic, as it rather prejudices the reader than convinces him, and is capable of making a beauty, as well as a blemish, the subject of derision. A man who cannot write with wit on a proper subject, is dull and stupid, but one who shows it in an improper place, is as impertinent and absurd. Besides, a man who has the gift of ridicule, is apt to find fault with anything that gives him an opportunity of exerting his beloved talent, and very often censures a passage, not because there is any fault in it, but because he can be merry upon it. Such kinds of pleasantry are very unfair, and disingenuous, in works of criticism, in which the greatest masters, both ancient and modern, have always appeared with a serious and instructive air.

As I intend in my next paper to show the defects in Milton's *Paradise Lost,* I thought fit to premise these few particulars, to the end that the reader may know I enter upon it, as on a very ungrateful work, and that I shall just point at the imperfections, without endeavouring to inflame them with ridicule. I must also observe with Longinus, that the productions of a great genius, with many lapses and inadvertencies, are infinitely preferable to the works of an inferior kind of author, which are scrupulously exact and conformable to all the rules of correct writing.

I shall conclude my paper with a story out of Boccalini, which sufficiently shows us the opinion that judicious author entertained of the sort of critics I have been here mentioning. A famous critic, says he, having gathered together all the faults of an eminent poet, made a present of them to Apollo, who received them very graciously, and resolved to make the author a suitable return for the trouble he had been at in collecting them. In order to this, he set before him a sack of wheat, as it had been just threshed out of the sheaf. He then bid him pick out the chaff from among the corn, and lay it aside by itself. The critic applied himself to the task with great industry and pleasure, and after having made the due separation, was presented by Apollo with the chaff for his pains.

No. 297. Saturday, February 9.

—VELUT SI
EGREGIO INSPERSOS REPRENDAS CORPORE NAEVOS · HORACE

AFTER what I have said in my last Saturday's paper, I shall enter on the subject of this without further preface, and remark the several defects which appear in the fable, the characters, the sentiments, and the language of Milton's *Paradise Lost;* not doubting but the reader will pardon me, if I allege at the same time, whatever may be said for the extenuation of such defects. The first imperfection which I shall observe in the fable is, that the event of it is unhappy.

The fable of every poem is, according to Aristotle's division, either Simple or Implex. It is called simple when there is no change of fortune in it: implex, when the fortune of the chief actor changes from bad to good, or from good to bad. The implex fable is thought the most perfect; I suppose, because it is more proper to stir up the passions of the reader, and to surprise him with a greater variety of accidents.

The implex fable is therefore of two kinds: in the first the chief actor makes his way through a long series of dangers and difficulties, till he arrives at honour and prosperity, as we see in the story of Ulysses. In the second, the chief actor in the poem falls from some eminent pitch of honour and prosperity, into misery and disgrace. Thus we see Adam and Eve sinking from a state of innocence and happiness into the most abject condition of sin and sorrow.

The most taking tragedies among the ancients were built on this last sort of implex fable, particularly the tragedy of Oedipus, which proceeds upon a story, if we may believe Aristotle, the most proper for tragedy that could be invented by the wit of man. I have taken some pains in a former paper to show, that this kind of implex fable, wherein the event is unhappy, is more apt to affect an audience than that of the first kind; notwithstanding many excellent pieces among the ancients, as well as most of those which have been written of late years in our own country, are raised upon contrary plans. I must, however, own, that I think this kind of fable, which is the most perfect in tragedy, is not so proper for an heroic poem.

Milton seems to have been sensible of this imperfection in his fable, and has therefore endeavoured to cure it by several expedients; particularly by the mortification which the great adversary of mankind meets with upon his return to the assembly of infernal spirits, as it is described in a beautiful passage of the tenth book; and likewise by the vision, wherein Adam at the close of the poem sees his offspring triumphing over his great enemy, and himself restored to a happier Paradise than that from which he fell.

There is another objection against Milton's fable, which is indeed almost the same with the former, though placed in a different light, namely, That the hero in the *Paradise Lost* is unsuccessful, and by no means a match for his enemies. This gave occasion to Mr. Dryden's reflection, that the devil was in reality Milton's hero. I think I have obviated this objection in my first paper. The *Paradise Lost* is an epic, or a narrative poem, and he that looks for an hero in it, searches for that which Milton never intended; but if he will needs fix the name of an hero upon any person in it, it is certainly the Messiah who is the hero, both in the principal action, and in the chief episodes. Paganism could not furnish out a real action for a fable greater than that of the *Iliad* or *Aeneid,* and therefore an heathen could not form a higher notion of a poem than one of that kind which they call an heroic. Whether Milton's is not of a sublimer nature I will not presume to determine: it is sufficient, that I show there is in the *Paradise Lost* all the greatness of plan, regularity of design, and masterly beauties which we discover in Homer and Virgil.

I must in the next place observe, that Milton has interwoven in the texture of his fable some particulars which do not seem to have probability enough for an epic poem, particularly in the actions which he ascribes to Sin and Death, and the picture which he draws of the Limbo of Vanity, with other passages in the second book. Such allegories rather savour of the spirit of Spenser and Ariosto, than of Homer and Virgil.

In the structure of his poem he has likewise admitted of too many digressions. It is finely observed by Aristotle, that the author of an heroic poem should seldom speak himself, but throw as much of his work as he can into the mouths of those who are his principal actors. Aristotle has given no reason for this precept; but I presume it is because the mind of the reader is more awed and elevated when he hears Aeneas or Achilles speak, than when Virgil or Homer talk in their own persons. Besides that assuming the character of an eminent man is apt to fire the imagination, and raise the ideas of an author. Tully tells us, mentioning his dialogue of old age, in which Cato is the chief speaker, that upon a review of it he was agreeably imposed upon, and fancied that it was Cato, and not he himself, who uttered his thoughts on that subject.

If the reader would be at the pains to see how the story of the *Iliad* and *Aeneid* is delivered by those persons who act in it, he will be surprised to find how little in either of these poems proceeds from the authors. Milton has, in the general disposition of his fable, very finely observed this great rule; insomuch, that there is scarce a third part of it which comes from the poet; the rest is spoken either by Adam and Eve, or by some good or evil spirit who is engaged either in their destruction or defence.

From what has been here observed, it appears that digressions are by no means to be allowed of in an epic poem. If the poet, even in the ordinary course of his narration, should speak as little as possible, he should certainly never let his narration sleep for the sake of any reflections of his own. I have often observed, with a secret admiration, that the longest reflection in the *Aeneid* is in that passage of the tenth book, where Turnus is represented as dressing himself in the spoils of Pallas, whom he had slain. Virgil here lets his fable stand still for the sake of the following remark. "How is the mind of man ignorant of futurity, and unable to bear prosperous fortune with moderation! The time will come when Turnus shall wish that he had left the body of Pallas untouched, and curse the day on which he dressed himself in these spoils." As the great event of the *Aeneid,* and the death of Turnus, whom Aeneas slew because he saw him adorned with the spoils of Pallas, turns upon this incident, Virgil went out of his way to make this reflection upon it, without which so small a circumstance might possibly have slipped out of his reader's memory. Lucan, who was an injudicious poet, lets drop his story very frequently for the sake of his unnecessary digressions, or his Diverticula, as Scaliger calls them. If he gives us an account of the prodigies which preceded the civil war, he declaims upon the occasion, and shows how much happier it would be for man, if he did not feel his evil fortune before it comes to pass, and suffer not only by its real weight, but by the apprehension of it. Milton's complaint for his blindness, his panegyric on marriage, his reflections on Adam and Eve's going naked, of the angels' eating, and several other passages in his poem, are liable to the same exception, though I must confess there is so great a beauty in these very digressions, that I would not wish them out of his poem.

I have, in a former paper, spoken of the characters of Milton's *Paradise Lost,* and declared my opinion, as to the allegorical persons who are introduced in it.

If we look into the sentiments, I think they are sometimes defective under the following heads; first, as there are several of them too much pointed, and some that degenerate even into puns. Of this last kind, I am afraid is that in the first book, where speaking of the pigmies, he calls them—

—The small infantry
Warr'd on by cranes—

Another blemish that appears in some of his thoughts, is his frequent allusion to heathen fables, which are not certainly of a piece with the divine subject of which he treats. I do not find fault with these allusions, where the poet himself represents them as fabulous, as he does in some places, but where he mentions them as truths and matters of fact. The limits of my paper will not give me leave to be particular in instances of this kind: the reader will easily remark them in his perusal of the poem.

A third fault in his sentiments, is an unnecessary ostentation of learning, which likewise occurs very frequently. It is certain that both Homer and Virgil were masters of all the learning of their times, but it shows itself in their works, after an indirect and concealed manner. Milton seems ambitious of letting us know, by his excursions on free-will and predestination, and his many glances upon history, astronomy, geography, and the like, as well as by the terms and phrases he sometimes makes use of, that he was acquainted with the whole circle of arts and sciences.

If, in the last place, we consider the language of this great poet, we must allow what I have hinted in a former paper, that it is often too much laboured, and sometimes obscured by old words, transpositions, and foreign idioms. Seneca's objection to the style of a great author, *Riget ejus oratio, nihil in ea placidum, nihil lene,* is what many critics make to Milton: as I cannot wholly refute it, so I have already apologized for it in another paper; to which I may further add, that Milton's sentiments and ideas were so wonderfully sublime, that it would have been impossible for him to have represented them in their full strength and beauty, without having recourse to these foreign assistances. Our language sunk under him, and was unequal to that greatness of soul which furnished him with such glorious conceptions.

A second fault in his language is, that he often affects a kind of jingle in his words, as in the following passages, and many others:

And brought into the *world* a *world* of woe.

—Begirt th' Almighty throne
Beseeching or *besieging*—

This *tempted* our *attempt*—

At one slight *bound* high over-leapt all *bound.*

I know there are figures for this kind of speech, that some of the greatest ancients have been guilty of it, and that Aristotle himself has given it a place in his *Rhetoric* among the beauties of that art. But as it is in itself poor and trifling, it is I think at present universally exploded by all the masters of polite writing.

The last fault which I shall take notice of in Milton's style, is the frequent use of what the learned call technical words, or terms of art. It is one of the great beauties of poetry, to make hard things intelligible, and to deliver what is abstruse of itself in such easy language as may be understood by ordinary readers: besides, that the knowledge of a poet should rather seem born with him, or inspired, than drawn from books and systems. I have often wondered, how Mr. Dryden could translate a passage out of Virgil, after the following manner,

Tack to the larboard, and stand off to sea,
Veer starboard sea and land.—

Milton makes use of larboard in the same manner. When he is upon building, he mentions Doric Pillars, Pilasters, Cornice, Freeze, Architrave. When he talks of heavenly bodies, you meet with Ecliptic, and Eccentric, the Trepidation, Stars dropping from the Zenith, Rays culminating from the Equator. To which might be added many instances of the like kind in several other arts and sciences.

I shall in my next papers give an account of the many particular beauties in Milton, which would have been too long to insert under those general heads I have already treated of, and with which I intend to conclude this piece of criticism.

JONATHAN RICHARDSON

EXPLANATORY NOTES AND REMARKS ON MILTON'S PARADISE LOST (1734)*

THERE is music in all language; the meanest peasant varies the sound as he speaks, though in that he is easily known from a gentleman. Sound is abundantly more expressive of the sense than is commonly imagined; animals who have not the use of words, that we understand at least, express their minds by sounds as well as by gestures, looks and actions; and we know their meaning as we know that of a man whose language we are absolute strangers to. Verse and prose have each their peculiar music, and whether one or the other, 'tis different according to the subject. All kinds of verses have sounds of their own; blank verse comes nearest to prose, and as the prose of some writers approaches verse, Milton's blank verse, that of *Paradise Lost,* has the beauty of both; it has the sweetness of measure, without stopping the voice at the end of the line, or any where else but as the sense requires; one verse runs into another, and the period concludes in any part of a line indifferently, and as if 'twas his choice 'tis very often not at the end of one or of a couplet, as is too frequent with those who write in rhyme. He has frequently eleven syllables in a verse, but 'tis rarely so unless those are no more in quantity than the ten of another.

---

* Approximately one-tenth of the essay is here reprinted. The sections on Milton's life and the external history of the composition and publication of *Paradise Lost* are omitted, but most of the critical material is included. In order to spare the reader Richardson's typographical eccentricities, the spelling has been modernized.

> Fall'n Cherube, to be Weak is Miserable
> Doing or Suffering: but of This be Sure,

the *e* in the middle of the word *Suff'ring* must be melted in the pronunciation, as if written without it as here; and the two syllables made by that vowel, and the *a* that follows in *Miserable* are so short as to be equal to but one in any part of the line. So

> Assur'd me and still Assure. Though what thou tell'st

here *me* and *and* are both so short as to be no more in quantity than if they were but one syllable. To read right requires some judgment, and some experience in Milton's manner who abounds more with these instances than most English poets; but, well read, the music of his verse is exceeding delicate and noble, though somewhat peculiar to himself; for he (as in his language) has profited himself of the Greeks and Latins; his ictus, or cadence, or music bears towards them, as he has formed himself upon their examples into something of his own, by his own ear, and which was a very musical, experienced, and judicious one. . . .

Milton's language is English, but 'tis Milton's English; 'tis Latin, 'tis Greek English; not only the words, the phraseology, the transpositions, but the ancient idiom is seen in all he writes, so that a learned foreigner will think Milton the easiest to be understood of all the English writers. This peculiar English is most conspicuously seen in *Paradise Lost,* for this is the work which he long before intended should enrich and adorn his native tongue. . . .

As his mind was rich in ideas, and in words of various languages to clothe them with, and as he had a vast fire, vigor and zeal of imagination, his style must necessarily distinguish itself; it did so; and even in his younger days, his juvenile poems, English, Latin, and Italian, have a brilliance not easily found elsewhere; nor is it not seen in his controversial prose works; *Paradise Lost* wants it not, in which there are specimens of all his kinds of styles, the tender, the fierce, the narrative, the reasoning, the lofty, &c. . . . There is something in every man's style whereby he is known, as by his voice, face, gait, &c. In Milton there is a certain vigor, whether versing or prosing, which will awaken attention be she never so drowsy, and then persuade her to be thankful though she was disturbed.

A reader of Milton must be always upon duty; he is surrounded with sense, it rises in every line, every word is to the purpose; there are no lazy intervals, all has been considered, and demands, and merits observation. Even in the best writers you sometimes find words and sentences which hang on so loosely you may blow 'em off; Milton's are all substance and weight; fewer would not have served the turn, and more would have been superfluous.

His silence has the same effect, not only that he leaves work for the imagination when he has entertained it, and furnished it with noble materials; but he expresses himself so concisely, employs words so sparingly, that whoever will possess his ideas must dig for them, and oftentimes pretty far below the surface. If this is called obscurity, let it be remembered 'tis such a one as is complaisant to the reader, not mistrusting his ability, care, diligence, or the candidness of his temper; not that vicious obscurity which proceeds from a muddled inaccurate head, not accustomed to clear, well separated and regularly ordered ideas, or from want of words and method and skill to convey them to another, from whence always arises uncertainty, ambiguity, and a sort of a moon-light prospect over a landscape at best not beautiful. Whereas, if a good writer is not understood, 'tis because his reader is unacquainted with or incapable of the subject or will not submit to do the duty of a reader, which is to attend carefully to what he reads.

What Macrobius says of Virgil is applicable to Milton. "He keeps his eye fixed and intent upon Homer and emulates alike his greatness and simplicity, his readiness of speech and silent majesty." By *silent majesty* he seems to mean, with Longinus, "his leaving more to the imagination than is expressed."

And now 'tis of no great importance whether this be called

an heroic or a divine poem, or only, as the author himself has called it in his title-page, a poem. What if it were a composition entirely new, and not reducible under any known denomination? But 'tis properly and strictly heroic, and such Milton intended it, as he has intimated in his short discourse concerning the kind of verse, and which is prefixed to it, as also in his entrance on the ninth book. And 'tis not his fault if there have been those who have not found a hero, or who he is. 'Tis Adam, Adam the first, the representative of human race. He is the hero in this poem, though as in other heroic poems, superior beings are introduced. The business of it is to conduct man through variety of conditions of happiness and distress, all terminating in the utmost good: from a state of precarious innocence, through temptation, sin, repentance, and finally a secure recumbency upon and interest in the Supreme Good by the mediation of His Son. He is not such a hero as Achilles, Ulysses, Aeneas, Orlando, Godfrey, &c., all romantic worthies and incredible performers of fortunate, savage cruelties; he is one of a nobler kind, such as Milton chose to write of, and found he had a genius for the purpose. He is not such a conqueror as subdued armies or nations, or enemies in single combat, but his conquest was what justly gave heroic name to person and to poem. His hero was more than a conqueror through Him that loved us (as Rom. viii. 37).

This was declared to be the subject of the poem at the entrance on it, man's first disobedience and misery till our restoration to a more happy state. The design of it is also declared: 'twas to justify providence, all which is done. The moral we are also directed to, and this the poet has put into the mouth of an angel. Many moral reflections are excited throughout the whole work, but the great one is marked strongly (XII. 745. &c.): "Piety and virtue, all comprised in one word charity, is the only way to happiness."

If the sublimity and peculiarity of the matter of this poem, if its superiority in that respect has raised it above some of the rules given by Aristotle or whatever other critics (and gathered from or founded on the *Iliad, Odyssey,* or *Aeneid*), it has distinguished it to its greater glory. 'Tis not only an heroic poem, but the most so that ever was wrote. Milton did not despise rules, such as were built upon reason, so far as those established reached; but as his free and exalted genius aspired beyond what had yet been attempted in the choice of his subject, himself was his own rule when in heights where none had gone before, and higher than which none can ever go.

Milton's true character as a writer is that he is an ancient, but born two thousand years after his time. His language indeed is modern, but the best (next to Greek and Latin) to convey those images himself conceived—and that moreover Greeked and Latinized and made as uncommon and expressive as our tongue could be, and yet intelligible to us for whom he wrote. But all his images are pure antique, so that we read Homer and Virgil in reading him. We hear them in our own tongue, as we see what they conceived when Milton speaks. Yes, and we find ourselves amongst persons and things of a more exalted character. Connoisseurs in painting and sculpture can best tell what is the difference of taste in ancient and modern work and can therefore best understand what I am now saying; it must suffice that I tell others that there is a certain grace, majesty and simplicity in the antique which is its distinguishing character. The same kind of taste is seen in writing; and Milton has it, I think, to a degree beyond what we have ever found in any modern painter or sculptor, not excepting Raphael himself.

Those who are unaccustomed to this train of thinking may only please to dip into Chaucer, Spenser, Ariosto, even Tasso or any of the moderns and observe what gothic figures and things present themselves to their imagination, or what are comparatively mean. Let them read even the ancients, the best of them (always excepting the most ancient of all, the Pentateuch, Job, and some other of the Sacred Books), and they will find even these fill not nor enrich the mind as Milton does. His Eden, his Chaos, Hell, Heaven; His human figures, his angels, good and evil, his Mediator, his God—all is superior to what is elsewhere to be found. All are with regard to the rest like what Raphael's pictures exhibit, compared with what we see in those of any other master. Or (to speak more familiarly to common observation) they are as Westminster Abbey, or even St. Paul's, compared with the Pantheon, the Coliseum, the Temple of Theseus, or other remains of architecture of the purest antiquity; even the prints of them (those I mean done by the best hands, and which are not very rare) will explain and prove what I advance. . . .

Whatever Milton has woven into his poem of others, still his sublimest passages are more so than could enter the heart of Orpheus, Hesiod, Homer, Pindar, Callimachus, &c. Such as the heathen world were incapable of by infinite degrees, such as none but the noblest genius could attain to, and that assisted by a religion revealed by God himself. We have then in *Paradise Lost* a collection, the quintessence of all that is excellent in writing; frequently improved and explained better than by the best of their professed commentators, but never debased; and a sublimity which all other human writings put together have not. To complete all, he has made use of all these, so as to be subservient to the great end of poetry, which is to please and enrich the imagination, and to mend the heart, and make the man happy. . . .

Were I called upon to define poetry in general, . . . I would do it by saying 'tis ornament. This implies fiction, for dress, lace, gold, jewels, &c. is not the body. Poetry therefore is not truth, but something more agreeable, at least than mere truth.

And its business is, consequently, to awaken, to please, to allure. 'Tis addressed to the imagination, to the passions, and this supposes energy as well as beauty. . . .

As we are most easily led or enticed by pleasure, poetry has proportionable influence on the mind, whether to carry it to good or evil. Whether 'tis made subservient to one or the other, 'tis no less or more poetry still. If you ask what is the most excellent, the most amiable poetry, the answer is easy: 'Tis that whose elevation of language, arrangement of words, its sentiments and images are directed and made subservient to, not only the delight, but the improvement of mankind. And this after all terminates in pleasure, as true wisdom and goodness has the greatest tendency to our happiness. In this use of poetry, and not its power over us, consists its real, its most important dignity.

Poetry pleases by a peculiarity and majesty of style and language. Its numbers, its rhyme (if used, and skilfully) pleases as music does, and as painting, the imagery of things not only real but fictitious. For poetry is a sort of new creation, not only as it produces to the imagination what is unknown to nature (such as Harpies, Sphinxes, Gorgons, Hydras, Centaurs &c. or a sort of men as Shakespeare's Caliban, or the people of romances, men better or worse than ever were), but as it raises and embellishes (where 'tis possible) what is seen in nature, or related in history, and by so doing shows things otherwise than they really are, or ever were. And this not only agreeably entertains the mind ('tis a sort of new acquisition), but it helps us ofttimes to see real beauties, and which would else have passed unregarded and perhaps makes us fancy we see what in truth we do not.

There is another pleasure in poetry, oftener felt perhaps than placed to its account. 'Tis this. Much of art is essential to this kind of writing, and to observe the address and capacity of the poet is vastly pleasing. 'Tis so for example when we meet with a true poetical word, phrase or expression, an apt simile, a beautiful allusion, a noble sentiment, a sublime image, &c.

Besides the pleasure we have in these particulars, 'tis some addition to it when we reflect (as self-love will teach us) on our own ability to discover, and lift up ourselves to the perception of the brilliance of these beauties. And thus, as it were, become sharers in the honor of them. There is yet a further pleasure in thinking this is the work of our friend, our country-man, at least of one of our species. 'Tis true this kind of pleasure is to be had from prose, but not the degree.

Thought is the life of the mind, 'tis the "intellectual being"

(II. 147) and has the universe, and beyond what is real, even the immense regions of fancy to range and wander in. And as it cannot be limited by time, it expatiates eternity. The soul's natural vigor produces a constant succession of ideas; but these are improvable by art, by frequent reflection, observation of what is offered to our senses, or by conversation. Reading is conversing only in somewhat a different manner from discourse *viva voce*. When we take a book in hand 'tis to supply ourselves with thoughts which we could not suggest from within, or did not expect would arise spontaneously. We read for amusement, delight, information, instruction, edification, to awaken or to put our passions into a more vigorous motion—in short, to rouse up the intellectual fire which then gives us a kindly warmth, a wholesome glow, a lucid and noble flame; or it pollutes the mind with black exhalations, and scorches, or torments us. Always the mind is fed with its proper nourishment, ideas. Thus the Scripture, the best of books, is said to be "Profitable for doctrine, for reproof, for correction, for instruction in righteousness." But none are destitute of some juice, something to feed the mind; though those where 'tis richest and in greatest abundance are to be chosen.

'Tis of no small consequence towards the happiness of life to have a lively, inventive, a great and beautiful imagination. 'Twill always furnish us with delight, fill up all the chasms in time, and intervals of business, and sweeten even those which most people seem to consider but as the offals if not the incumbrance of life; but the happiest in this particular may be made happier by assistance from abroad, by conversation and reading.

Paradise Lost is such a fountain in this case as the sun (VII. 364.), whence even these may in their golden urns draw light. Here the morning planet may "gild its horns"; those too who are not so expert at this poetical imagery may richly "augment their small peculiar" here. All may gather something that will adorn and delight their minds.

If ever any book was truly poetical, if ever any abounded with poetry, 'tis *Paradise Lost*. What an expansion of facts from a small seed of history! What worlds are invented, what embellishments of nature upon what our senses present us with? Divine things are more nobly, more divinely represented to the imagination than by any other poem, a more beautiful idea is given of nature than any poet has pretended to, nature as just come out of the hand of God, in its virgin loveliness, glory, and purity. And the human race is shown, not as Homer's, more gigantic, more robust, more valiant, but without comparison more truly amiable, more so than by the pictures and statues of the greatest masters. And all these sublime ideas are conveyed to us in the most effectual and engaging manner. The mind of the reader is tempered and prepared by pleasure, 'tis drawn and allured, 'tis awakened and invigorated to receive such impressions as the poet intended to give it. It opens the fountains of knowledge, piety and virtue, and pours along full streams of peace, comfort and joy to such as can penetrate the true sense of the writer and obediently listen to his song.

In reading the *Iliad* or *Aeneid* we treasure up a collection of fine imaginative pictures as when we read *Paradise Lost*. Only that from thence we have (to speak like a connoisseur) more Raphaels, Correggios, Guidos, &c. Milton's pictures are more sublimely great, divine and lovely than Homer's or Virgil's or those of any other poet or of all the poets ancient or modern.

To have the mind thus stored, besides the advantage of it intended by the poet, is of no small importance to us. The works of the best masters in painting or sculpture deserve the great price they bear upon account of the fine ideas they give us whenever we please to have recourse to them, or as we happen to remember them. A well-chosen collection of poetical pictures, to such as know how to form them, answers much the same purposes, but more may possess such and at a much easier price.

Paradise Lost not only aims at a more noble and more extensive moral, not only leads the mind towards it by the way of pleasantness. All the flowers in that way are not only fragrant, but wholesome and balsamic; all is interesting, all not only delight the mind, but contribute to make it better.

What's Hecuba to him, or he to Hecuba?

What does the War of Troy, or the original of the Roman name, say it was that of Britain, concern you and me? The original of things, the first happy, but precarious condition of mankind, his deviation from rectitude, his lost state, his restoration to the favor of God by repentance and imputed righteousness—and that upon a foundation which cannot be shaken. The great doctrines of the Christian religion, regeneration, adoption and glorification, happiness here and forever: these concern us all equally, and equally with our first parents, whose story, and that of the whole Church of God, this poem sets before us. That is, these things are of the utmost importance, such importance as that what all the world calls great are comparatively trifles, and known to be so upon the least serious reflection. Without a solid establishment of mind in these sublime truths, all comprehended in a just idea of God (so far as we are enabled to conceive of Him, and He has sufficiently revealed Himself to us for that purpose, more we need not), whatever happiness anyone may seem to enjoy, 'tis a cheat, precarious, and will fail when the mind is itself, when awakened by its own vigor, or by some adventitious circumstance. Whereas whoever profits, as he may, by this poem will, as Adam in the Garden, enjoy the pleasures of sense to the utmost, with temperance and purity of heart, the truest and fullest enjoyment of them; and will moreover perceive his happiness is established upon a better foundation than that of his own impeccability, and thus possess a Paradise within far more happy than that of Eden.

O Milton, thou hast employed all thy vast treasure of wit, learning, and ability, all the beauty, energy, and propriety of words our language was capable of, all the sweetness and harmony of numbers thy musical and judicious ear furnished thee with, all the fire and beauty and sublimity of imagination peculiar to thyself, added to what could be supplied by those who have most excelled in that angelical faculty, in whatever ages or languages, all the firmness, force and dignity of mind thy virtue and piety excited in thee, or rewarded thee with. And together with all these, a genius perfectly poetical, if ever any man's was, and that regulated by a most solid judgment. All these thou hast consecrated to produce a poem, more instrúmental than any other human composition, to calm and purify the mind, and through the delightful regions of poetry to exalt and fix it to the mysteries, sublimities and practice of religion, to a state of tranquillity and happiness, the utmost mortality is capable of.

SAMUEL JOHNSON

MILTON (1779)*

IN THE examination of Milton's poetical works, I shall pay so much regard to time as to begin with his juvenile productions. For his early pieces he seems to have had a degree of fondness not very laudable: what he has once written he resolves to preserve, and gives to the publick an unfinished poem, which he broke off because he was *nothing satisfied with what he had done,* supposing his readers less nice than himself. These preludes to his future labours are in Italian, Latin, and English. Of the Italian I cannot pretend to speak as a critick; but I have heard them commended by a man well qualified to decide their merit. The Latin pieces are lusciously elegant; but the delight which they afford is rather by the exquisite imitation of the ancient writers, by the purity of the diction, and the harmony of the numbers, than by any power of invention, or vigour of sentiment. They are not all of equal value; the elegies excell the odes; and some of the exercises on Gunpowder Treason might have been spared.

The English poems, though they make no promises of *Paradise Lost,* have this evidence of genius, that they have a cast original and unborrowed. But their peculiarity is not excellence: if they differ from verses of others, they differ for the worse; for they are too often distinguished by repulsive harshness; the combination of words are new, but they are not pleasing; the rhymes and epithets seem to be laboriously sought, and violently applied.

---

* From *The Lives of the English Poets.* The last third of the Milton essay is here reprinted; the omitted portion deals with Milton's life.

That in the early parts of his life he wrote with much care appears from his manuscripts, happily preserved at Cambridge, in which many of his smaller works are found as they were first written, with the subsequent corrections. Such reliques shew how excellence is acquired; what we hope ever to do with ease, we may learn first to do with diligence.

Those who admire the beauties of this great poet, sometimes force their own judgement into false approbation of his little pieces, and prevail upon themselves to think that admirable which is only singular. All that short compositions can commonly attain is neatness and elegance. Milton never learned the art of doing little things with grace; he overlooked the milder excellence of suavity and softness; he was a *Lion* that had no skill *in dandling the Kid.*

One of the poems on which much praise has been bestowed is *Lycidas;* of which the diction is harsh, the rhymes uncertain, and the numbers unpleasing. What beauty there is, we must therefore seek in the sentiments and images. It is not to be considered as the effusion of real passion; for passion runs not after remote allusions and obscure opinions. Passion plucks no berries from the myrtle and ivy, nor calls upon Arethuse and Mincius, nor tells of rough *satyrs* and *fauns with cloven heel.* Where there is leisure for fiction there is little grief.

In this poem there is no nature, for there is no truth; there is no art, for there is nothing new. Its form is that of a pastoral, easy, vulgar, and therefore disgusting: whatever images it can supply, are long ago exhausted; and its inherent improbability always forces dissatisfaction on the mind. When Cowley tells of Hervey that they studied together, it is easy to suppose how much he must miss the companion of his labours, and the partner of his discoveries; but what image of tenderness can be excited by these lines!

> We drove a field, and both together heard
> What time the grey fly winds her sultry horn,
> Battening our flocks with the fresh dews of night.

We know that they never drove a field, and that they had no flocks to batten; and though it be allowed that the representation may be allegorical, the true meaning is so uncertain and remote, that it is never sought because it cannot be known when it is found.

Among the flocks, and copses, and flowers, appear the heathen deities; Jove and Phoebus, Neptune and Aeolus, with a long train of mythological imagery, such as a College easily supplies. Nothing can less display knowledge, or less exercise invention, than to tell how a shepherd has lost his companion, and must now feed his flocks alone, without any judge of his skill in piping; and how one god asks another god what is become of Lycidas, and how neither god can tell. He who thus grieves will excite no sympathy; he who thus praises will confer no honour.

This poem has yet a grosser fault. With these trifling fictions are mingled the most awful and sacred truths, such as ought never to be polluted with such irreverent combinations. The shepherd likewise is now a feeder of sheep, and afterwards an ecclesiastical pastor, a superintendent of a Christian flock. Such equivocations are always unskilful; but here they are indecent, and at least approach to impiety, of which, however, I believe the writer not to have been conscious.

Such is the power of reputation justly acquired, that its blaze drives away the eye from nice examination. Surely no man could have fancied that he read *Lycidas* with pleasure, had he not known its author.

Of the two pieces, *L'Allegro* and *Il Penseroso,* I believe opinion is uniform; every man that reads them, reads them with pleasure. The author's design is not, what Theobald has remarked, merely to shew how objects derived their colours from the mind, by representing the operation of the same things upon the gay and the melancholy temper, or upon the same man as he is differently disposed; but rather how, among the successive variety of appearances, every disposition of mind takes hold on those by which it may be gratified.

The *chearful* man hears the lark in the morning; the *pensive* man hears the nightingale in the evening. The *chearful* man sees the cock strut, and hears the horn and hounds echo in the wood; then walks *not unseen* to observe the glory of the rising sun, or listen to the singing milk-maid, and view the labours of the plowman and the mower; then casts his eyes about him over scenes of smiling plenty, and looks up to the distant tower, the residence of some fair inhabitant; thus he pursues rural gaiety through a day of labour or of play, and delights himself at night with the fanciful narratives of superstitious ignorance.

The *pensive* man, at one time, walks *unseen* to muse at midnight; and at another hears the sullen curfew. If the weather drives him home, he sits in a room lighted only by *glowing embers;* or by a lonely lamp outwatches the North Star, to discover the habitation of separate souls, and varies the shades of meditation, by contemplating the magnificent or pathetick scenes of tragick and epick poetry. When the morning comes, a morning gloomy with rain and wind, he walks into the dark trackless woods, falls asleep by some murmuring water, and with melancholy enthusiasm expects some dream of prognostication, or some musick played by aerial performers.

Both Mirth and Melancholy are solitary, silent inhabitants of the breast that neither receive nor transmit communication; no mention is therefore made of a philosophical friend, or a pleasant companion. The seriousness does not arise from any participation of calamity, nor the gaiety from the pleasures of the bottle.

The man of *chearfulness,* having exhausted the country, tries what *towered cities* will afford, and mingles with scenes of splendor, gay assemblies, and nuptial festivities; but he mingles a mere spectator, as, when the learned counsels of Jonson, or the wild dramas of Shakespeare, are exhibited, he attends the theatre.

The *pensive* man never loses himself in crowds, but walks the cloister, or frequents the cathedral. Milton probably had not yet forsaken the Church.

Both his characters delight in musick; but he seems to think that chearful notes would have obtained from Pluto a compleat dismission of Eurydice, of whom solemn sounds only procured a conditional release.

For the old age of Chearfulness he makes no provision; but Melancholy he conducts with great dignity to the close of life. His Chearfulness is without levity, and his Pensiveness without asperity.

Through these two poems the images are properly selected, and nicely distinguished; but the colours of the diction seem not sufficiently discriminated. I know not whether the characters are kept sufficiently apart. No mirth can, indeed, be found in his melancholy; but I am afraid that I always meet some melancholy in his mirth. They are two noble efforts of imagination.

The greatest of his juvenile performances is the *Mask of Comus;* in which may very plainly be discovered the dawn or twilight of *Paradise Lost.* Milton appears to have formed very early that system of diction, and mode of verse, which his maturer judgement approved, and from which he never endeavoured nor desired to deviate.

Nor does *Comus* afford only a specimen of his language; it exhibits likewise his power of description and his vigour of sentiment, employed in the praise and defence of virtue. A work more truly poetical is rarely found; allusions, images, and descriptive epithets, embellish almost every period with lavish decoration. As a series of lines, therefore, it may be considered as worthy of all the admiration with which the votaries have received it.

As a drama it is deficient. The action is not probable. A Masque, in those parts where supernatural intervention is admitted, must indeed be given up to all the freaks of imagination; but, so far as the action is merely human, it ought to be reasonable, which can hardly be said of the conduct of the two brothers; who, when their sister sinks with fatigue in a pathless wilderness, wander both away together in search of berries too far to find their way back, and leave a helpless Lady to all the sadness and danger of solitude. This however is a defect over-balanced by its convenience.

What deserves more reprehension is, that the prologue spoken in the wild wood by the attendant Spirit is addressed to the audience; a mode of communication so contrary to the nature of dramatick representation, that no precedents can support it.

The discourse of the Spirit is too long: an objection that may be made to almost all the following speeches: they have not the spriteliness of a dialogue animated by reciprocal contention, but seem rather declamations deliberately composed, and formally repeated, on a moral question. The auditor therefore listens as to a lecture, without passion, without anxiety.

The song of Comus has airiness and jollity; but, what may recommend Milton's morals as well as his poetry, the invitations to pleasure are so general, that they excite no distinct images of corrupt enjoyment, and take no dangerous hold on the fancy.

The following soliloquies of Comus and the Lady are elegant, but tedious. The song must owe much to the voice, if it ever can delight. At last the Brothers enter, with too much tranquillity; and when they have feared lest their sister should be in danger, and hoped that she is not in danger, the Elder makes a speech in praise of chastity, and the Younger finds how fine it is to be a philosopher.

Then descends the Spirit in form of a shepherd; and the Brother, instead of being in haste to ask his help, praises his singing, and enquires his business in that place. It is remarkable, that at this interview the Brother is taken with a short fit of rhyming. The Spirit relates that the Lady is in the power of Comus; the Brother moralises again; and the Spirit makes a long narration, of no use because it is false, and therefore unsuitable to a good Being.

In all these parts the language is poetical, and the sentiments are generous; but there is something wanting to allure attention.

The dispute between the Lady and Comus is the most animated and affecting scene of the drama, and wants nothing but a brisker reciprocation of objections and replies, to invite attention, and detain it.

The songs are vigorous, and full of imagery; but they are harsh in their diction, and not very musical in their numbers.

Throughout the whole, the figures are too bold, and the language too luxuriant for dialogue. It is a drama in the epick style, inelegantly splendid, and tediously instructive.

The *Sonnets* were written in different parts of Milton's life, upon different occasions. They deserve not any particular criticism; for of the best it can only be said, that they are not bad; and perhaps only the eighth and the twenty-first are truly entitled to this slender commendation. The fabrick of a sonnet, however adapted to the Italian language, has never succeeded in ours, which, having greater variety of termination, requires the rhymes to be often changed.

Those little pieces may be dispatched without much anxiety; a greater work calls for greater care. I am now to examine *Paradise Lost;* a poem, which, considered with respect to design, may claim the first place, and with respect to performance the second, among the productions of the human mind.

By the general consent of criticks, the first praise of genius is due to the writer of an epick poem, as it requires an assemblage of all the powers which are singly sufficient for other compositions. Poetry is the art of uniting pleasure with truth, by calling imagination to the help of reason. Epick poetry undertakes to teach the most important truths by the most pleasing precepts, and therefore relates some great event in the most affecting manner. History must supply the writer with the rudiments of narration, which he must improve and exalt by a nobler art, must animate by dramatick energy, and diversify by retrospection and anticipation; morality must teach him the exact bounds, and different shades, of vice and virtue; from policy, and the practice of life, he has to learn the discriminations of character, and the tendency of the passions, either single or combined; and physiology must supply him with illustrations and images. To put these materials to poetical use, is required an imagination capable of painting nature, and realizing fiction. Nor is he yet a poet till he has attained the whole extension of his language, distinguished all the delicacies of phrase, and all the colours of words, and learned to adjust their different sounds to all the varieties of metrical modulation.

Bossu is of opinion that the poet's first work is to find a *moral,* which his fable is afterwards to illustrate and establish. This seems to have been the process only of Milton; the moral of other poems is incidental and consequent; in Milton's only it is essential and intrinsick. His purpose was the most useful and the most arduous; *to vindicate the ways of God to man;* to shew the reasonableness of religion, and the necessity of obedience to the Divine Law.

To convey this moral, there must be a *fable,* a narration artfully constructed, so as to excite curiosity, and surprise expectation. In this part of his work, Milton must be confessed to have equalled every other poet. He has involved in his account of the Fall of Man the events which preceded, and those that were to follow it: he has interwoven the whole system of theology with such propriety, that every part appears to be necessary; and scarcely any recital is wished shorter for the sake of quickening the progress of the main action.

The subject of an epick poem is naturally an event of great importance. That of Milton is not the destruction of a city, the conduct of a colony, or the foundation of an empire. His subject is the fate of worlds, the revolutions of heaven and of earth; rebellion against the Supreme King, raised by the highest order of created beings; the overthrow of their host, and the punishment of their crime; the creation of a new race of reasonable creatures; their original happiness and innocence, their forfeiture of immortality, and their restoration to hope and peace.

Great events can be hastened or retarded only by persons of elevated dignity. Before the greatness displayed in Milton's poem, all other greatness shrinks away. The weakest of his agents are the highest and noblest of human beings, the original parents of mankind; with whose actions the elements consented; on whose rectitude, or deviation of will, depended the state of terrestrial nature, and the condition of all the future inhabitants of the globe.

Of the other agents in the poem, the chief are such as it is irreverence to name on slight occasions. The rest are lower powers;

> —— of which the least could wield
> Those elements, and arm him with the force
> Of all their regions;

powers, which only the control of Omnipotence restrains from laying creation waste, and filling the vast expanse of space with ruin and confusion. To display the motives and actions of being thus superiour, so far as human reason can examine them, or human imagination represent them, is the task which this mighty poet has undertaken and performed.

In the examination of epick poems much speculation is commonly employed upon the *characters*. The characters in the *Paradise Lost,* which admit of examination, are those of angels and of man; of angels good and evil; of man in his innocent and sinful state.

Among the angels, the virtue of Raphael is mild and placid, of easy condescension and free communication; that of Michael is regal and lofty, and, as may seem, attentive to the dignity of his own nature. Abdiel and Gabriel appear occasionally, and act as every incident requires; the solitary fidelity of Abdiel is very amiably painted.

Of the evil angels the characters are more diversified. To Satan, as Addison observes, such sentiments are given as suit *the most exalted and most depraved being.* Milton has been censured, by Clarke, for the impiety which sometimes breaks from Satan's mouth. For there are thoughts, as he justly remarks, which no observation of character can justify, because no good man would willingly permit them to pass, however transiently, through his own mind. To make Satan speak as a rebel, without any such expressions as might taint the reader's imagination, was indeed one of the great difficulties in Milton's undertaking, and I cannot but think that he has extricated himself with great happiness. There is in Satan's speeches little that can give pain to a pious ear. The language of rebellion cannot be the same with that of obedience. The malignity of Satan foams in haughtiness and obstinacy; but his expressions are commonly general, and no otherwise offensive than as they are wicked.

The other chiefs of the celestial rebellion are very judiciously discriminated in the first and second books; and the ferocious character of Moloch appears, both in the battle and the council, with exact consistency.

To Adam and to Eve are given, during their innocence, such sentiments as innocence can generate and utter. Their love is pure benevolence and mutual veneration; their repasts are without luxury, and their diligence without toil. Their addresses to their Maker have little more than the voice of admiration and gratitude. Fruition left them nothing to ask, and Innocence left them nothing to fear.

But with guilt enter distrust and discord, mutual accusation, and stubborn self-defence; they regard each other with alienated minds, and dread their Creator as the avenger of their transgression. At last they seek shelter in his mercy, soften to repentance, and melt in supplication. Both before and after the Fall, the superiority of Adam is diligently sustained.

Of the *probable* and the *marvellous,* two parts of a vulgar epick poem, which immerge the critick in deep consideration, the *Paradise Lost* requires little to be said. It contains the history of a miracle, of Creation and Redemption; it displays the power and the mercy of the Supreme Being; the probable therefore is marvellous, and the marvellous is probable. The substance of the narrative is truth; and as truth allows no choice, it is, like necessity, superior to rule. To the accidental or adventitious parts, as to every thing human, some slight exceptions may be made. But the main fabrick is immovably supported.

It is justly remarked by Addison, that this poem has, by the nature of its subject, the advantage above all others, that it is universally and perpetually interesting. All mankind will, through all ages, bear the same relation to Adam and to Eve, and must partake of that good and evil which extend to themselves.

Of the *machinery*, so called from Θεὸς ἀπὸ μηχανῆς, by which is meant the occasional interposition of supernatural power, another fertile topic of critical remarks, here is no room to speak, because every thing is done under the immediate and visible direction of Heaven; but the rule is so far observed, that no part of the action could have been accomplished by any other means.

Of *episodes*, I think there are only two, contained in Raphael's relation of the war in heaven, and Michael's prophetick account of the changes to happen in this world. Both are closely connected with the great action; one was necessary to Adam as a warning, the other as a consolation.

To the compleatness or *integrity* of the design nothing can be objected; it has distinctly and clearly what Aristotle requires, a beginning, a middle, and an end. There is perhaps no poem, of the same length, from which so little can be taken without apparent mutilation. Here are no funeral games, nor is there any long description of a shield. The short digressions at the beginning of the third, seventh, and ninth books, might doubtless be spared; but superfluities so beautiful, who would take away? or who does not wish that the author of the *Iliad* had gratified succeeding ages with a little knowledge of himself? Perhaps no passages are more frequently or more attentively read than those extrinsick paragraphs; and, since the end of poetry is pleasure, that cannot be unpoetical with which all are pleased.

The questions, whether the action of the poem be strictly

one, whether the poem can be properly termed *heroick,* and who is the hero, are raised by such readers as draw their principles of judgement rather from books than from reason. Milton, though he intituled *Paradise Lost* only a *poem,* yet calls it himself *heroick song.* Dryden, petulantly and indecently, denies the heroism of Adam, because he was overcome; but there is no reason why the hero should not be unfortunate, except established practice, since success and virtue do not go necessarily together. Cato is the hero of Lucan; but Lucan's authority will not be suffered by Quintilian to decide. However, if success be necessary, Adam's deceiver was at last crushed; Adam was restored to his Maker's favour, and therefore may securely resume his human rank.

After the scheme and fabrick of the poem, must be considered its component parts, the sentiments and the diction.

The *sentiments,* as expressive of manners, or appropriated to characters, are, for the greater part unexceptionably just.

Splendid passages, containing lessons of morality, or precepts of prudence, occur seldom. Such is the original formation of this poem, that as it admits no human manners till the Fall, it can give little assistance to human conduct. Its end is to raise the thoughts above sublunary cares or pleasures. Yet the praise of that fortitude, with which Abdiel maintained his singularity of virtue against the scorn of multitudes, may be accommodated to all times; and Raphael's reproof of Adam's curiosity after the planetary motions, with the answer returned by Adam, may be confidently opposed to any rule of life which any poet has delivered.

The thoughts which are occasionally called forth in the progress, are such as could only be produced by an imagination in the highest degree fervid and active, to which materials were supplied by incessant study and unlimited curiosity. The heat of Milton's mind might be said to sublimate his learning, to throw off into his work the spirit of science, unmingled with its grosser parts.

He had considered creation in its whole extent, and his descriptions are therefore learned. He had accustomed his imagination to unrestrained indulgence, and his conceptions therefore were extensive. The characteristick quality of his poem is sublimity. He sometimes descends to the elegant, but his element is the great. He can occasionally invest himself with grace; but his natural port is gigantick loftiness. He can please when pleasure is required; but it is his peculiar power to astonish.

He seems to have been well acquainted with his own genius, and to know what it was that Nature had bestowed upon him more bountifully than upon others; the power of displaying the vast, illuminating the splendid, enforcing the awful, darkening the gloomy, and aggravating the dreadful: he therefore chose a subject on which too much could not be said, on which he might tire his fancy without the censure of extravagance.

The appearances of nature, and the occurrences of life, did not satiate his appetite of greatness. To paint things as they are, requires a minute attention, and employs the memory rather than the fancy. Milton's delight was to sport in the wide regions of possibility; reality was a scene too narrow for his mind. He sent his faculties out upon discovery, into worlds where only imagination can travel, and delighted to form new modes of existence, and furnish sentiment and action to superior beings, to trace the counsels of hell, or accompany the choirs of heaven.

But he could not be always in other worlds: he must sometimes revisit earth, and tell of things visible and known. When he cannot raise wonder by the sublimity of his mind, he gives delight by its fertility.

Whatever be his subject, he never fails to fill the imagination. But his images and descriptions of the scenes or operations of Nature do not seem to be always copied from original form, nor to have the freshness, raciness, and energy of immediate observation. He saw Nature, as Dryden expresses it, *through the spectacles of books;* and on most occasions calls learning to his assistance. The garden of Eden brings to his mind the vale of *Enna,* where Proserpine was gathering flowers. Satan makes his way through fighting elements, like *Argo* between the *Cyanean* rocks, or *Ulysses* between the two *Sicilian* whirlpools, when he shunned *Charybdis* on the *larboard*. The mythological allusions have been justly censured, as not being always used with notice of their vanity; but they contribute variety to the narration, and produce an alternate exercise of the memory and the fancy.

His similes are less numerous, and more various, than those of his predecessors. But he does not confine himself within the limits of rigorous comparison: his great excellence is amplitude, and he expands the adventitious image beyond the dimensions which the occasion required. Thus, comparing the shield of Satan to the orb of the Moon, he crowds the imagination with the discovery of the telescope, and all the wonders which the telescope discovers.

Of his moral sentiments it is hardly praise to affirm that they excel those of all other poets; for this superiority he was indebted to his acquaintance with the sacred writings. The ancient epick poets, wanting the light of Revelation, were very unskilful teachers of virtue: their principal characters may be great, but they are not amiable. The reader may rise from their works with a greater degree of active or passive fortitude, and sometimes of prudence; but he will be able to carry away few precepts of justice, and none of mercy.

From the Italian writers it appears, that the advantages of even Christian knowledge may be possessed in vain. Ariosto's pravity is generally known; and though the *Deliverance of Jerusalem* may be considered as a sacred subject, the poet has been very sparing of moral instruction.

In Milton every line breathes sanctity of thought, and purity of manners, except when the train of the narration requires the introduction of the rebellious spirits; and even they are compelled to acknowledge their subjection to God, in such a manner as excites reverence, and confirms piety.

Of human beings there are but two; but those two are the parents of mankind, venerable before their fall for dignity and innocence, and amiable after it for repentance and submission. In their first state their affection is tender without weakness, and their piety sublime without presumption. When they have sinned, they shew how discord begins in mutual frailty, and how it ought to cease in mutual forbearance; how confidence of the divine favour is forfeited by sin, and how hope of pardon may be obtained by penitence and prayer. A state of innocence we can only conceive, if indeed, in our present misery, it be possible to conceive it; but the sentiments and worship proper to a fallen and offending being, we have all to learn, as we have all to practise.

The poet, whatever be done, is always great. Our progenitors, in their first state, conversed with angels, even when folly and sin had degraded them, they had not in their humiliation *the port of mean suitors;* and they rise again to reverential regard, when we find that their prayers were heard.

As human passions did not enter the world before the Fall, there is in the *Paradise Lost* little opportunity for the pathetick; but what little there is has not been lost. That passion which is peculiar to rational nature, the anguish arising from the consciousness of transgression, and the horrours attending the sense of the Divine Displeasure, are very justly described and forcibly impressed. But the passions are moved only on one occasion; sublimity is the general and prevailing quality in this poem; sublimity variously modified, sometimes descriptive, sometimes argumentative.

The defects and faults of *Paradise Lost,* for faults and defects every work of man must have, it is the business of impartial criticism to discover. As, in displaying the excellence of Milton, I have not made long quotations, because of selecting beauties there had been no end, I shall in the same general manner mention that which seems to deserve censure; for what Englishman can take delight in transcribing passages, which, if they lessen the reputation of Milton, diminish in some degree the honour of our country?

The generality of my scheme does not admit the frequent notice of verbal inaccuracies; which Bentley, perhaps better skilled in grammar than poetry, has often found, though he sometimes made them, and which he imputed to the obtrusions of a reviser whom the author's blindness obliged him to employ. A supposition rash and groundless, if he thought it true; and vile and pernicious, if, as is said, he in private allowed it to be false.

The plan of *Paradise Lost* has this inconvenience, that it comprises neither human actions nor human manners. The man and woman who act and suffer, are in a state which no other man or woman can ever know. The reader finds no transaction in which he can be engaged; beholds no condition in which he can by any effort of imagination place himself; he has, therefore, little natural curiosity or sympathy.

We all, indeed, feel the effects of Adam's disobedience; we all sin like Adam, and like him must all bewail our offences; we have restless and insidious enemies in the fallen angels, and in the blessed spirits we have guardians and friends; in the Redemption of mankind we hope to be included; in the description of heaven and hell we are surely interested, as we are all to reside hereafter either in the regions of horrour or of bliss.

But these truths are too important to be new; they have been taught to our infancy; they have mingled with our solitary thoughts and familiar conversation, and are habitually interwoven with the whole texture of life. Being therefore not new, they raise no unaccustomed emotion in the mind; what we knew before, we cannot learn; what is not unexpected, cannot surprise.

Of the ideas suggested by these awful scenes, from some we recede with reverence, except when stated hours require their association; and from others we shrink with horrour, or admit them only as salutary inflictions, as counterpoises to our interests and passions. Such images rather obstruct the career of fancy than incite it.

Pleasure and terrour are indeed the genuine sources of poetry; but poetical pleasure must be such as human imagination can at least conceive, and poetical terrour such as human strength and fortitude may combat. The good and evil of Eternity are too ponderous for the wings of wit; the mind sinks under them in passive helplessness, content with calm belief and humble adoration.

Known truths, however, may take a different appearance, and be conveyed to the mind by a new train of intermediate images. This Milton has undertaken, and performed with pregnancy and vigour of mind peculiar to himself. Whoever considers the few radical positions which the Scriptures afforded him, will wonder by what energetick operation he expanded them to such extent, and ramified them to so much variety, restrained as he was by religious reverence from licentiousness of fiction.

Here is a full display of the united force of study and genius; of a great accumulation of materials, with judgement to digest, and fancy to combine them: Milton was able to select from nature, or from story, from ancient fable, or from modern science, whatever could illustrate or adorn his thoughts. An accumulation of knowledge impregnated his mind, fermented by study, and exalted by imagination.

It has been therefore said, without an indecent hyperbole, by one of his encomiasts, that in reading *Paradise Lost* we read a book of universal knowledge.

But original deficience cannot be supplied. The want of human interest is always felt. *Paradise Lost* is one of the books which the reader admires and lays down, and forgets to take up again. None ever wished it longer than it is. Its perusal is a duty rather than a pleasure. We read Milton for instruction, retire harassed and overburdened, and look elsewhere for recreation; we desert our master, and seek for companions.

Another inconvenience of Milton's design is, that it requires the description of what cannot be described, the agency of spirits. He saw that immateriality supplied no images, and that he could not show angels acting but by instruments of action; he therefore invested them with form and matter. This, being necessary, was therefore defensible; and he should have secured the consistency of his system, by keeping immateriality out of sight, and enticing his reader to drop it from his thoughts. But he has unhappily perplexed his poetry with his philosophy. His infernal and celestial powers are sometimes pure spirit, and sometimes animated body. When Satan walks with his lance upon the *burning marle,* he has a body; when, in his passage between hell and the new world, he is in danger of sinking in the vacuity, and is supported by a gust of rising vapours, he has a body; when he animates the toad, he seems to be mere spirit, that can penetrate matter at pleasure; when he *starts up in his own shape,* he has at least a determined form; and when he is brought before Gabriel, he has *a spear and a shield,* which he had the power of hiding in the toad, though the arms of the contending angels are evidently material.

The vulgar inhabitants of Pandaemonium, being *incorporeal spirits,* are *at large, though without number,* in a limited space; yet in the battle, when they were overwhelmed by mountains, their armour hurt them, *crushed in upon their substance, now grown gross by sinning.* This likewise happened to the uncorrupted angels, who were overthrown the *sooner for their arms, for unarmed they might easily as spirits have evaded by contraction or remove.* Even as spirits they are hardly spiritual; for *contraction* and *remove* are images of matter; but if they could have escaped without their armour, they might have escaped from it, and left only the empty cover to be battered. Uriel, when he rides on a sun-beam, is material; Satan is material when he is afraid of the prowess of Adam.

The confusion of spirit and matter which pervades the whole narration of the war of heaven fills it with incongruity; and the book, in which it is related, is, I believe, the favourite of children, and gradually neglected as knowledge is increased.

After the operation of immaterial agents, which cannot be explained, may be considered that of allegorical persons, which have no real existence. To exalt causes into agents, to invest abstract ideas with form, and animate them with activity, has always been the right of poetry. But such airy beings are, for the most part, suffered only to do their natural office, and retire. Thus Fame tells a tale, and Victory hovers over a general, or perches on a standard; but Fame and Victory can do no more. To give them any real employment, or ascribe to them any material agency, is to make them allegorical no longer, but to shock the mind by ascribing effects to nonentity. In the *Prometheus* of Aeschylus, we see *Violence* and *Strength,* and in the *Alcestis* of Euripides, we see *Death,* brough upon the stage, all as active persons of the drama; but no precedents can justify absurdity.

Milton's allegory of Sin and Death is undoubtedly faulty. Sin is indeed the mother of Death, and may be allowed to be the portress of hell; but when they stop the journey of Satan, a journey described as real, and when Death offers him battle, the allegory is broken. That Sin and Death should have shewn the way to hell, might have been allowed; but they cannot facilitate the passage by building a bridge, because the difficulty of Satan's passage is described as real and sensible, and the bridge ought to be only figurative. The hell assigned to the rebellious spirits is described as not less local than the residence of man. It is placed in some distant part of space, separated from the regions of harmony and order by a chaotick waste and an unoccupied vacuity; but *Sin* and *Death* worked up a *mole of aggravated soil,* cemented with *asphaltus;* a work too bulky for ideal architects.

This unskilful allegory appears to me one of the greatest faults of the poem; and to this there was no temptation, but the author's opinion of its beauty.

To the conduct of the narrative some objections may be made. Satan is with great expectation brought before Gabriel in Paradise, and is suffered to go away unmolested. The creation of man is represented as the consequence of the vacuity left in heaven by the expulsion of the rebels; yet Satan mentions it as a report *rife in heaven* before his departure.

To find sentiments for the state of innocence, was very difficult; and something of anticipation perhaps is now and then discovered. Adam's discourse of dreams seems not to be the speculation of a new-created being. I know not whether his answer to the angel's reproof for curiosity does not want something of propriety: it is the speech of a man acquainted with many other men. Some philosophical notions, especially when the philosophy is false, might have been better omitted. The angel, in a comparison, speaks of *timorous deer,* before deer were yet timorous, and before Adam could understand the comparison.

Dryden remarks, that Milton has some flats among his elevations. This is only to say, that all the parts are not equal. In every work, one part must be for the sake of others; a palace must have passages; a poem must have transitions. It is no more to be required that wit should always be blazing, than that the sun should always stand at noon. In a great work there is a vicissitude of luminous and opaque parts, as there is in the world a succession of day and night. Milton, when he has expatiated in the sky, may be allowed sometimes to revisit earth; for what other author ever soared so high, or sustained his flight so long?

Milton, being well versed in the Italian poets, appears to have borrowed often from them; and, as every man catches something from his companions, his desire of imitating Ariosto's levity has disgraced his work with the *Paradise of Fools;* a fiction not in itself ill-imagined, but too ludicrous for its place.

His play on words, in which he delights too often; his equivocations, which Bentley endeavours to defend by the example of the ancients; his unnecessary and ungraceful use of terms of art; it is not necessary to mention, because they are easily remarked, and generally censured, and at last bear so little proportion to the whole, that they scarcely deserve the attention of a critick.

Such are the faults of that wonderful performance *Paradise Lost;* which he who can put in balance with its beauties must be considered not as nice but as dull, as less to be censured for want of candour, than pitied for want of sensibility.

Of *Paradise Regained,* the general judgement seems now to

be right, that it is in many parts elegant, and every-where instructive. It was not to be supposed that the writer of *Paradise Lost* could ever write without great effusions of fancy, and exalted precepts of wisdom. The basis of *Paradise Regained* is narrow; a dialogue without action can never please like an union of the narrative and dramatick powers. Had this poem been written not by Milton, but by some imitator, it would have claimed and received universal praise.

If *Paradise Regained* has been too much depreciated, *Samson Agonistes* has in requital been too much admired. It could only be by long prejudice, and the bigotry of learning, that Milton could prefer the ancient tragedies, with their encumbrance of a chorus, to the exhibitions of the French and English stages; and it is only by a blind confidence in the reputation of Milton, that a drama can be praised in which the intermediate parts have neither cause nor consequence, neither hasten nor retard the catastrophe.

In this tragedy are however many particular beauties, many just sentiments and striking lines; but it wants that power of attracting the attention which a well-connected plan produces.

Milton would not have excelled in dramatick writing; he knew human nature only in the gross, and had never studied the shades of character, nor the combinations of concurring, or the perplexity of contending passions. He had read much, and knew what books could teach; but had mingled little in the world, and was deficient in the knowledge which experience must confer.

Through all his greater works there prevails an uniform peculiarity of *Diction,* a mode and cast of expression which bears little resemblance to that of any former writer, and which is so far removed from common use, that an unlearned reader, when he first opens his book, finds himself surprised by a new language.

This novelty has been, by those who can find nothing wrong in Milton, imputed to his laborious endeavours after words suitable to the grandeur of his ideas. *Our language,* says Addison, *sunk under him.* But the truth is, that, both in prose and verse, he had formed his style by a perverse and pedantick principle. He was desirous to use English words with a foreign idiom. This in all his prose is discovered and condemned; for there judgement operates freely, neither softened by the beauty, nor awed by the dignity of his thoughts; but such is the power of his poetry, that his call is obeyed without resistance, the reader feels himself in captivity to a higher and a nobler mind, and criticism sinks in admiration.

Milton's style was not modified by his subject: what is shown with greater extent in *Paradise Lost,* may be found in *Comus.* One source of his peculiarity was his familiarity with the Tuscan poets: the disposition of his words is, I think, frequently Italian; perhaps sometimes combined with other tongues. Of him, at last, may be said what Jonson says of Spenser, that *he wrote no language,* but has formed what Butler calls a *Babylonish Dialect,* in itself harsh and barbarous, but made by exalted genius and extensive learning, the vehicle of so much instruction and so much pleasure, that, like other lovers, we find grace in its deformity.

Whatever be the faults of his diction, he cannot want the praise of copiousness and variety: he was master of his language in its full extent; and has selected the melodious words with such diligence, that from his book alone the Art of English Poetry might be learned.

After his diction, something must be said of his *versification. The measure,* he says, *is the English heroick verse without rhyme.* Of this mode he had many examples among the Italians, and some in his own country. The Earl of Surrey is said to have translated one of Virgil's books without rhyme; and, besides our tragedies, a few short poems had appeared in blank verse; particularly one tending to reconcile the nation to Raleigh's wild attempt upon Guiana, and probably written by Raleigh himself. These petty performances cannot be supposed to have much influenced Milton, who more probably took his hint from Trisino's *Italia Liberata;* and, finding blank verse easier than rhyme, was desirous of persuading himself that it is better.

Rhyme, he says, and says truly, *is no necessary adjunct of true poetry.* But perhaps, of poetry as a mental operation, metre or musick is no necessary adjunct: it is however by the musick of metre that poetry has been discriminated in all languages; and in languages melodiously constructed with a due proportion of long and short syllables, metre is sufficient. But one language cannot communicate its rules to another: where metre is scanty and imperfect, some help is necessary. The musick of the English heroick line strikes the ear so faintly that it is easily lost, unless all the syllables of every line co-operate together: this co-operation can be only obtained by the preservation of every verse unmingled with another, as a distinct system of sounds; and this distinctness is obtained and preserved by the artifice of rhyme. The variety of pauses, so much boasted by the lovers of blank verse, changes the measures of an English poet to the periods of a declaimer; and there are only a few skilful and happy readers of Milton, who enable their audience to perceive where the lines end or begin. *Blank verse,* said an ingenious critick, *seems to be verse only to the eye.*

Poetry may subsist without rhyme, but English poetry will not often please; nor can rhyme ever be safely spared but where the subject is able to support itself. Blank verse makes some approach to that which is called the *lapidary style;* has neither the easiness of prose, nor the melody of numbers, and therefore tires by long continuance. Of the Italian writers without rhyme, whom Milton alleges as precedents, not one is popular; what reason could urge in its defence, has been confuted by the ear.

But, whatever be the advantage of rhyme, I cannot prevail on myself to wish that Milton had been a rhymer; for I cannot wish his work to be other than it is; yet, like other heroes, he is to be admired rather than imitated. He that thinks himself capable of astonishing, may write blank verse; but those that hope only to please, must condescend to rhyme.

The highest praise of genius is original invention. Milton

cannot be said to have contrived the structure of an epick poem, and therefore owes reverence to that vigour and amplitude of mind to which all generations must be indebted for the art of poetical narration, for the texture of the fable, the variation of incidents, the interposition of dialogue, and all the stratagems that surprise and enchain attention. But, of all the borrowers from Homer, Milton is perhaps the least indebted. He was naturally a thinker for himself, confident of his own abilities, and disdainful of help or hindrance: he did not refuse admission to the thought or images of his predecessors, but he did not seek them. From his contemporaries he neither courted nor received support; there is in his writings nothing by which the pride of other authors might be gratified, or favour gained; no exchange of praise, nor solicitation of support. His great works were performed under discountenance, and in blindness, but difficulties vanished at his touch; he was born for whatever is arduous; and his work is not the greatest of heroick poems, only because it is not the first.

SAMUEL TAYLOR COLERIDGE

MILTON (1818)*

I_{F WE} divide the period from the accession of Elizabeth to
the Protectorate of Cromwell into two unequal portions, the
first ending with the death of James I, the other comprehending the reign of Charles and the brief glories of the Republic,
we are forcibly struck with a difference in the character of the
illustrious actors, by whom each period is rendered severally
memorable. Or rather, the difference in the characters of the
great men in each period, leads us to make this division. Eminent as the intellectual powers were that were displayed in
both; yet in the number of great men, in the various sorts of
excellence, and not merely in the variety but almost diversity
of talents united in the same individual, the age of Charles falls
short of its predecessor; and the stars of the Parliament, keen as
their radiance was, in fulness and richness of lustre, yield to the
constellation at the court of Elizabeth;—which can only be
paralleled by Greece in her brightest moment, when the titles
of the poet, the philosopher, the historian, the statesman and
the general not seldom formed a garland round the same head,
as in the instances of our Sidneys and Raleighs. But then, on
the other hand, there was a vehemence of will, an enthusiasm
of principle, a depth and an earnestness of spirit, which the
charms of individual fame and personal aggrandisement could
not pacify,—an aspiration after reality, permanence, and general good,—in short, a moral grandeur in the latter period,
with which the low intrigues, Machiavellic maxims, and selfish

---

* From Lecture X, delivered in 1818, printed in *Literary Remains* (1836).

and servile ambition of the former, stand in painful contrast.

The causes of this it belongs not to the present occasion to detail at length; but a mere allusion to the quick succession of revolutions in religion, breeding a political indifference in the mass of men to religion itself, the enormous increase of the royal power in consequence of the humiliation of the nobility and the clergy—the transference of the papal authority to the crown,—the unfixed state of Elizabeth's own opinions, whose inclinations were as popish as her interests were protestant—the controversial extravagance and practical imbecility of her successor—will help to explain the former period; and the persecutions that had given a life and soul-interest to the disputes so imprudently fostered by James,—the ardour of a conscious increase of power in the commons, and the greater austerity of manners and maxims, the natural product and most formidable weapon of religious disputation, not merely in conjunction, but in closest combination, with newly awakened political and republican zeal, these perhaps account for the character of the latter aera.

In the close of the former period, and during the bloom of the latter, the poet Milton was educated and formed; and he survived the latter, and all the fond hopes and aspirations which had been its life; and so in evil days, standing as the representative of the combined excellence of both periods, he produced the *Paradise Lost* as by an after-throe of nature. "There are some persons (observes a divine, a contemporary of Milton's) of whom the grace of God takes early hold, and the good spirit inhabiting them, carries them on in an even constancy through innocence into virtue, their Christianity bearing equal date with their manhood, and reason and religion, like warp and woof, running together, make up one web of a wise and exemplary life. This (he adds) is a most happy case, wherever it happens; for, besides that there is no sweeter or more lovely thing on earth than the early buds of piety, which drew from our Saviour signal affection to the beloved disciple, it is better to have no wound than to experience the most sovereign balsam, which, if it work a cure, yet usually leaves a scar behind." Although it was and is my intention to defer the consideration of Milton's own character to the conclusion of this Lecture, yet I could not prevail on myself to approach the *Paradise Lost* without impressing on your minds the conditions under which such a work was in fact producible at all, the original genius having been assumed as the immediate agent and efficient cause; and these conditions I find in the character of the times and in his own character. The age in which the foundations of his mind were laid, was congenial to it as one golden aera of profound erudition and individual genius;—that in which the superstructure was carried up, was no less favourable to it by a sternness of discipline and a show of self-control, highly flattering to the imaginative dignity of an heir of fame, and which won Milton over from the dear-loved delights of academic groves and cathedral aisles to the anti-prelatic party. It acted on him, too, no doubt, and modified his studies by a controversial spirit, (his presentation of God is tinted with it)—a spirit not less busy indeed in political than in theological and ecclesiastical dispute, but carrying on the former almost always, more or less, in the guise of the latter. And so far as Pope's censure of our poet,—that he makes God the Father a school divine—is just, we must attribute it to the character of his age, from which the men of genius, who escaped, escaped by a worse disease, the licentious indifference of a Frenchified court.

Such was the *nidus* or soil, which constituted, in the strict sense of the word, the circumstances of Milton's mind. In his mind itself there were purity and piety absolute; an imagination to which neither the past nor the present were interesting, except as far as they called forth and enlivened the great ideal, in which and for which he lived; a keen love of truth, which, after many weary pursuits, found a harbour in a sublime listening to the still voice in his own spirit, and as keen a love of his country, which, after a disappointment still more depressive, expanded and soared into a love of man as a probationer of immortality. These were, these alone could be, the conditions under which such a work as the *Paradise Lost* could be conceived and accomplished. By a life-long study Milton had known—

> What was of use to know,
> What best to say could say, to do had done.
> His actions to his words agreed, his words
> To his large heart gave utterance due, his heart
> Contain'd of good, wise, fair, the perfect shape;

and he left the imperishable total, as a bequest to the ages coming, in the *Paradise Lost.*

Difficult as I shall find it to turn over these leaves without catching some passage, which would tempt me to stop, I propose to consider, 1st, the general plan and arrangement of the work;—2ndly, the subject with its difficulties and advantages; —3rdly, the poet's object, the spirit in the letter, the ἐνθύμιον ἐν μύθῳ, the true school-divinity; and lastly, the characteristic excellencies of the poem, in what they consist, and by what means they were produced.

1. As to the plan and ordonnance of the Poem.

Compare it with the *Iliad,* many of the books of which might change places without any injury to the thread of the story. Indeed, I doubt the original existence of the *Iliad* as one poem; it seems more probable that it was put together about the time of the Pisistratidae. The *Iliad*—and, more or less, all epic poems, the subjects of which are taken from history—have no rounded conclusion; they remain, after all, but single chapters from the volume of history, although they are ornamental chapters. Consider the exquisite simplicity of the *Paradise Lost.* It and it alone really possesses a beginning, a middle, and an end; it has the totality of the poem as distinguished from the *ab ovo* birth and parentage, or straight line, of history.

2. As to the subject.

In Homer, the supposed importance of the subject, as the first effort of confederated Greece, is an after-thought of the critics; and the interest, such as it is, derived from the events themselves, as distinguished from the manner of representing them, is very languid to all but Greeks. It is a Greek poem. The superiority of the *Paradise Lost* is obvious in this respect, that the interest transcends the limits of a nation. But we do not generally dwell on this excellence of the *Paradise Lost,* because it seems attributable to Christianity itself;—yet in fact the interest is wider than Christendom, and comprehends the Jewish and Mohammedan worlds;—nay, still further, inasmuch as it represents the origin of evil, and the combat of evil and good, it contains matter of deep interest to all mankind, as forming the basis of all religion, and the true occasion of all philosophy whatsoever.

The FALL of Man is the subject; Satan is the cause; man's blissful state the immediate object of his enmity and attack; man is warned by an angel who gives him an account of all that was requisite to be known, to make the warning at once intelligible and awful; then the temptation ensues, and the Fall; then the immediate sensible consequence; then the consolation, wherein an angel presents a vision of the history of men with the ultimate triumph of the Redeemer. Nothing is touched in this vision but what is of general interest in religion; anything else would have been improper.

The inferiority of Klopstock's *Messiah* is inexpressible. I admit the prerogative of poetic feeling, and poetic faith; but I cannot suspend the judgment even for a moment. A poem may in one sense be a dream, but it must be a waking dream. In Milton you have a religious faith combined with the moral nature; it is an efflux; you go along with it. In Klopstock there is a wilfulness; he makes things so and so. The feigned speeches and events in the *Messiah* shock us like falsehoods; but nothing of that sort is felt in the *Paradise Lost,* in which no particulars, at least very few indeed, are touched which can come into collision or juxtaposition with recorded matter.

But notwithstanding the advantages in Milton's subject, there were concomitant insuperable difficulties, and Milton has exhibited marvellous skill in keeping most of them out of sight. High poetry is the translation of reality into the ideal under the predicament of succession of time only. The poet is an historian, upon condition of moral power being the only force in the universe. The very grandeur of his subject ministered a difficulty to Milton. The statement of a being of high intellect, warring against the supreme Being, seems to contradict the idea of a supreme Being. Milton precludes our feeling this, as much as possible, by keeping the peculiar attributes of divinity less in sight, making them to a certain extent allegorical only. Again, poetry implies the language of excitement; yet how to reconcile such language with God? Hence Milton confines the poetic passion in God's speeches to the language of scripture; and once only allows the *passio vera*, or *quasihumana* to appear, in the passage, where the Father contemplates his own likeness in the Son before the battle:—

> Go then, thou Mightiest, in thy Father's might,
> Ascend my chariot, guide the rapid wheels
> That shake Heaven's basis, bring forth all my war,
> My bow and thunder; my almighty arms
> Gird on, and sword upon thy puissant thigh;
> Pursue these sons of darkness, drive them out
> From all Heaven's bounds into the utter deep:
> There let them learn, as likes them, to despise
> God and Messiah his anointed king.
>
> B. VI. v. 710.

3. As to Milton's object:—

It was to justify the ways of God to man! The controversial spirit observable in many parts of the poem, especially in God's speeches, is immediately attributable to the great controversy of that age, the origination of evil. The Arminians considered it a mere calamity. The Calvinists took away all human will. Milton asserted the will, but declared for the enslavement of the will out of an act of the will itself. There are three powers in us, which distinguish us from the beasts that perish;—1, reason; 2, the power of viewing universal truth; and 3, the power of contracting universal truth into particulars. Religion is the will in the reason, and love in the will.

The character of Satan is pride and sensual indulgence, finding in self the sole motive of action. It is the character so often seen *in little* on the political stage. It exhibits all the restlessness, temerity, and cunning which have marked the mighty hunters of mankind from Nimrod to Napoleon. The common fascination of men is, that these great men, as they are called, must act from some great motive. Milton has carefully marked in his Satan the intense selfishness, the alcohol of egotism, which would rather reign in hell than serve in heaven. To place this lust of self in opposition to denial of self or duty, and to show what exertions it would make, and what pains endure to accomplish its end, is Milton's particular object in the character of Satan. But around this character he has thrown a singularity of daring, a grandeur of sufferance, and a ruined splendour, which constitute the very height of poetic sublimity.

Lastly, as to the execution:—

The language and versification of the *Paradise Lost* are peculiar in being so much more necessarily correspondent to each than those in any other poem or poet. The connexion of the sentences and the position of the words are exquisitely artificial; but the position is rather according to the logic of passion or universal logic, than to the logic of grammar. Milton attempted to make the English language obey the logic of passion as perfectly as the Greek and Latin. Hence the occasional harshness in the construction.

Sublimity is the pre-eminent characteristic of the *Paradise Lost*. It is not an arithmetical sublime like Klopstock's, whose rule always is to treat what we might think large as contemptibly small. Klopstock mistakes bigness for greatness. There is a greatness arising from images of effort and daring, and also from those of moral endurance; in Milton both are united. The fallen angels are human passions, invested with a dramatic reality.

The apostrophe to light at the commencement of the third book is particularly beautiful as an intermediate link between Hell and Heaven; observe, how the second and third books support the subjective character of the poem. In all modern poetry in Christendom there is an under consciousness of a sinful nature, a fleeting away of external things, the mind or subject greater than the object, the reflective character predominant. In the *Paradise Lost* the sublimest parts are the revelations of Milton's own mind, producing itself and evolving its own greatness; and this is so truly so, that when that which is merely entertaining for its objective beauty is introduced, it at first seems a discord.

In the description of Paradise itself you have Milton's sunny side as a man; here his descriptive powers are exercised to the utmost, and he draws deep upon his Italian resources. In the description of Eve, and throughout this part of the poem, the poet is predominant over the theologian. Dress is the symbol of the Fall, but the mark of intellect; and the metaphysics of dress are, the hiding what is not symbolic and displaying by discrimination what is. The love of Adam and Eve in Paradise is of the highest merit—not phantomatic, and yet removed from every thing degrading. It is the sentiment of one rational being towards another made tender by a specific difference in that which is essentially the same in both; it is a union of opposites, a giving and receiving mutually of the permanent in either, a completion of each in the other.

Milton is not a picturesque, but a musical, poet; although he has this merit that the object chosen by him for any particular foreground always remains prominent to the end, enriched, but not incumbered, by the opulence of descriptive details furnished by an exhaustless imagination. I wish the *Paradise Lost* were more carefully read and studied than I can see any ground for believing it is, especially those parts which, from the habit of always looking for a story in poetry, are scarcely read at all—as for example, Adam's vision of future events in the 11th and 12th books. No one can rise from the perusal of this immortal poem without a deep sense of the grandeur and the purity of Milton's soul, or without feeling how susceptible of domestic enjoyments he really was, notwithstanding the discomforts which actually resulted from an apparently unhappy choice in marriage. He was, as every truly great poet has ever been, a good man; but finding it impossible to realize his own aspirations, either in religion, or politics, or society, he gave up his heart to the living spirit and light within him, and avenged himself on the world by enriching it with this record of his own transcendent ideal.

WILLIAM HAZLITT

ON SHAKSPEARE AND MILTON (1818)*

SHAKSPEARE discovers in his writings little religious enthusiasm, and an indifference to personal reputation; he had none of the bigotry of his age, and his political prejudices were not very strong. In these respects, as well as in every other, he formed a direct contrast to Milton. Milton's works are a perpetual invocation to the Muses; a hymn to Fame. He had his thoughts constantly fixed on the contemplation of the Hebrew theocracy, and of a perfect commonwealth; and he seized the pen with a hand just warm from the touch of the ark of faith. His religious zeal infused its character into his imagination; so that he devotes himself with the same sense of duty to the cultivation of his genius, as he did to the exercise of virtue, or the good of his country. The spirit of the poet, the patriot, and the prophet, vied with each other in his breast. His mind appears to have held equal communion with the inspired writers, and with the bards and sages of ancient Greece and Rome;—

> Blind Thamyris, and blind Maeonides,
> And Tiresias, and Phineus, prophets old.

He had a high standard, with which he was always comparing himself, nothing short of which could satisfy his jealous ambition. He thought of nobler forms and nobler things than those he found about him. He lived apart, in the solitude of his own thoughts, carefully excluding from his mind whatever might

---

* The last half of Lecture III (omitting the part on Shakespeare), delivered and published in 1818.

distract its purposes or alloy its purity, or damp its zeal. "With darkness and with dangers compassed round," he had the mighty models of antiquity always present to his thoughts, and determined to raise a monument of equal height and glory, "piling up every stone of lustre from the brook," for the delight and wonder of posterity. He had girded himself up, and as it were, sanctified his genius to this service from his youth. "For after," he says, "I had from my first years, by the ceaseless diligence and care of my father, been exercised to the tongues, and some sciences as my age could suffer, by sundry masters and teachers, it was found that whether aught was imposed upon me by them, or betaken to of my own choice, the style by certain vital signs it had, was likely to live; but much latelier, in the private academies of Italy, perceiving that some trifles which I had in memory, composed at under twenty or thereabout, met with acceptance above what was looked for; I began thus far to assent both to them and divers of my friends here at home, and not less to an inward prompting which now grew daily upon me, that by labour and intense study (which I take to be my portion in this life), joined with the strong propensity of nature, I might perhaps leave something so written to after-times as they should not willingly let it die. The accomplishment of these intentions, which have lived within me ever since I could conceive myself anything worth to my country, lies not but in a power above man's to promise; but that none hath by more studious ways endeavoured, and with more unwearied spirit that none shall, that I dare almost aver of myself, as far as life and free leisure will extend. Neither do I think it shame to convenant with any knowing reader, that for some few years yet, I may go on trust with him toward the payment of what I am now indebted, as being a work not to be raised from the heat of youth or the vapours of wine; like that which flows at waste from the pen of some vulgar amourist, or the trencher fury of a rhyming parasite, nor to be obtained by the invocation of Dame Memory and her Siren daughters, but by devout prayer to that eternal spirit who can enrich with

all utterance and knowledge, and sends out his Seraphim with
the hallowed fire of his altar, to touch and purify the lips of
whom he pleases: to this must be added industrious and select
reading, steady observation, and insight into all seemly and
generous arts and affairs. Although it nothing content me to
have disclosed thus much beforehand; but that I trust hereby
to make it manifest with what small willingness I endure to
interrupt the pursuit of no less hopes than these, and leave a
calm and pleasing solitariness, fed with cheerful and confident
thoughts, to embark in a troubled sea of noises and hoarse
disputes, from beholding the bright countenance of truth in
the quiet and still air of delightful studies."

So that of Spenser:

> The noble heart that harbours virtuous thought,
>   And is with child of glorious great intent,
> Can never rest until it forth have brought
>   The eternal brood of glory excellent.

Milton, therefore, did not write from casual impulse, but
after a severe examination of his own strength, and with a
resolution to leave nothing undone which it was in his power
to do. He always labours, and almost always succeeds. He strives
hard to say the finest things in the world, and he does say them.
He adorns and dignifies his subject to the utmost: he surrounds
it with every possible association of beauty or grandeur, whether
moral, intellectual, or physical. He refines on his descriptions
of beauty; loading sweets on sweets, till the sense aches at them;
and raises his images of terror to a gigantic elevation, that
"makes Ossa like a wart." In Milton, there is always an appearance of effort: in Shakspeare, scarcely any.

Milton has borrowed more than any other writer, and exhausted every source of imitation, sacred or profane; yet he is
perfectly distinct from every other writer. He is a writer of
centos, and yet in originality scarcely inferior to Homer. The
power of his mind is stamped on every line. The fervour of his

imagination melts down and renders malleable, as in a furnace, the most contradictory materials. In reading his works, we feel ourselves under the influence of a mighty intellect, that the nearer it approaches to others, becomes more distinct from them. The quantity of art in him shews the strength of his genius: the weight of his intellectual obligations would have oppressed any other writer. Milton's learning has the effect of intuition. He describes objects, of which he could only have read in books, with the vividness of actual observation. His imagination has the force of nature. He makes words tell as pictures.

> Him followed Rimmon, whose delightful seat
> Was fair Damascus, on the fertile banks
> Of Abbana and Pharphar, lucid streams.

The word *lucid* here gives to the idea all the sparkling effect of the most perfect landscape.

And again:

> As when a vulture on Imaus bred,
> Whose snowy ridge the roving Tartar bounds,
> Dislodging from a region scarce of prey,
> To gorge the flesh of lambs and yeanling kids
> On hills where flocks are fed, flies towards the springs
> Of Ganges or Hydaspes, Indian streams;
> But in his way lights on the barren plains
> Of Sericana, where Chineses drive
> With sails and wind their cany waggons light.

If Milton had taken a journey for the express purpose, he could not have described this scenery and mode of life better. Such passages are like demonstrations of natural history. Instances might be multiplied without end.

We might be tempted to suppose that the vividness with which he describes visible objects, was owing to their having acquired an unusual degree of strength in his mind, after the privation of his sight; but we find the same palpableness and truth in the descriptions which occur in his early poems. In *Lycidas* he speaks of "the great vision of the guarded mount," with that preternatural weight of impression with which it would present itself suddenly to "the pilot of some small night-foundered skiff": and the lines in the *Penseroso*, describing "the wandering moon,"

> Riding near her highest noon,
> Like one that had been led astray
> Through the heaven's wide pathless way,

are as if he had gazed himself blind in looking at her. There is also the same depth of impression in his descriptions of the objects of all the different senses, whether colours, or sounds, or smells—the same absorption of his mind in whatever engaged his attention at the time. It has been indeed objected to Milton, by a common perversity of criticism, that his ideas were musical rather than picturesque, as if because they were in the highest degree musical, they must be (to keep the sage critical balance even, and to allow no one man to possess two qualities at the same time) proportionably deficient in other respects. But Milton's poetry is not cast in any such narrow, commonplace mould; it is not so barren of resources. His worship of the Muse was not so simple or confined. A sound arises "like a steam of rich distilled perfumes"; we hear the pealing organ, but the incense on the altars is also there, and the statues of the gods are ranged around! The ear indeed predominates over the eye, because it is more immediately affected, and because the language of music blends more immediately with, and forms a more natural accompaniment to, the variable and indefinite associations of ideas conveyed by words. But where the associations of the imagination are not the principal thing, the individual object is given by Milton with equal force and beauty. The strongest and best proof of this, as a characteristic power of his mind, is, that the persons of Adam and Eve, of Satan, &c. are always accompanied, in our imagination, with the grandeur of the naked figure; they convey to us the ideas of sculpture. As an instance take the following:

> —————————He soon
> Saw within ken a glorious Angel stand,
> The same whom John saw also in the sun:
> His back was turned, but not his brightness hid;
> Of beaming sunny rays a golden tiar
> Circled his head, nor less his locks behind
> Illustrious on his shoulders fledge with wings
> Lay waving round; on some great charge employ'd
> He seem'd, or fix'd in cogitation deep.
> Glad was the spirit impure, as now in hope
> To find who might direct his wand'ring flight
> To Paradise, the happy seat of man,
> His journey's end, and our beginning woe.
> But first he casts to change his proper shape,
> Which else might work him danger or delay
> And now a stripling cherub he appears,
> Not of the prime, yet such as in his face
> Youth smiled celestial, and to every limb
> Suitable grace diffus'd, so well he feign'd:
> Under a coronet his flowing hair
> In curls on either cheek play'd; wings he wore
> Of many a colour'd plume sprinkled with gold,
> His habit fit for speed succinct, and held
> Before his decent steps a silver wand.

The figures introduced here have all the elegance and precision of a Greek statue; glossy and impurpled, tinged with golden light, and musical as the strings of Memnon's harp!

Again, nothing can be more magnificent than the portrait of Beelzebub:

> With Atlantean shoulders fit to bear
> The weight of mightiest monarchies:

Or the comparison of Satan, as he "lay floating many a rood," to "that sea beast,"

> Leviathan, which God of all his works
> Created hugest that swim the ocean-stream!

What a force of imagination is there in this last expression! What an idea it conveys of the size of that hugest of created beings, as if it shrunk up the ocean to a stream, and took up the sea in its nostrils as a very little thing? Force of style is one of Milton's greatest excellences. Hence, perhaps, he stimulates us more in the reading, and less afterwards. The way to defend Milton against all impugners, is to take down the book and read it.

Milton's blank verse is the only blank verse in the language (except Shakspeare's) that deserves the name of verse. Dr. Johnson, who had modelled his ideas of versification on the regular sing-song of Pope, condemns the *Paradise Lost* as harsh and unequal. I shall not pretend to say that this is not sometimes the case; for where a degree of excellence beyond the mechanical rules of art is attempted, the poet must sometimes fail. But I imagine that there are more perfect examples in Milton of musical expression, or of an adaptation of the sound and movement of the verse to the meaning of the passage, than in all our other writers, whether of rhyme or blank verse, put together, (with the exception already mentioned). Spenser is the most harmonious of our stanza writers, as Dryden is the most sounding and varied of our rhymists. But in neither is there any thing like the same ear for music, the same power of approximating the varieties of poetical to those of musical rhythm, as there is in our great epic poet. The sound of his lines is moulded into the expression of the sentiment, almost of the very image. They rise or fall, pause or hurry rapidly on, with exquisite art, but without the least trick or affectation, as the occasion seems to require.

The following are some of the finest instances:

> ————————His hand was known
> In Heaven by many a tower'd structure high;—
> Nor was his name unheard or unador'd

In ancient Greece: and in the Ausonian land
Men called him Mulciber: and how he fell
From Heaven, they fabled, thrown by angry Jove
Sheer o'er the chrystal battlements; from morn
To noon he fell, from noon to dewy eve,
A summer's day; and with the setting sun
Dropt from the zenith like a falling star
On Lemnos, the Aegean isle: thus they relate,
Erring.—

——————But chief the spacious hall
Thick swarm'd, both on the ground and in the air,
Brush'd with the hiss of rustling wings. As bees
In spring time, when the sun with Taurus rides,
Pour forth their populous youth about the hive
In clusters; they among fresh dews and flow'rs
Fly to and fro: or on the smoothed plank,
The suburb of their straw-built citadel,
New rubb'd with balm, expatiate and confer
Their state affairs. So thick the airy crowd
Swarm'd and were straiten'd; till the signal giv'n,
Behold a wonder! They but now who seem'd
In bigness to surpass earth's giant sons,
Now less than smallest dwarfs, in narrow room
Throng numberless, like that Pygmean race
Beyond the Indian mount, or fairy elves,
Whose midnight revels by a forest side
Or fountain, some belated peasant sees,
Or dreams he sees, while over-head the moon
Sits arbitress, and nearer to the earth
Wheels her pale course: they on their mirth and dance
Intent, with jocund music charm his ear;
At once with joy and fear his heart rebounds.

I can only give another instance, though I have some difficulty
in leaving off.

Round he surveys (and well might, where he stood
So high above the circling canopy
Of night's extended shade) from th' eastern point

> Of Libra to the fleecy star that bears
> Andromeda far off Atlantic seas
> Beyond the horizon: then from pole to pole
> He views in breadth, and without longer pause
> Down right into the world's first region throws
> His flight precipitant, and winds with ease
> Through the pure marble air his oblique way
> Amongst innumerable stars that shone
> Stars distant, but nigh hand seem'd other worlds;
> Or other worlds they seem'd or happy isles, &c.

The verse, in this exquisitely modulated passage, floats up and down as if it had itself wings. Milton has himself given us the theory of his versification—

> Such as the meeting soul may pierce
> In notes with many a winding bout
> Of linked sweetness long drawn out.

Dr. Johnson and Pope would have converted his vaulting Pegasus into a rocking-horse. Read any other blank verse but Milton's,—Thomson's, Young's, Cowper's, Wordsworth's,—and it will be found, from the want of the same insight into "the hidden soul of harmony," to be mere lumbering prose.

To proceed to a consideration of the merits of *Paradise Lost,* in the most essential point of view, I mean as to the poetry of character and passion. I shall say nothing of the fable, or of other technical objections or excellences; but I shall try to explain at once the foundation of the interest belonging to the poem. I am ready to give up the dialogues in Heaven, where, as Pope justly observes, "God the Father turns a school-divine"; nor do I consider the battle of the angels as the climax of sublimity, or the most successful effort of Milton's pen. In a word, the interest of the poem arises from the daring ambition and fierce passions of Satan, and from the account of the paradisaical happiness, and the loss of it by our first parents. Three-fourths of the work are taken up with these characters, and nearly all that relates to them is unmixed sublimity and beauty.

The two first books alone are like two massy pillars of solid gold.

Satan is the most heroic subject that ever was chosen for a poem; and the execution is as perfect as the design is lofty. He was the first of created beings, who, for endeavouring to be equal with the highest, and to divide the empire of heaven with the Almighty, was hurled down to hell. His aim was no less than the throne of the universe; his means, myriads of angelic armies bright, the third part of the heavens, whom he lured after him with his countenance, and who durst defy the Omnipotent in arms. His ambition was the greatest, and his punishment was the greatest; but not so his despair, for his fortitude was as great as his sufferings. His strength of mind was matchless as his strength of body; the vastness of his designs did not surpass the firm, inflexible determination with which he submitted to his irreversible doom, and final loss of all good. His power of action and of suffering was equal. He was the greatest power that was ever overthrown, with the strongest will left to resist or to endure. He was baffled, not confounded. He stood like a tower; or

> —————————As when Heaven's fire
> Hath scathed the forest oaks or mountain pines.

He was still surrounded with hosts of rebel angels, armed warriors, who own him as their sovereign leader, and with whose fate he sympathises as he views them round, far as the eye can reach; though he keeps aloof from them in his own mind, and holds supreme counsel only with his own breast. An outcast from Heaven, Hell trembles beneath his feet, Sin and Death are at his heels, and mankind are his easy prey.

> All is not lost; th' unconquerable will,
> And study of revenge, immortal hate,
> And courage never to submit or yield,
> And what else is not to be overcome,

are still his. The sense of his punishment seems lost in the magnitude of it; the fierceness of tormenting flames is qualified and made innoxious by the greater fierceness of his pride; the loss of infinite happiness to himself is compensated in thought, by the power of inflicting infinite misery on others. Yet Satan is not the principle of malignity, or of the abstract love of evil —but of the abstract love of power, of pride, of self-will personified, to which last principle all other good and evil, and even his own, are subordinate. From this principle he never once flinches. His love of power and contempt for suffering are never once relaxed from the highest pitch of intensity. His thoughts burn like a hell within him; but the power of thought holds dominion in his mind over every other consideration. The consciousness of a determined purpose, of "that intellectual being, those thoughts that wander through eternity," though accompanied with endless pain, he prefers to nonentity, to "being swallowed up and lost in the wide womb of uncreated night." He expresses the sum and substance of all ambition in one line. "Fallen cherub, to be weak is miserable, doing or suffering!" After such a conflict as his, and such a defeat, to retreat in order, to rally, to make terms, to exist at all, is something; but he does more than this—he founds a new empire in hell, and from it conquers this new world, whither he bends his undaunted flight, forcing his way through nether and surrounding fires. The poet has not in all this given us a mere shadowy outline; the strength is equal to the magnitude of the conception. The Achilles of Homer is not more distinct; the Titans were not more vast; Prometheus chained to his rock was not a more terrific example of suffering and of crime. Wherever the figure of Satan is introduced, whether he walks or flies, "rising aloft incumbent on the dusky air," it is illustrated with the most striking and appropriate images: so that we see it always before us, gigantic, irregular, portentous, uneasy, and disturbed—but dazzling in its faded splendour, the clouded ruins of a god. The deformity of Satan is only in the depravity of his will; he has no bodily deformity to excite our loathing or disgust. The horns and tail are not there, poor emblems of the unbending, unconquered spirit, of the writhing agonies within. Milton was too magnanimous and open an antagonist to support his argument by the bye-tricks of a hump and cloven foot; to bring into the fair field of controversy the good old catholic prejudices of which Tasso and Dante have availed themselves, and which the mystic German critics would restore. He relied on the justice of his cause, and did not scruple to give the devil his due. Some persons may think that he has carried his liberality too far, and injured the cause he professed to espouse by making him the chief person in his poem. Considering the nature of his subject, he would be equally in danger of running into this fault, from his faith in religion, and his love of rebellion; and perhaps each of these motives had its full share in determining the choice of his subject.

Not only the figure of Satan, but his speeches in council, his soliloquies, his address to Eve, his share in the war in heaven, or in the fall of man, shew the same decided superiority of character. To give only one instance, almost the first speech he makes:

> Is this the region, this the soil, the clime,
> Said then the lost archangel, this the seat
> That we must change for Heaven; this mournful gloom
> For that celestial light? Be it so, since he
> Who now is sov'rain can dispose and bid
> What shall be right: farthest from him is best,
> Whom reason hath equal'd, force hath made supreme
> Above his equals. Farewel happy fields,
> Where joy for ever dwells: Hail horrors, hail
> Infernal world, and thou profoundest Hell,
> Receive thy new possessor: one who brings
> A mind not to be chang'd by place or time.
> The mind is its own place, and in itself
> Can make a Heav'n of Hell, a Hell of Heav'n.
> What matter where, if I be still the same,
> And what I should be, all but less than he
> Whom thunder hath made greater? Here at least
> We shall be free; th' Almighty hath not built
> Here for his envy, will not drive us hence:

Here we may reign secure, and in my choice
To reign is worth ambition, though in Hell:
Better to reign in Hell, than serve in Heaven.

The whole of the speeches and debates in Pandemonium are well worthy of the place and the occasion—with Gods for speakers, and angels and archangels for hearers. There is a decided manly tone in the arguments and sentiments, an eloquent dogmatism, as if each person spoke from thorough conviction; an excellence which Milton probably borrowed from his spirit of partisanship, or else his spirit of partisanship from the natural firmness and vigour of his mind. In this respect Milton resembles Dante, (the only modern writer with whom he has any thing in common) and it is remarkable that Dante, as well as Milton, was a political partisan. That approximation to the severity of impassioned prose which has been made an objection to Milton's poetry, and which is chiefly to be met with in these bitter invectives, is one of its great excellences. The author might here turn his philippics against Salmasius to good account. The rout in Heaven is like the fall of some mighty structure, nodding to its base, "with hideous ruin and combustion down." But, perhaps, of all the passages in *Paradise Lost,* the description of the employments of the angels during the absence of Satan, some of whom "retreated in a silent valley, sing with notes angelical to many a harp their own heroic deeds and hapless fall by doom of battle," is the most perfect example of mingled pathos and sublimity.—What proves the truth of this noble picture in every part, and that the frequent complaint of want of interest in it is the fault of the reader, not of the poet, is that when any interest of a practical kind takes a shape that can be at all turned into this, (and there is little doubt that Milton had some such in his eye in writing it,) each party converts it to its own purposes, feels the absolute identity of these abstracted and high speculations; and that, in fact, a noted political writer of the present day has exhausted nearly the whole account of Satan in the *Paradise Lost,* by applying it to a character whom he considered as after the devil, (though I do not know whether he would make even that exception) the greatest enemy of the human race. This may serve to shew that Milton's Satan is not a very insipid personage.

Of Adam and Eve it has been said, that the ordinary reader can feel little interest in them, because they have none of the passions, pursuits, or even relations of human life, except that of man and wife, the least interesting of all others, if not to the parties concerned, at least to the by-standers. The preference has on this account been given to Homer, who, it is said, has left very vivid and infinitely diversified pictures of all the passions and affections, public and private, incident to human nature—the relations of son, of brother, parent, friend, citizen, and many others. Longinus preferred the *Iliad* to the *Odyssey*, on account of the greater number of battles it contains; but I can neither agree to his criticism, nor assent to the present objection. It is true, there is little action in this part of Milton's poem; but there is much repose, and more enjoyment. There are none of the every-day occurrences, contentions, disputes, wars, fightings, feuds, jealousies, trades, professions, liveries, and common handicrafts of life; "no kind of traffic; letters are not known; no use of service, of riches, poverty, contract, succession, bourne, bound of land, tilth, vineyard none; no occupation, no treason, felony, sword, pike, knife, gun, nor need of any engine." So much the better; thank Heaven, all these were yet to come. But still the die was cast, and in them our doom was sealed. In them

> The generations were prepared; the pangs,
> The internal pangs, were ready, the dread strife
> Of poor humanity's afflicted will,
> Struggling in vain with ruthless destiny.

In their first false step we trace all our future woe, with loss of Eden. But there was a short and precious interval between, like the first blush of morning before the day is overcast with tempest, the dawn of the world, the birth of nature from "the unapparent deep," with its first dews and freshness on its cheek, breathing odours. Theirs was the first delicious taste of life, and on them depended all that was to come of it. In them hung trembling all our hopes and fears. They were as yet alone in the world, in the eye of nature, wondering at their new being, full of enjoyment and enraptured with one another, with the voice of their Maker walking in the garden, and ministering angels attendant on their steps, winged messengers from heaven like rosy clouds descending in their sight. Nature played around them her virgin fancies wild; and spread for them a repast where no crude surfeit reigned. Was there nothing in this scene, which God and nature alone witnessed, to interest a modern critic? What need was there of action, where the heart was full of bliss and innocence without it! They had nothing to do but feel their own happiness, and "know to know no more." "They toiled not, neither did they spin; yet Solomon in all his glory was not arrayed like one of these." All things seem to acquire fresh sweetness, and to be clothed with fresh beauty in their sight. They tasted as it were for themselves and us, of all that there ever was pure in human bliss. "In them the burthen of the mystery, the heavy and the weary weight of all this unintelligible world, is lightened." They stood awhile perfect, but they afterwards fell, and were driven out of Paradise, tasting the first fruits of bitterness as they had done of bliss. But their pangs were such as a pure spirit might feel at the sight—their tears "such as angels weep." The pathos is of that mild contemplative kind which arises from regret for the loss of unspeakable happiness, and resignation to inevitable fate. There is none of the fierceness of intemperate passion, none of the agony of mind and turbulence of action, which is the result of the habitual struggles of the will with circumstances, irritated by repeated disappointment, and constantly setting its desires most eagerly on that which there is an impossibility of attaining. This would have destroyed the beauty of the whole picture. They had received their unlooked-for happiness as a free gift from their Creator's hands, and they submitted to its loss, not without sorrow, but without impious and stubborn repining.

> In either hand the hast'ning angel caught
> Our ling'ring parents, and to th' eastern gate
> Led them direct, and down the cliff as fast
> To the subjected plain; then disappear'd.
> They looking back, all th' eastern side beheld
> Of Paradise, so late their happy seat,
> Wav'd over by that flaming brand, the gate
> With dreadful faces throng'd, and fiery arms:
> Some natural tears they dropt, but wip'd them soon;
> The world was all before them, where to choose
> Their place of rest, and Providence their guide.

SIR WALTER ALEXANDER RALEIGH

THE STYLE OF MILTON (1900)*

To approach the question of Milton's poetic style thus late in the course of this treatise is to fall into the absurdity of the famous art-critic, who, lecturing on the Venus of Milo, devoted the last and briefest of his lectures to the shape of that noble work of art. In truth, since Milton died, his name is become the mark, not of a biography nor of a theme, but of a style—the most distinguished in our poetry. But the task of literary criticism is, at the best, a task of such disheartening difficulty, that those who attempt it should be humoured if they play long with the fringes of the subject, and wait for courageous moments to attack essentials. . . .

Consider first his choice of subject. Ever since the Renaissance had swept modern poetry back to the pagan world, some voices of protest had been raised, some swimmers, rather bold than strong, had attempted to stem the tide. . . . Nevertheless, the seventeenth century, which stirred so many questions in politics and criticism, stirred this also; the fitness of sacred subjects for heroic poetry was debated long and ardently both in France and England, and many experiments were made. . . . By the force of his genius and the magic of his style, Milton succeeded in an attempt thought hopeless by the best critical judges of his century, and won his way through a ravine that was strewn with the corpses of his epic predecessors.

---

* From *Milton,* London, Edward Arnold & Co., copyright 1900, from Chaps. V-VI. Reprinted by permission of Edward Arnold & Co.

His courage and originality are witnessed also by the metre that he chose for his poem. To us blank verse seems the natural metre for a long serious poem. Before Milton's day, except in the drama, it had only once been so employed—in an Elizabethan poem of no mark or likelihood, called *A Tale of Two Swannes.* While Milton was writing *Paradise Lost* the critics of his time were discussing whether the rhymed couplet or some form of stanza was fitter for narrative poetry, and whether the couplet or blank verse better suited the needs of drama. As no one, before Milton, had maintained in argument that blank verse was the best English measure for narrative poetry dealing with lofty themes, so no critic had ever been at the pains to refute that opinion. In the year of the publication of *Paradise Lost,* Dryden delivered his judgment, that the rhymed couplet was best suited for tragic passages in the drama, and that blank verse should be employed chiefly for the lighter and more colloquial purposes of comedy. Some echo of the courtly dispute then in progress between Dryden and his brother-in-law, Sir Robert Howard, probably reached Milton's ear through his bookseller, Samuel Simmons; for it was at the request of his bookseller that he added the three Miltonic sentences on "The Verse," by way of preface. With his accustomed confidence and directness of attack he begs the question in his first words:—"The measure is English heroic verse without rime"; and in his closing words he takes credit to himself for his "example set, the first in English, of ancient liberty recovered to heroic poem from the troublesome and modern bondage of riming."

In these two cardinal points, then—the matter and the form of his poem—Milton was original. For the one there was no true precedent in English; for the other there was no precedent that might not rather have been called a warning. His matter was to be arranged and his verse handled by his own ingenuity and at his own peril. He left a highroad behind him, along which many a tuneful pauper has since limped; but before him he found nothing but the jungle and false fires. In considering his style, therefore, it is well to treat the problem as it presented itself to him, and to follow his achievement as he won step by step out of the void.

There were two great influences in English poetry, other than the drama, when Milton began to write: the influence of Spenser and the influence of Donne. Only the very slightest traces of either can be discerned in Milton's early verse. There are some Spenserian cadences in the poem *On the Death of a Fair Infant,* written in his seventeenth year:—

> Or wert thou of the golden-wingèd host
> Who, having clad thyself in human weed,
> To earth from thy prefixèd seat didst post,
> And after short abode fly back with speed,
> As if to show what creatures Heaven doth breed;
>   Thereby to set the hearts of men on fire
> To scorn the sordid world, and unto Heaven aspire?

The later verses on *The Passion,* written in the same metre, are perhaps the last in which Milton echoes Spenser, however faintly. Meanwhile, in the hymn *On the Morning of Christ's Nativity,* he had struck a note that was his own, and it is not surprising that he left the poem on *The Passion* unfinished, "nothing satisfied with what was begun."

As for the great Dean of St. Paul's, there is no evidence that Milton was touched by him, or, for that matter, that he had read any of his poems. In the verses written *At a Vacation Exercise,* he expressly sets aside

> Those new-fangled toys and trimming slight
> Which takes our late fantastics with delight;

and he very early came to dislike the fashionable conceits that ran riot in contemporary English verse. A certain number of conceits, few and poor enough, is to be found scattered here and there in his early poems. Bleak Winter, for instance, is represented in three cumbrous stanzas, as the slayer of the Fair Infant:—

> For he, being amorous on that lovely dye
>> That did thy cheek envermeil, thought to kiss,
> But killed, alas! and then bewailed his fatal bliss.

In the lines on Shakespeare the monument promised to the dead poet is a marvel of architecture and sculpture, made up of all his readers, frozen to statues by the wonder and astonishment that they feel when they read the plays. But perhaps the nearest approach to a conceit of the metaphysical kind is to be found in that passage of *Comus,* where the Lady accuses Night of having stolen her brothers:—

> O thievish Night,
> Why shouldst thou, but for some felonious end,
> In thy dark lantern thus close up the stars
> Which Nature hung in heaven, and filled their lamps
> With everlasting oil to give due light
> To the misled and lonely traveller?

When Milton does fall into a vein of conceit, it is generally both trivial and obvious, with none of the saving quality of Donne's remoter extravagances. In Donne they are hardly extravagances; the vast overshadowing canopy of his imagination seems to bring the most wildly dissimilar things together with ease. . . . The virtues of the metaphysical school were impossible virtues for one whose mind had no tincture of the metaphysic. Milton, as has been said already, had no deep sense of mystery. One passage of *Il Penseroso,* which might be quoted against this statement, is susceptible of an easier explanation:—

> And if aught else great bards beside
> In sage and solemn tunes have sung
> Of turneys, and of trophies hung,
> Of forests, and enchantments drear,
> Where more is meant than meets the ear.

He alludes no doubt to Spenser, and by the last line intends only allegory—a definite moral signification affixed to certain characters and stories—not the mystic correspondences that Donne loves. The most mysterious lines in *Comus* are these:—

                        A thousand fantasies
            Begin to throng into my memory,
            Of calling shapes, and beckoning shadows dire,
            And airy tongues that syllable men's names
            On sands and shores and desert wildernesses.

They are purely Elizabethan and reminiscent. But if the
stranger beauties of the metaphysical school were beyond his
reach, its vices touched him wonderfully little, so that his conceits are merely the rare flaws of his early work.

The dramatists were a much more potent influence than
either Spenser or the metaphysical school. He learned his blank
verse from the dramatists. . . . But his tendencies and ambitions were not dramatic, so he escaped the diseases that af-
flicted the drama in its decadence. When he began to write
blank verse, the blank verse of the dramatists, his contemporaries, was fast degenerating into more or less rhythmical prose.
Suckling and Davenant and their fellows not only used the
utmost license of redundant syllables at the end of the line,
but hustled and slurred the syllables in the middle till the line
was a mere gabble, and interspersed broken lines so plentifully
that it became impossible even for the most attentive ear to follow the metre. . . . At the time when blank verse was yielding to decay, Milton took it up, and used it neither for con-
versational nor for rhetorical purposes. In the interests of pure
poetry and melody he tightened its joints, stiffened its texture,
and one by one gave up almost all the licenses that the dramatists had used. From the first he makes a sparing use of the
double ending. The redundant syllable in the middle of the
line, which he sometimes allows himself in *Comus*, does not
occur in *Paradise Lost*. In the later poem he adopts strict prac-
tices with regard to elision, which, with some trifling exceptions, he permits only in the case of contiguous open vowels,
and of short unstressed vowels separated by a liquid conso-
nant, in such words, for instance, as "dissolute," or "amorous."
By a variety of small observances, which, when fully stated,

make up a formidable code, he mended the shambling gait of the loose dramatic blank verse, and made of it a worthy epic metre.

In a long poem variety is indispensable, and he preserved the utmost freedom in some respects. He continually varies the stresses in the line, their number, their weight, and their incidence, letting them fall, when it pleases his ear, on the odd as well as on the even syllables of the line. The pause or caesura he permits to fall at any place in the line, usually towards the middle, but, on occasion, even after the first or ninth syllables. His chief study, it will be found, is to vary the word in relation to the foot, and the sentence in relation to the line. No other metre allows of anything like the variety of blank verse in this regard, and no other metrist makes so splendid a use of its freedom. He never forgets the pattern; yet he never stoops to teach it by the repetition of a monotonous tattoo. Hence there are, perhaps, fewer one-line quotations to be found in the works of Milton than in the works of any other master of blank verse. De Quincey speaks of the "slow planetary wheelings" of Milton's verse, and the metaphor is a happy one; the verse revolves on its axis at every line, but it always has another motion, and is related to a more distant centre.

It may well be doubted whether Milton could have given a clear exposition of his own prosody. In the only place where he attempts it he finds the elements of musical delight to consist in "apt numbers, fit quantity of syllables, and the sense variously drawn out from one verse into another." By "apt numbers" he probably meant the skilful handling of stress-variation in relation to the sense. But the last of the three is the essential of Miltonic blank verse. There lies the secret for whoso can divine it.

Every well-marked type of blank verse has a natural gait or movement of its own, which it falls into during its ordinary uninspired moods. Tennyson's blank verse, when it is not carefully guarded and varied, drops into a kind of fluent sing-song. . . . [Milton's] verse, even in its least admirable passages, does not sing, nor trip with regular alternate stress; its movement suggests neither dance nor song, but rather the advancing march of a body of troops skilfully handled, with incessant changes in their disposition as they pass over broken ground. He can furnish them with wings when it so pleases him. No analysis of his prosody can explain the wonders of his workmanship. But it is not idle to ask for a close attention to the scansion of lines like these, wherein he describes the upward progress of the Son of God and his escort after the Creation:—

> The heavens and all the constellations rung,
> The planets in their station listening stood,
> While the bright pomp ascended jubilant.

In the last line the first four words marshal the great procession in solid array; the last two lift it high into the empyrean. Let any one attempt to get the same upward effect with a stress, however light, laid on the last syllable of the line, or with words of fewer than three syllables apiece, and he will have to confess that, however abstruse the rules of its working may be, there is virtue in metrical cunning. The passage in the Seventh Book from which these lines are quoted would justify an entire treatise. The five regular alternate stresses first occur in a line describing the progress over the wide plain of Heaven:—

> He through Heaven,
> That opened wide her blazing portals, led
> To God's eternal house direct the way.

But, indeed, the examination of the music of Milton involves so minute a survey of technical detail as to be tedious to all but a few lovers of theory. The laws of music in verse are very subtle, and, it must be added, very imperfectly ascertained; so that those who dogmatise on them generally end by slipping into fantasy or pedantry. How carefully and incessantly Milton

adjusted the sound to the sense is known to every reader of
Paradise Lost. The dullest ear is caught by the contrast between the opening of the gates of Heaven—

>   Heaven opened wide
> Her ever-during gates, harmonious sound
> On golden hinges moving—

and the opening of those other gates—

>   On a sudden open fly,
> With impetuous recoil and jarring sound,
> The infernal doors, and on their hinges grate
> Harsh thunder, that the lowest bottom shook
> Of Erebus.

But there are many more delicate instances than these. In the
choruses of *Samson Agonistes,* where he reaches the top of his
skill, Milton varies even the length of the line. So he has hardly
a rule left, save the iambic pattern, which he treats merely as
a point of departure or reference, a background or framework
to carry the variations imposed upon it by the luxuriance of a
perfectly controlled art. The great charm of the metre of
Wither, which Charles Lamb admired and imitated, lies in its
facile combination of what, for the sake of brevity, may be
called the iambic and trochaic movements. In *L'Allegro* and *Il
Penseroso* Milton had proved his mastery of both its resources.
The gaiety of these lines—

> Haste thee, Nymph, and bring with thee
> Jest, and youthful Jollity—

passes easily into the solemnity of these—

> But let my due feet never fail
> To walk the studious cloister's pale.

In *Samson Agonistes* he sought to extend something of the same
liberty to the movement of blank verse. He freely intermixes
the falling with the rising stress, shifting the weights from
place to place, and often compensating a light patter of syl-

lables in the one half of the line by the introduction of two or three consecutive strong stresses in the other half. Under this treatment the metre of *Gorboduc* breaks into blossom and song:—

> O, how comely it is, and how reviving
> To the spirits of just men long oppressed,
> When God into the hands of their deliverer
> Puts invincible might.

To try to explain this marvel of beauty is to beat the air.

By his deliberate attention to the elements of verbal melody Milton gave a new character to English blank verse. But this is not all. Quite as important is the alteration that he made in the character of English poetic diction.

The essence of the lyric is that it is made up of phrases, not of words. The lines run easily because they run on tracks chosen for their ease by the instinct of generations and worn smooth by use. The lyrical phrase, when the first two or three words of it have been pronounced, finishes itself. From Carew's "Ask me no more," with its long train of imitations, to the latest banality of the music-halls, the songs that catch the ear catch it by the same device. The lyric, that is to say, is almost always dependent for its music on easy idiomatic turns of speech. The surprising word occurs rarely; with all the greater effect inasmuch as it is embedded in phrases that slip from the tongue without a trace of thought or effort. These phrases naturally allow of little diversity of intonation; they have the unity of a single word, a single accepted emphasis, and a run of lightly-stressed syllables more or less musical in sequence.

All this Milton changed. He chooses his every word. You cannot guess the adjective from the substantive, nor the end of the phrase from its beginning. He is much given to inverting the natural English order of epithet and noun, that he may gain a greater emphasis for the epithet. His style is not a simple loose-flowing garment, which takes its outline from its natural fall over the figure, but a satin brocade, stiff with gold, exactly fitted to the body. There is substance for it to clothe; but, as his imitators quickly discovered, it can stand alone. He packs his meaning into the fewest possible words, and studies economy in every trifle. In his later poetry there are no gliding connectives; no polysyllabic conjunctive clauses, which fill the mouth while the brain prepares itself for the next word of value; no otiose epithets, and very few that court neglect by their familiarity. His poetry is like the eloquence of the Lord Chancellor Bacon, as described by Ben Jonson:— "No man ever spake more neatly, more pressly, more weightily, or suffered less emptiness, less idleness in what he uttered. No member of his speech but consisted of his own graces. His hearers could not cough, or look aside from him, without loss." It is this quality of Milton's verse that makes the exercise of reading it aloud a delight and a trial. Every word is of value. There is no mortar between the stones, each is held in place by the weight of the others, and helps to uphold the building. In reading, every word must be rendered clearly and articulately; to drop one out, or to slur it over, is to take a stone from an arch. Indeed, if Lamb and Hazlitt are right in thinking that Shakespeare's greatest plays cannot be acted, by the same token, Milton's greatest poems cannot be read aloud. For his most sonorous passages the human voice is felt to be too thin an instrument; the lightest word in the line demands some faint emphasis, so that the strongest could not be raised to its true value unless it were roared through some melodious megaphone.

The carefully jewelled mosaic style was practised very early by Milton. It occurs already in the hymn on the Nativity:—

> See how from far upon the eastern road
> The star-led wizards haste with odours sweet:
> O run, prevent them with thy humble ode
> And lay it lowly at his blessed feet.

The same deliberateness and gentle pause of words one after another rounding and falling like clear drops is found in the song of the Spirit in *Comus*:—

> Sabrina fair,
>   Listen where thou art sitting
> Under the glassy, cool, translucent wave,
>   In twisted braids of lilies knitting
> The loose train of thy amber-dropping hair.

This is the effect which Sir Henry Wotton, Milton's earliest critic, speaks of, in a letter to Milton, as "a certain Doric delicacy in your songs and odes, whereunto I must plainly confess to have seen yet nothing parallel in our language."

There are poems, and good poems among the number, written on a more diffuse principle. If you miss one line you find the idea repeated or persisting in the next. It is quite possible to derive pleasure from the *Fairie Queene* by attending to the leading words, and, for the rest, floating onward on the melody. You can catch the drift with ease. The stream circles in so many eddies that to follow it laboriously throughout its course is felt to be hardly necessary: miss it once and you can often join it again at very near the same point. "But a reader of Milton," as an early critic of Milton remarks, "must be always upon duty; he is surrounded with sense; it rises in every line, every word is to the purpose. There are no lazy intervals: all has been considered, and demands and merits observation. Even in the best writers you sometimes find words and sentences which hang on so loosely, you may blow them off. Milton's are all substance and weight: fewer would not have served his turn, and more would have been superfluous. His silence has the same effect, not only that he leaves work for the imagination, when he has entertained it and furnished it with noble materials; but he expresses himself so concisely, employs words so sparingly, that whoever will possess his ideas must dig for them, and oftentimes pretty far below the surface."

An illustration and contrast may serve to point the moral. Here is an example of Spenser's diffuser style, taken from the second book of the *Faerie Queene*. Guyon, escaped from the cave of Mammon, is guarded, during his swoon, by an angel:—

> Beside his head there satt a faire young man,

(This announces the theme, as in music.)

> Of wondrous beauty and of freshest yeares,

(The fair young man was fair and young.)

> Whose tender bud to blossom new began,

(The fair young man was young.)

> And florish faire above his equal peers.

(The fair young man was fair, fairer even than his equals, who were also his peers.)

In the remaining lines of the stanza the comparison of his hair to the rays of the sun is played with in the same way:—

> His snowy front curled with golden heares,
> Like Phoebus' face adorned with sunny rayes,
> Divinely shone; and two sharp winged sheares,
> Decked with diverse plumes, like painted Jayes,
> Were fixed at his back to cut his ayery wayes.

The whole stanza is beautiful, and musical with the music of redundance. Nothing could be less like Milton's mature style. His verse, "with frock of mail, Adamantean proof," advances proudly and irresistibly, gaining ground at every step. He brings a situation before us in two lines, every word contributing its share:—

> Betwixt these rocky pillars Gabriel sat,
> Chief of the angelic guards, awaiting night.

With as decisive a touch he sketches the story of Jacob—

> In the field of Luz,
> Dreaming by night under the open sky,
> And waking cried, *This is the gate of Heaven.*

Or the descent of Raphael:—

> Like Maia's son he stood,
> And shook his plumes, that heavenly fragrance filled
> The circuit wide.

The packed line introduced by Milton is of a greater density and conciseness than anything to be found in English literature before it. It is our nearest native counterpart to the force and reserve of the high Virgilian diction. . . . The necessities of rhyme sometimes hamper both Dryden and Pope; and the nearest parallel to the manner of Virgil is to be sought in Milton. The famous line describing Samson—

> Eyeless, in Gaza, at the mill, with slaves—

is a good example; the sense of humiliation and abasement is intensified at every step. Or, to take a passage in a very different key of feeling, the same quality is seen in the description of the obedience of Eve:—

> Required with gentle sway
> And by her yielded, by him best received,
> Yielded with coy submission, modest pride,
> And sweet, reluctant, amorous delay.

The slight stress and pause needed after each word, to render the full meaning, produce, when the words are short as well as emphatic, a line of terrific weight and impact. What more heartbreaking effect of weariness and eternity of effort could be produced in a single line than this, descriptive of the dolorous march of the fallen angels?—

> O'er many a frozen, many a fiery Alp,
> Rocks, caves, lakes, fens, bogs, dens, and shades of death.

It would be difficult to match this line. . . .

All superfluous graces are usually discarded by Milton. He steers right onward, and gives the reader no rest. . . . His epithets are chosen to perform one exploit, and are dismissed when it is accomplished. As with single epithets, so with lines

and phrases; he does not employ conventional repetitions either for their lyrical value or for wafting the story on to the next point of interest. He seeks no effects such as Marlowe obtained by the lyrical repetition of the line:—

> To entertain divine Zenocrate.

He arrests the attention at every word; and when the thing is once said, he has done with it. . . .

Milton seldom allows his verse to play in eddies; he taxes every line to its fullest capacity, and wrings the last drop of value from each word. A signal characteristic of his diction has its origin in this hard dealing. He is often not satisfied with one meaning from a word, but will make it do double duty. Here the Latin element in our language gave him his opportunity. Words borrowed from the Latin always change their usage and value in English air. To the ordinary intelligence they convey one meaning; to a scholar's memory they suggest also another. It became the habit of Milton to make use of both values, to assess his words in both capacities. Any page of his work furnishes examples of his delicate care for the original meaning of Latin words, such as *intend*—"intend at home . . . what best may ease the present misery"; *arrive* —"ere he arrive the happy Isle"; *obnoxious*—"obnoxious more to all the miseries of life"; *punctual*—"this opacous Earth, this punctual spot"; *sagacious*—"sagacious of his quarry from so far"; *explode*—"the applause they meant turned to exploding hiss"; *retort*—"with retorted scorn his back he turned"; *infest*—"find some occasion to infest our foes." The Speaker of the House of Commons had to determine, some years ago, whether it is in order to allude to the Members as "infesting" the House. Had Milton been called upon for such a decision he would doubtless have ruled that the word is applicable only to Members whose deliberate intention is to maim or destroy the constitution of Parliament.

But he was not content to revive the exact classical meaning in place of the vague or weak English acceptation; he often kept both senses, and loaded the word with two meanings at once. When Samson speaks of Dalila as

> That specious monster, my accomplished snare—

something of this double sense resides in both epithets. In two words we are told that Dalila was both beautiful and deceitful, that she was skilled in the blandishments of art, and successful in the work of her husband's undoing. With a like double reference Samson calls the secret of his strength "my capital secret." Where light, again, is called the "prime work of God," or where we are told that Hell saw "Heaven ruining from Heaven," the original and derivative senses of the words "prime" and "ruin" are united in the conception. These words, and many others similarly employed, are of Latin origin; but Milton carried his practice over into the Saxon part of our vocabulary. The word "uncouth" is used in a double-barrelled sense in the Second Book of *Paradise Lost*—

> Who shall tempt with wandering feet
> The dark, unbottomed, infinite Abyss,
> And through the palpable obscure find out
> His uncouth way?

And when Satan's eyes are called "baleful," the word, besides indicating the "huge affliction and dismay" that he feels, gives a hint of the woes that are in store for the victims on whom those eyes have not yet lit.

It was this habit of "verbal curiosity" and condensation which seduced Milton into punning. Some of his puns are very bad. There is a modern idea that a pun is a thing to laugh at. Milton's puns, like Shakespeare's, give no smallest countenance to this theory. Sometimes he plays with what is merely a chance identity of sound, as where Satan, entering Paradise—

> At one slight bound high overleapt all bound.

But in most of these cases it seems likely that he believed in an etymological relation between the two words, and so fancied that he was drawing attention to an original unity of meaning. Some such hypothesis is needful to mitigate the atrocity of his worst pun, in *Paradise Regained,* where he describes

> The ravens with their horny beaks
> Food to Elijah bringing even and morn—
> Though ravenous, taught to abstain from what they brought.

Milton was no philologist, and we may be permitted in charity to suppose that he derived "raven" and "ravenous" from the same root.

Some of his puns are to be justified for another reason—that they are made the weapons of mockery. So when Satan rails against Abdiel he says—

> Thou shalt behold
> Whether by supplication we intend
> Address, and to begirt the Almighty Throne
> Beseeching or besieging.

The long punning-bout between Satan and Belial in the Sixth Book exemplifies the more usual form of the Miltonic pun. When he introduces the newly-invented artillery, Satan makes a speech, "scoffing in ambiguous words"—

> Ye, who appointed stand,
> Do as you have in charge, and briefly touch
> What we propound, and loud that all may hear.

And again, when it has taken effect, scattering the heavenly host in unseemly disorder, he says—

> If our proposals once again were heard,
> We should compel them to a quick result.

Belial, "in like gamesome mood," replies to the jests of his leader, until, by the providence of Heaven, his wit and his artillery are buried under a weight heavier than themselves. On this whole scene Landor remarks that "the first overt crime of the refractory angels was punning"; and adds, with true Miltonic conciseness, "they fell rapidly after that."

Some minor flaws, which may be found in Milton by those

who give a close examination to his works, are to be attributed to the same cause—his love of condensed statement. Mixture of metaphors in poetry is often caused merely by the speed of thought, which presents a subject in a new aspect without care taken to adjust or alter the figure. In these cases the obscurity or violence of expression arises not from defect, but from excess of thought. Some few instances occur in Milton, who, in *Lycidas,* writes thus—

> But now my oat proceeds,
> And listens to the Herald of the Sea.

The syntax of the thought is sufficiently lucid and orderly, but it is compressed into too few words. In the Fifth Book of *Paradise Lost* is described how—

> The Eternal Eye, whose sight discerns
> Abstrusest thoughts, from forth his holy mount,
> And from within the golden lamps that burn
> Nightly before him, saw without their light
> Rebellion rising—saw in whom, how spread
> Among the Sons of Morn, what multitudes
> Were banded to oppose his high decree;
> And, smiling, to his only Son thus said.

Here, it is true, "the Eternal Eye" smiles and speaks to his only Son. But Milton has really discarded the figure after the words "his high decree," which bring in a new order of thoughts. He trusts the reader to follow his thought without grammatical readjustment—to drop the symbol and remember only the thing symbolised. His trust was warranted, until Landor detected the solecism. The clearest case of mixed metaphor ever charged against Milton occurs in the Eleventh Book, where the lazar-house is described—

> Sight so deform what heart of rock could long
> Dry-eyed behold?

Rogers pointed this out to Coleridge, who told Wordsworth that he could not sleep all the next night for thinking of it.

What months of insomnia must he not have suffered from the perusal of Shakespeare's works!

The close-wrought style of Milton makes the reading of *Paradise Lost* a hard task in this sense, that it is a severe intellectual exercise, without relaxation. The attention that it demands, word by word, and line by line, could not profitably be given to most books; so that many readers, trained by a long course of novel-reading to nibble and browse through the pastures of literature, find that Milton yields little or no delight under their treatment, and abandon him in despair.

And yet, with however great reluctance, it must be admitted that the close study and admiring imitation of Milton bring in their train some lesser evils. Meaning may be arranged too compactly in a sentence; for perfect and ready assimilation some bulk and distention are necessary in language as in diet. Now the study of Milton, if it teaches anything, teaches to discard and abhor all superfluity. He who models himself upon this master will never "go a-begging for some meaning, and labour to be delivered of the great burden of nothing." But he may easily fall into the opposite error of putting "riddles of wit, by being too scarce of words." He will be so intent upon the final and perfect expression of his thought, that his life may pass before he finds it, and even if, in the end, he should say a thing well, he is little likely to say it in due season.

*   *   *

Of all English styles Milton's is best entitled to the name of Classic. In his poems may be found every device that belongs to the Classic manner, as in Shakespeare's plays may be found every device that belongs distinctively to the Romantic. Perhaps the two manners are best compared by the juxtaposition of descriptive passages. In description it is impossible for literature to be exhaustive; a choice must be made, an aspect emphasised, and by far the greater part left to the imagination of the reader. A man, for instance, has stature, feature, bones, muscles, nerves, entrails; his eyes, hair, and skin are of certain colours; he stands in a particular attitude at a particular spot on the surface of the earth; he is agitated by certain passions and ideas; every movement that he makes is related to his constitution and his past history; he has affinity with other men by the ties of the family, the society, the State; he thinks and acts more in a minute than a hundred writers can describe and explain in a year; he is a laughing, weeping, money-making, clothes-wearing, lying, reasoning, worshipping, amorous, credulous, sceptical, imitative, combative, gregarious, prehensile, two-legged animal. He does not cease to be all this and more, merely because he happens to be at one of his thousand tricks, and you catch him in the act. How do you propose to describe him?

Broadly speaking, there are two methods available. You may begin with the more general and comprehensive of the relations that fall in with your purpose, securing breadth of view and truth in the larger values, leaving the imagination to supply the more particular and personal details on the barest of hints from you: or you may fix your gaze exclusively on some vivid cluster of details, indicating their remoter relations and their place in a wider perspective by a few vague suggestions.

The first of these ways is Milton's. He maps out his descriptions in bold outline, attending always to the unity of the picture and the truth of the larger relations. He is chary of detail, and what he adds is added for its own immediate importance rather than for its remoter power of suggestion. Adam and Eve when they are first introduced, are thus described:—

> Two of far nobler shape, erect and tall,
> Godlike erect, with native honour clad
> In naked majesty, seemed lords of all,
> And worthy seemed; for in their looks divine
> The image of their glorious Maker shone,
> Truth, wisdom, sanctitude severe and pure,—
> Severe, but in true filial freedom placed,
> Whence true authority in men.

As pictorial description this is all but completely empty. It tells you only that they stood upright, that they were like their Maker, and that they were possessed of the virtues that their appearance would lead you to expect. Their physical delineation is to be accommodated by the imagination of the reader to this long catalogue of moral qualities,—nobility, honour, majesty, lordliness, worth, divinity, glory, brightness, truth, wisdom, sanctitude, severity, and purity. In the following lines the poet proceeds to distinguish the one figure from the other, adding a few details with regard to each. The epithets he chooses are still vague. Adam's forehead is "fair" and "large," his eye is "sublime," his locks are "hyacinthine," and (a detail that has escaped the notice of many illustrators of *Paradise Lost*) they fall in clusters as low as his shoulders. From beginning to end of the description the aim of the poet is to preserve the right key of large emotion, and the words that he chooses are chosen chiefly for their emotional value. The emotions are given; the portraiture is left to be filled in by the imagination.

Shakespeare commonly works in the reverse way. He does not, like Crabbe, describe "as if for the police"; he chooses his detail with consummate skill, but he makes use of it to suggest the emotions. It is impossible to set his description of persons over against Milton's; for the drama does not describe persons, it presents them in action; and a description, where it occurs, is often designed merely to throw light on the character and feelings of the speaker. "Her voice was ever soft, gentle, and low" is a description rather of Lear, as he hangs over the dead body of Cordelia, refusing to believe that she is dead, than of Cordelia herself. "An excellent thing in woman" is not a doctrine, but a last heartbreaking movement of defiance, as if to refute any stander-by who dares to think that there is something amiss, that a voice should not be so low as to be inaudible.

The contrast of the methods may, therefore, be better noted

in the description of scenes. There is no very close parallel obtainable; but the two passages compared by Lessing are not wholly dissimilar in theme, and serve well enough to illustrate the difference of the styles. The first, taken from the Seventh Book of *Paradise Lost,* tells how the King of Glory, from the verge of his heavenly domain, beholds the gulf of Chaos:—

> On Heavenly ground they stood, and from the shore
> They viewed the vast immeasurable Abyss,
> Outrageous as a sea, dark, wasteful, wild,
> Up from the bottom turned by furious winds
> And surging waves, as mountains to assault
> Heaven's highth, and with the centre mix the pole.

The other is the imaginary view from Dover Cliff, described by Edgar in *King Lear*:—

> How fearful
> And dizzy 'tis, to cast one's eyes so low!
> The crows and choughs that wing the midway air
> Show scarce so gross as beetles: half way down
> Hangs one that gathers samphire, dreadful trade!
> Methinks he seems no bigger than his head;
> The fishermen, that walk upon the beach,
> Appear like mice; and yond tall anchoring bark,
> Diminish'd to her cock; her cock, a buoy
> Almost too small for sight: the murmuring surge
> That on th' unnumbered idle pebbles chafes,
> Cannot be heard so high. I'll look no more;
> Lest my brain turn and the deficient sight
> Topple down headlong. . . .

Shakespeare sets a scene before your eyes, and by his happy choice of vivid impression makes you giddy. The crows help, rather than impede your fall; for to look into illimitable vacuum is to look at nothing, and therefore to be unmoved. But the classic manner is so careful for unity of emotional impression that it rejects these humble means for attaining even to so great an end. It refuses to work by mice and beetles, lest the sudden intrusion of trivial associations should mar the main impression. No sharp discords are allowed, even though they should be resolved the moment after. Every word and every image must help forward the main purpose. Thus, while the besetting sin of the Romantics is the employment of excessive, or irrelevant, or trivial or grotesque detail, the besetting sin of the Classics is so complete an omission of realistic detail that the description becomes inflated, windy and empty, and the strongest words in the language lose their vital force because they are set fluttering hither and thither in multitudes, with no substantial hold upon reality. There is nothing that dies sooner than an emotion when it is cut off from the stock on which it grows. The descriptive epithet or adjective, if only it be sparingly and skilfully employed, so that the substantive carry it easily, is the strongest word in a sentence. But when once it loses its hold upon concrete reality it becomes the weakest, and not all the protests of debility, superlative degrees, and rhetorical insistence, can save it from neglect.

It is apparent, therefore, how necessary to Milton were the concrete epic realities with which his poem deals,—the topographical scheme of things, and the definite embodiment of all his spiritual essences. Keats' *Hyperion* fails largely for want of an exact physical system such as Milton devises. Keats works almost wholly with vague Romantic suggestion, and there is nothing for the poem to hang on by. Something is happening; but it is difficult to say what, for we see only dream-imagery, and hear only muffled echoes. Had Milton made unsparing use of abstraction and suggestion, his poem would have fallen into windy chaos. . . . He uses abstract terms magnificently, but almost always with a reference to concrete realities, not as the names of separate entities. By the substitution of abstract nouns for concrete he achieves a wonderful effect of majesty. He does not name, for instance, the particular form of wind instrument that the heralds blew in Hell:—

> Four speedy Cherubim
> Put to their mouths the sounding alchymy.

He avoids defining his creatures by names that lend themselves to definite picture: of Death he says—

> So spake the grisly Terror;

and he makes Raphael, at the call of Heaven's king, rise

> from among
> Thousand celestial Ardours.

In the Tenth Book, Death, snuffing the distant scent of
mortality, becomes all nose—

> So scented the grim Feature, and upturned
> His nostril wide into the murky air.

A superb example of this powerful use of abstract terms is
contained in the First Book of *Paradise Regained*, where is
described how Satan, disguised as an old man, took his leave
of the Son of God, and

> Bowing low
> His gray dissimulation, disappeared
> Into thin air diffused.

The word "dissimulation" expresses the fact of the gray
hairs assumed, the purpose of deceit, the cringing attitude,
and adds a vague effect of power. The same vagueness is habitually studied by Milton in such phrases as "the vast abrupt,"
"the palpable obscure," "the void immense," "the wasteful
deep," where, by the use of an adjective in place of a substantive, the danger of a definite and inadequate conception
is avoided.

Milton, therefore, describes the concrete, the specific, the
individual, using general and abstract terms for the sake of
the dignity and scope that they lend. The best of our Romantic
poets follow the opposite course: they are much concerned
with abstract conceptions and general truths, but they bring
them home by the employment of concrete and specific terms,
and figures so familiar that they cannot easily avoid grotesque
associations. . . .

The mean associations, . . . in so far as they exist, help Shakespeare's purpose. Milton had no purpose that could be furthered by such help. The omissions in his descriptions cannot be supplied by an appeal to experience, for what he describes is outside the pale of human experience, and is, in that sense, unreal. His descriptions do not so much remind us of what we have seen as create for us what we are to see. He is bound, therefore, to avoid the slightest touch of unworthy association; the use of even a few domestic figures and homely phrases would bring his hanging palace about his ears. What dangers he escaped may be well seen in Cowley's *Davideis*, which fell into them all. This is how Cowley describes the attiring of his Gabriel, who is commissioned to bear a message to David—

> He took for skin a cloud most soft and bright,
> That e'er the midday Sun pierced through with light:
> Upon his cheeks a lively blush he spred;
> Washt from the morning beauties deepest red.
> An harmless flaming *Meteor* shone for haire,
> And fell adown his shoulders with loose care.
> He cuts out a silk *Mantle* from the skies,
> Where the most sprightly azure pleas'd the eyes.
> This he with starry vapours spangles all,
> Took in their prime ere they grow *ripe* and *fall*,—

—and so on. The whole business suggests the arming of Pigwiggin; or the intricacies of Belinda's toilet in *The Rape of the Lock*. Such a Gabriel should add the last touch of adornment from a patch-box filled with sun-spots; and then is fit only to be—

> Drawn with a team of little atomies
> Athwart men's noses as they lie asleep.

Milton was not in the least likely to fall into this fantastic-familiar vein. But he was also debarred from dealing freely in realism; from carrying conviction by some sudden startling piece of fidelity to the mixed texture of human experience

and human feeling. When the feast is spread in Eden he remarks, it is true,—"No fear lest dinner cool"; but a lapse like
this is of the rarest. His success—and he knew it—depended
on the untiring maintenance of a superhuman elevation. His
choice of subject had therefore not a little to do with the nature of his diction; and, through the influence of his diction,
as shall be shown hereafter, with the establishment of the poetic tradition that dominated Eighteenth Century poetry.

The same motives and tendencies, the same consistent care
for remoteness and loftiness, may be seen in the character of
the similes that he most frequently employs. Almost all his
figures and comparisons illustrate concrete objects by concrete
objects, and occurrences in time by other occurrences later in
time. The essentially Romantic sort of figure, scarcely used by
Milton, illustrates subtle conceptual relations by parable—

> Now at the last gasp of Love's latest breath,
> When, his pulse failing, Passion speechless lies,
> And Faith is kneeling by his bed of death,
> And Innocence is closing up his eyes,—
> Now, if thou would'st, when all have given him over,
> From death to life thou might 'st him yet recover.

Sometimes, by a curious reversal, poets, especially the more
sophisticated poets of the Romantic Revival, describe a perfectly definite outward object or scene by a figure drawn from
the most complex abstract conceptions. So Shelley, with whom
these inverted figures are habitual, compares the skylark to

> A poet hidden
> In the light of thought;

and Byron, describing the rainbow over a waterfall, likens it to

> Love watching Madness with unalterable mien.

Both ways are foreign to the epic manner of Milton. His
figures may be called historic parallels, whereby the names and
incidents of human history are made to elucidate and ennoble
the less familiar names and incidents of his pre-historic theme.

Sometimes, following Homer, he borrows a figure from rustic life, as where, for instance, he compares the devils, crowding into Pandemonium, to a swarm of bees. But he perceived clearly enough that he could not, for the reasons already explained, afford to deal largely in this class of figure: he prefers to maintain dignity and distance by choosing comparisons from ancient history and mythology, or from those great and strange things in Nature which repel intimacy—the sun, the moon, the sea, planets in opposition, a shooting star, an evening mist, a will-o'-the-wisp, a vulture descending from the Himalayas, the ice-floes on the North-East passage, the sea-beast leviathan, Xerxes' Hellespontic bridge, the gryphon pursuing the Arimaspian, the madness of Alcides in Oeta, the rape of Proserpine, and a hundred more reminiscences of the ancient world.

Even the great events of ancient history seemed to him at times too familiar, too little elevated and remote to furnish a resting-place for a song that intended "no middle flight." He transforms his proper names, both to make them more melodious, and to make them more unfamiliar to the ear. No praise is too high for his art and skill in this matter. An example may be found in those four lines—the earliest that have the full Miltonic resonance—describing the fate of Lycidas carried by the tide southward to the Cornish coast:—

> Or whether thou, to our moist vows denied,
> Sleep'st by the fable of Bellerus old,
> Where the great Vision of the guarded mount
> Looks toward Namancos and Bayona's hold.

"Bellerus" seems to be a name of Milton's coinage. He had written "Corineus," and probably disliked the sound, for in this case it can hardly have been that the name was too familiar. Both reasons concurred in prompting the allusion to Pharaoh and his Egyptian squadrons as—

> Busiris and his Memphian chivalry.

One would think "Italy" a pleasant enough sound, and "Vulcan" a good enough name for poetry. Neither was musical enough for Milton; both perhaps had associations too numerous, familiar, and misleading. Vulcan is mentioned, by that name, in *Comus;* but in *Paradise Lost,* where the story of his fall from Heaven is told, and the architect of Pandemonium is identified with him, both names, "Italy" and "Vulcan," are heightened and improved:—

> In Ausonian land
> Men called him Mulciber.

"Hephaistos," the name dear to moderns, could have found no place in Milton's works, unless it had been put in a description of the God's smithy, or, perhaps, in the sonnet where are pilloried those harsh-sounding Presbyterian names:—

> Colkitto, or Macdonnel, or Galasp.

Milton's use of proper names is a measure of his poetic genius. He does not forego it even in the lyric. Was there ever so learned a lyric as that beginning "Sabrina fair"—with its rich stores of marine mythology? History, not philosophy, was the source that he drew on for his splendours; and history, according to Milton, had, since the Fall of Man, furnished nothing but fainter and weaker repetitions of those stupendous events which filled the early theatre of universal space.

His epic catalogues, which are few in number, show the same predominant interest in history and geography. The story of the Creation gave him an excellent opportunity of enumerating the kinds and properties of birds, beasts, fishes, and reptiles, plants and trees, after the manner of Chaucer and Spenser. This opportunity he refuses, or, at any rate, turns to but small account. His general descriptions are highly picturesque, but he spends little time on enumeration and detail. Of vegetables, only the vine, the gourd, and the corn are mentioned by name; of the inhabitants of the sea only the seal, the dolphin, and the whale. Natural knowledge, although he made a fair place for it in his scheme of education, was not one of his dearer studies. It was enough for him, as for Raphael, that Adam knew the natures of the beasts, and gave them appropriate names. The mere mention, on the other hand, of historic and geographic names rouses all the poet in him. The spendid roll-call of the devils, in the First Book of *Paradise Lost,* and the only less splendid enumeration, in the Eleventh Book, of the Kingdoms of the Earth, shown to Adam in vision, are a standing testimony to his powers. Compared with these, the list of human diseases and maladies in the Eleventh Book, suggested perhaps by Du Bartas, is rehearsed in a slighter and more perfunctory fashion.

One last point in Milton's treatment must not be left unnoticed. Much adverse criticism has been spent on his allegorical figures of Sin and Death. There is good classical precedent for the introduction of such personified abstractions among the actors of a drama; and, seeing that the introduction of sin and death into the world was the chief effect of his main action, Milton no doubt felt that this too must be handled in right epic fashion, and must not be left to be added to the theme as a kind of embroidery of moral philosophy. In no other way could he have treated the topic half so effectively. There is enough of his philosophy in Milton's Heaven to damp our desire for more of it on his Earth or in his Hell. And when once we have given him license to deal only in persons, we are amply rewarded. His management of the poetic figure of personification is superb. It is a figure difficult to handle, and generally fails of effect through falling into one of two extremes. Either the quality, or the person, is forgotten. The figures in the *Romaunt of the Rose* are good examples of the one type, of the minute materialistic personifications of the Middle Ages, pictorial rather than literary in essence, like the illuminated figures in a psalter. The feeble abstractions that people Gray's Odes, where, as Coleridge remarked, the personification depends wholly on the use of an initial capital, are examples of the other. Neither has the art of combining the vastness and vagueness of the abstract with the precise and definite conception of person, as is done in the great figure of Religion drawn by Lucretius, as is done also in those other figures—the only creations of English poetry which approach the Latin in grandeur—the horrible phantoms of Sin and Death.

These, then, here outlined slightly and imperfectly, are some of the most noteworthy features of Milton's style. By the measured roll of his verse, and the artful distribution of stress and pause to avoid monotony and to lift the successive lines in a climax; by the deliberate and choice character of his diction, and his wealth of vaguely emotional epithets; by the intuition which taught him to use no figures that do not heighten the majesty, and no names that do not help the music of his poem; by the vivid outlines of the concrete imaginations that he imposes on us for real, and the cloudy brilliance that he weaves for them out of all great historical memories, and all far-reaching abstract conceptions, he attained to a finished style of perhaps a more consistent and unflagging elevation than is to be found elsewhere in literature. There is nothing to put beside him. "His natural port," says Johnson, "is gigantick loftiness." And Landor: "After I have been reading the *Paradise Lost,* I can take up no other poet with satisfaction. I seem to have left the music of Handel for the music of the streets, or, at best, for drums and fifes." The secret of the style is lost; and no poet, since Milton's day, has recaptured the solemnity and beauty of the large utterance of Gabriel, or Belial, or Satan.

JAMES HOLLY HANFORD

MILTON AND THE RETURN
TO HUMANISM (1919)*

———————

IT IS now some two centuries and a half since John Milton
gave forth his greatest poem to an alien world, consoling himself in the isolation of his evil days with the thought that,
whatever its immediate reception might prove to be, *Paradise Lost* was a work of lofty thinking and uncompromising art which would always find "fit audience though few" and
which "after times" would not willingly let die. Time has
amply justified his faith. Through all revolutions of taste and
thought, despite much "barbarous noise" of controversy and
"detraction rude," the chorus of praise has risen in ever increasing volume. It would seem paradoxical to say that Milton
has received less than his due measure of that lasting fame
which was for him, though in his sterner thought he held it
vanity, an object of intense desire. Yet, looking back upon the
history of Milton's triumph over the judgment of mankind,
one is tempted to affirm that he has fared but ill even at the
hands of his most devoted friends. The mass of critical appreciation seems in large measure to have missed its mark, to
have been, on the whole, perversely directed to aspects of his
work which he himself would have deemed of secondary importance. It is not strange that it has been so. For the appeal of
Milton, as of all the great forces in the literature of the past,

———————

* From *Studies in Philology*, XVI (1919) , 126-147. Reprinted through the
generous permission of the author and the kindness of the editor of *Studies
in Philology*.

has been conditioned by the moral and intellectual outlook of successive generations of readers, and in so far as the atmosphere of the later age has differed, vitally, from that in which Milton lived, criticism has inevitably suffered limitations. It has suffered, also, from the character of polemic which so much of it has assumed. The ardent defense of Milton against one charge after another levelled against him by enemies of his art or thought has led of necessity to partial views. And as the dust of controversy has subsided the discussions which have grown out of it have come to seem unsatisfactory and incomplete. For the present generation even the "standard" interpretations and estimates of the Victorian era savor too much of the special bias of the time. Meanwhile the signs multiply of an important departure in Milton investigation and criticism. The number of studies which have dealt anew with the themes of *Paradise Lost* and *Paradise Regained,* have re-examined Milton's relations with Spenser and the Elizabethans, have overhauled his doctrines in both his poetry and his prose, have subjected to analysis his political as well as his moral and religious philosophy, are evidence that the effects of an altered viewpoint, which is itself the fruit of a new age of experience, are beginning to be felt.[1] These studies are in the main scholarly rather than controversial in character. They aim at interpretation rather than defense. Out of them we are about to write a new chapter in Milton criticism which, without altogether invalidating the old, will testify to the enduring vitality of the supreme works of human genius not for their art alone, and will reaffirm the principle that poetry is a higher and more philosophical thing than prose. It is perhaps an appropriate

---

[1] A few of the more significant contributions are: E. N. S. Thompson, *Essays on Milton;* Alden Sampson, *Studies in Milton;* A. H. Gilbert, "The Temptation Motive in *Paradise Regained"* (*Journal of English and Germanic Philology,* 1916) ; Edwin Greenlaw, "A Better Teacher than Aquinas" (*Studies in Philology,* 1917) ; H. W. Peck, "The Theme of *Paradise Lost"* (*Publications of the Modern Language Association,* 1914) ; John Erskine, "The Theme of Death in *Paradise Lost"* (*ibid.,* 1917) ; and "Was Paradise Well Lost?" (*ibid.,* 1918); and R. L. Ramsay, "Morality Themes in Milton's Poetry" (*Studies in Philology,* 1918) .

moment to pass in brief review the Miltonism of the past in its chief phases, with the aim of defining more clearly the special character of the new approach. Materials for such a review are already at hand in recent monographs and articles devoted to the history of Milton's reputation.[2] Discussion naturally centers in *Paradise Lost,* for in that poem, by common consent, the influences which shaped Milton's art and thought met in the most perfect balance, and it is by *Paradise Lost* that his position in English literature is determined.

By a strange fatality the audience for which *Paradise Lost* was ideally intended had at the moment of its publication already ceased to exist. Conceived and partly executed in a time when the forces of the Renaissance had not altogether lost their potency and when a synthesis of the two great movements of the age was still possible, the poem was not actually given to the world until years of conflict had made an irremediable breach in the soul of man. Puritanism, indeed, out-lived the Restoration, but it was a Puritanism narrowed and hardened into opposition to poetry, a Puritanism committed solely to conduct and no longer capable of being blended with art and thought. Its literary forms are the sermon and the tract and the didactic allegory. Such a Puritanism had existed in the earlier period, but until the civil wars it had existed simply as a check upon and protest against the more extreme secular tendencies of the Renaissance. Milton's true kinship is not with Bunyan or Baxter, nor yet altogether with Cromwell and the heroes of the battle for religious and political liberty, but with those men of the older day, whose spiritual aspirations were united with the human passion for truth and beauty and who trusted the imagination as an important medium for the attainment of their ideals. Of the Elizabethans Spenser might have read *Paradise Lost* with a comprehending soul. So too in their degree might Taylor, the Fletchers, Herbert,

[2] R. D. Havens, "Seventeenth Century Notices of Milton," and "Early Reputation of *Paradise Lost*" (*Englische Studien,* 1909, 40: 175 ff.) ; John W. Good, *Studies in the Milton Tradition* (*University of Illinois Studies in Language and Literature,* 1915) .

Donne. Even in Milton's own day there were perhaps a few whose outlook was sufficiently akin to his—men like Marvel or the gentle and humane Colonel Hutchinson, or the musician Lawes, or Lawrence "of virtuous father virtuous son." But Puritans like this were rare and becoming rarer. In the Restoration period Milton stood alone, as unintelligible in his point of view to the author of *Pilgrim's Progress* as he was to Dryden and the literary wits of the court of Charles II. The point is often overlooked by those who, focusing their view on his Puritanism, conceive of him as a poet for the Puritans. Orthodox theology in the eighteenth century did indeed derive some support from *Paradise Lost,* but no one surely will claim that Milton came to his own as a champion of the dying cause of Calvinism.

In the end it was, paradoxically enough, the wits and not the Puritans who first seriously undertook the criticism of *Paradise Lost,* and in their appreciations and discussions we may discover the initial phase of the perverted emphasis which has dominated Miltonic interpretation to our own day. Their efforts were directed primarily to an examination of Milton's poetic art in the light of the principles of poetry set forth by Aristotle and reinterpreted by the theorists of the neo-classic school. The process had already begun during the Restoration period when Dryden, taking a narrow view, finds in the "unprosperous event," the disproportion between the divine and human personages, and other technical shortcomings, a violation of epic principles. But the condemnation of Milton on these grounds could not satisfy the better sense of the critics themselves. Possessed of a more genuine responsiveness to sincere and lofty poetry than we sometimes give them credit for, they recognized the genius of Milton as they did of Shakespeare and desired to justify him on some valid and accepted critical basis. It was in this spirit that Addison in the next generation wrote the famous critique in the *Spectator,* vindicating Milton's epic art by a sympathetic analysis of *Paradise Lost* according to the method of Aristotle, with comparison of Homer and Virgil. Other critics fell back on the standard conclusion that Milton, like Shakespeare, was a great irregular genius, rising superior to rule. Dennis founded the poet's claims on the higher inspiration due to his Christian theme, and finally Warburton defined *Paradise Lost* as a new species of epic poem, deserving a place independent of but equal to the epic forms invented by Homer and Virgil.[3]

It is unnecessary in this place to pronounce on the respective merits of these viewpoints. We have only to note that the discussion centered in questions of literary art. With the great controversy over Milton's blank verse which raged throughout the period it is the same. For the eighteenth century critic the major point at issue regarding Milton was the basis of aesthetic theory on which his fame must rest.

Now we must recognize that the attitude assumed in these discussions was perfectly valid as far as it went, and later critics along this line have had little to do but to choose and amplify one or the other methods of approach as their critical creed or temperament inclines them to the classical or romantic estimate of aesthetic values. Milton himself invited consideration of his works from this angle, in his frequent claims of artistic relationship with the ancients, in his defense of blank verse against the "modern bondage of rhyme," and in his obvious consciousness of the formulated theories of epic and dramatic poetry which the Renaissance inherited from antiquity. Progress, therefore, was real enough in the critical treatment of

---

[3] "Milton produced a third species of poetry; for just as Virgil rivalled Homer, so Milton emulated both. He found Homer possessed of the province of Morality, Virgil of Politics, and nothing was left for him but that of Religion. This he seized as aspiring to share with them in the Government of the Poetic world; and by means of the superior dignity of his subject, got to the head of that Triumvirate which took so many ages in forming. These are the species of the Epic poem; for its largest province is human action, which can be considered but in a moral, a political or a religious view; and these the three great creators of them; for each of these poems was struck out at a heat, and came to perfection from its first Essay. Here then the grand scene is closed, and all further improvement of the Epic is at an end." Quoted by Good, *op. cit.*, p. 160.

Paradise Lost in the eighteenth century, but if it constituted in the end a pretty complete vindication of Milton's art, it contributed little to a fuller comprehension of his substance, led to no real interpretation of his greatest work, and furnishes no evidence as to whether this work was actually read in the spirit and from the point of view from which it was written.

Meanwhile, however, other notes were struck in eighteenth century Milton appreciation which concern themselves rather with substance and spirit than with form. A consideration of these developments will bring us forcibly to the conclusion that the dominant spiritual outlook of the period resulted in the playing up in Milton's work of values which were not the essential values and rendered the age incapable of seeing *Paradise Lost* in its true light.

In so far as the currents of eighteenth century thought set toward rationalism, Milton, with his faith in the supernatural governance of the world and his recognition of the authority of the divine imperative within the soul, could waken little real sympathy. To the philosophers of the scientific dispensation the moral and theological system which had held sway in Milton's mind and with which he would have believed the poem bound to stand or fall, was dead. No longer valuing him for his ideas they were obliged, if they regarded him at all, to fall back upon his art. But the immense popularity of Milton in the eighteenth century and the high esteem in which *Paradise Lost* was held, were not primarily based on an aesthetic appreciation. Writers like Addison did not create the fame of Milton; they found him already in the field, holding his place against all comers. Their service was, by exploring the grounds of admiration, at once to increase its volume and to determine its direction. The *Spectator* papers, with their popular adaptation of the critical technique of the day, tended to justify the public in their instinctive choice. But already in Addison's critique much space is devoted to other aspects of the poet's work. In his running commentary on the separate books, as well as incidentally in the course of the formal analysis to which the earlier papers in the series are devoted, Addison emphasizes deeper values in the poem, the recognition of which came ultimately to make Milton seem like the prophet of a new era.

The turn of the century had seen an important change in the position of Milton in relation to the dominant thought and feeling of the age. During the Restoration the reaction against Puritan "enthusiasm," the cynical scorn of virtue, the repression of emotion in all its forms had resulted in a general lack of sympathy with the substance of Milton's poetry, while the unpopularity of the poet's politics served also to throw his merits into collapse. The political revolution of 1688 and the revolution in moral sentiment which attended it called his work again into esteem. Religion and virtue being no longer unfashionable, a religious poem commending virtue might be read with approval by a gentleman. The poetical tributes, with their emphasis on the poet's pure morality and on the divinely inspired character of his imagination fall in with the traditional admirations of the "sublimity" of his subject and the majesty of his style. There is, too, an increasing tendency to stress the emotional and human elements in *Paradise Lost,* in so far as these fall within the perceptions of its readers of those days. In a social age, as Good points out, the social features of the epic came in for particular attention, the more so because Milton had portrayed society in its elements and in an idealized form. It would appear from Steele that *Paradise Lost* in this aspect had already been introduced on terms of familiarity into the drawing-room life of the time. He represents a party of women remarking that Milton had said "some of the tenderest things ever heard" in the love speeches of Adam and Eve, and on. another occasion he speaks of a fan on which was painted "our first parents asleep in each others arms." Steele himself never tires of quoting passages and commending "beauties" of *Paradise Lost,* selecting almost invariably scenes and speeches from the domestic life of the first lovers. And Addison, with a somewhat wider range, does the same. Much is said in the Critique of the "justice" and "beauty" of Milton's "sentiments." He is claimed to have "filled a great part of his Poem with that kind of writing which the French critics call the Tender and which is in a particular manner engaging to all sorts of readers." In his discussion of the character and relations of Adam and Eve Addison writes almost entirely from this standpoint. The representation is said to be "wonderfully contrived to influence the Reader with Pity and Compassion." The characters are drawn "with such sentiments as do not only interest the Reader in their afflictions, but raise in him the most melting passions of Humanity and Commiseration." Detailed illustrations follow, particular emphasis being placed on the reconcilement of the sinning pair.

These passages should be read in the light of those other *Spectator* essays which comment on the domestic virtues, sentimentalize over conjugal affection, and look with indulgent commiseration on the weaknesses of man and woman which so often make their common pathway through the world a vale of tears.

We recognize at once that the emotional expansion of the era had opened new gateways of Miltonic appreciation, and we do not wonder at the degree to which he became an ally of the forward movements of the age. If, however, we consider for a moment the philosophical postulates which were behind the sentimental attitude we shall see why it was impossible for anyone deeply touched by the new creed to grasp the central reality of Milton's view of life. The cardinal fact is that the doctrine of original sin, with all its implications, had given way to the theory of the natural goodness of the human heart. The evil of the world is evil of circumstances only, and as such it is apparent rather than real, an inevitable part of the perfect system of the universe formed by divine intelligence. The logical consequence of such a view is the weakening of conviction regarding human responsibility, and with it the disappearance of all ideas of the tragedy of character. We see the operation of this principle in the eighteenth century drama of pity, in which the great-

est crimes are condoned and attention distracted from the momentous consequences of moral choice to the misfortunes of
those persons who because of wrong education or the overwhelming pressure of temptation pursue the wretched path
which leadeth to the gallows. The effect of this attitude is apparent everywhere in eighteenth century comment on *Paradise
Lost*. We feel it, for example, in Addison when he speaks of
"the miserable aspects of eternal infelicity," and it gives ludicrous results in Bentley's cheerful alteration of the last two lines
of Milton's epic from

> They hand in hand with wandering steps and slow,
> Through Eden took their solitary way.

to

> Then hand in hand with social steps their way
> Through Eden took, with Heavenly comfort cheered.

We may note also a final fruit of the softening of Milton's grim
realities in Burns's humorous commiseration of Satan in the
Address to the Deil:

> But, fare you weel, Auld Nickie-ben!
> O, wad ye take a thought an' men!
> Ye aiblins might—I dinna ken—
>   Still hae a stake:
> I'm wae to think upo' yon den,
>   Ev'n for your sake!

Obviously it would be impossible for the eighteenth century
man of feeling to enter into the heroic consciousness of John
Milton; for him the Puritan poet's central theme of the operation of divine justice through which Paradise was lost to man
as the consequence of his own sin and restored to him again by
the exercise of the righteous will, could mean nothing. We find
in the characteristic eighteenth century rhapsodies on Milton a
steadfast avoidance of this issue. A perusal of the long list of
poetic tributes quoted by Good will show that Milton lovers

throughout the period praise everything about the poet but the strength and fidelity of his handling of the fundamental problem which he set out to treat.

An intensification and a deepening of eighteenth century feeling for Milton was brought about by the rise of emotional religion. Men like Wesley found an important source of inspiration in *Paradise Lost,* while to Cowper Milton, congenial both in his art and in his religious thought, became an ever present companion in the daily meditations of the heart. The religious use of Milton, which caused *Paradise Lost* as a devotional work to retain even to the present day a place coordinate with *Pilgrim's Progress* and second only to the Bible, hardly produces a critical interpretation, but it does involve a shift of attention to the spiritual and meditative aspects of the poem. Thus the loves of Adam and Eve received less attention than their pure devotions in Eden and their ultimate reconciliation to the will of God. A closer sympathy with Milton's deeper interests results, but it must be admitted that in so far as the new religion partakes of the unchecked emotionalism of the sentimental movement it is foreign to Milton's balanced and temperate philosophy of life. The stern yet hopeful outlook of the poet's creed had given way to a morbid melancholy. The idea of man's struggle toward moral freedom, the sober consciousness of difficulties and dangers which might yet be overcome by the exercise of the firm and enlightened will was lost in the subjectivism of the Methodist revival, with its insistence on sudden conversion (an idea quite alien to Milton's thought) and its tendency to emphasize salvation by grace rather than by character.

The true measure of the eighteenth century reading of *Paradise Lost* is clearly given by a consideration of the various forms of the Miltonic influence in the literature of the period. Natural admiration for the poet's genius, the spell exercised by his exalted utterance, the fact that with all his irregularities he yet afforded the one great English model of epic poetry on classical lines, combined to make him a major force in eighteenth century poetry. In one aspect the Miltonism of the age is to be interpreted as a phase of classicism. The doctrine of imitation was extended to include the use of older English authors and Milton became a favorite model of style and form. As a pattern of the epic *Paradise Lost* completely dominated the eighteenth century. Thus the *Rape of the Lock,* despite its professed adherence to ancient models, owes perhaps more to Milton than it does to Homer or Virgil. With the serious epics of Blackmore it is the same. In style Milton is the father of eighteenth century blank verse, and here the influence joins with the currents which set toward the romantic movement. The deeper effects of the study of Milton are to be seen in Thomson and Cowper, who found in him the serious feeling, the reverent attitude, the sincerity and warmth of poetic utterance which they missed in the writings of the school of Pope. It is impossible to discuss this subject at any length. The point is that the influence of Milton was felt first of all in matters of style and form by poets who were utterly removed from him in spirit; and that even where it counted for the deepening of poetic sensibility it produced no re-embodiment of his philosophy of life, no attempt to carry further his imaginative presentation of the problem of evil, no echo, in short, of the humanistic attitude which he inherited from the Renaissance both on its intellectual and moral side. Alienated in interest and aim from the whole period the poet finds neither in its intellectual elite nor in its deeper emotional and religious natures more than a partial comprehension.

From the eighteenth century view of Milton to the nineteenth the transition is direct but strongly marked. The close of the century saw, on the one hand, an increased emphasis on the spiritual values in *Paradise Lost,* and, on the other, a tendency to make the poet a champion of radicalism in politics, religion, and art. Details of the romantic application need not be given here.[4] We may, however, note its most significant phases, and

---

[4] A discussion of the romantic use of Milton in the eighteenth century is to be found in Good, *op. cit.*, 208 ff.

again raise the question whether it affords a view sufficiently in accord with Milton's purposes to be acceptable as a basis for critical interpretation.

The beginnings of a more liberally conceived justification of Milton's art we have already noted. The new romantic criticism revolted sharply against neo-classic standards and prided itself upon having rescued Milton, with Shakespeare, from the Procrustean bed of eighteenth century formalism. Setting a supreme value on the imagination as opposed to form or thought the romantic writers saw in Milton the English poet who above all others

> rode sublime
> Upon the seraph wings of ecstacy,

and they made, more emphatically than the eighteenth century appreciators had made, Milton's imaginative sublimity the true criterion of his greatness. They expatiate on the grandeur of his characters, his images, his verse, illuminating the Miltonic quality with a rich abundance of qualifying phrase. A typical essay is that of Hazlitt, whose treatment of Satan, for instance, considered as a piece of purely descriptive appreciation, can hardly be surpassed:

> The poet has not in all this given us a mere shadowy outline; the strength is equal to the magnitude of the conception. The Achilles of Homer is not more distinct; the Titans were not more vast; Prometheus chained to his rock was not a more terrific example of suffering and of crime. Wherever the figure of Satan is introduced, whether he walks or flies, "rising aloft incumbent on the dusky air," it is illustrated with the most striking and appropriate images: so that we see it always before us, gigantic, irregular, portentous, uneasy and disturbed—but dazzling in its faded splendor, the clouded ruins of a god.

Such a passage suggests the changed relationship of the new age to the poetry of Milton, on the aesthetic side. But the true secret of the Miltonic "revival" of the late eighteenth and early nineteenth centuries lies not solely, not primarily, in a revised estimate of his poetic quality, but in a new interpretation of the moral and spiritual content of his work—a new reading of his "message" to the generations of mankind. It is here that the Romanticists give us a new Milton constituted in their own image and worshipped as they believed, at last in spirit and in truth. This new Milton is first of all a seer, a mystic. His imagination is not so much a quality of literary excellence as it is an instrument wherewith the spirit of man is enabled to pass "the flaming bounds of time and space" and be at one with supersensuous and divine reality. Such he was to Blake, who, notwithstanding his abhorrence of Milton's fundamental creed, had impregnated himself with *Paradise Lost* as he had with Scripture and had fed his own distorted imagination with the poet's creations, unconscious of the impassable gulf which yawned between himself and one whose most rapt imagination never led him for a moment to trespass beyond the bounds of sanity. But more characteristically, perhaps, the romantic Milton is an individual. Admiration for his art is lost in admiration for his personality. His poetry becomes a sublime embodiment of will and passion, an expression of the grandeur of soul which elevated him above the pettiness of his human environment and made him stand firm against the shock of circumstances. For Shelley and Byron he is the type of the free personality, a hero in the warfare against the tyranny of law. It is thus that Shelley apostrophizes him in *Adonais:*

> He died,—
> Who was the sire of an immortal strain,
> Blind, old, and lonely, when his country's pride,
> The priest, the slave, and the liberticide,
> Trampled and mocked with many a loathed rite
> Of lust and blood; he went, unterrified,
> Into the gulf of death; but his clear Sprite
> Yet reigns o'er earth; the third among the sons of light.

And Byron in the Dedication to *Don Juan:*

> If, fallen in evil days on evil tongues,
> Milton appealed to the Avenger, Time,
> If Time, the Avenger, execrates his wrongs,
> And makes the word "Miltonic" mean "sublime,"
> He deign'd not to belie his soul in songs,
> Nor turn his very talent to a crime;
> He did not loathe the Sire to laud the Son
> But closed the tyrant-hater he begun.

The "sublimity" of Milton thus becomes a personal quality—sublimity of soul. His works are interpreted in the light of his career, and are read as the record of his life-struggle. This attitude marks an important advance over the sentimental or the purely literary approach of the eighteenth century; its limitation is to be sought in the essential contradiction between the Miltonic and the romantic ideal of character. For Byron, and, to a large extent, Shelley, make Milton what he assuredly was not, an individualist like themselves, averting their eyes from the fact that the controlling principle of his life was after all not rebellion but free obedience. The official morality of *Paradise Lost* is discountenanced; Milton's insistent condemnation of Satan as the inversion of all good is ignored. The poet becomes a witness in spite of himself to the absolute value of "the will not to be changed by time or place" and a chief assailant of the moral and theological system of which he had innocently supposed himself to be a chief defender. Thus *Paradise Lost* is made the text of works and the source of sentiments the purport of which its author would not even have comprehended. From such discipleship as that of the creator of Cain and Manfred the great Puritan would surely have prayed to be delivered. The "fit audience though few" would not have included Byron, and the fame arising from his praise would have sounded something worse distorted than the vain plaudits of the "herd confused" who extol things vulgar and admire they know not what. The poet has himself pronounced the fitting condemnation:

> Licence they mean when they cry liberty;
> For who loves that, must first be wise and good.

With Shelley the case stands somewhat differently. Inspired to resistance, not by mere passion and expansive egoism, but by a clearly discerned ideal of good, he saw Milton engaged, like himself, in a heroic conflict with the principle of evil in its earthly manifestations of tyranny and injustice. But for Shelley the principle of evil is incarnated in tradition and comes dangerously near to being identical with law itself. Hence in *Prometheus Unbound,* which more than any other of his works was written under the inspiration of *Paradise Lost,* the typical utterance of the enchained Titan has a Satanic ring. His protest is against government itself, and not solely against government which is tyrannical and corrupt; and, what is more serious, he is an uncompromising enemy of historical Christianity, particularly on its Hebraic side. With such an attitude Milton could have had nothing in common. Had Shelley been less inclined to look in the works of poets he admired as in a mirror, finding there solely an image of himself, he might have remembered that his hero's ideal of government was embodied in the regime of Oliver Cromwell and that his personal religion and morality were squarely founded on the Hebrew Scriptures. Evidence of Shelley's complete inversion of the Miltonic viewpoint is to be found in the following judgment on the morality of *Paradise Lost:* "Milton's Devil, as a moral being, is as far superior to his God as one who perseveres in some purpose which he has conceived to be excellent in spite of adversity and torture, is to one who in the cold security of undoubted triumph, inflicts the most horrible revenge upon his enemy, not from any mistaken notion of inducing him to repent of a perseverance in enmity, but with the alleged design of exasperating him to deserve new torments." In other words Satan and God stand in exactly the relation of Prometheus and Jupiter, and it is in Satan that Shelley finds the true embodiment of Milton's personality and of his moral ideal.

Wordsworth takes a saner view of Milton's personality. He has little to say of his rebellion, much of his stern righteousness and uncompromising idealism. To him the "sublimity" of

Milton is a sublimity of character and spiritual insight, not one of passion and will. He invokes the poet's influence against the selfishness and base materialism of the times, crying, as every age has done and will do:

> Milton, thou should'st be living at this hour.

In the noble ode in which he formally renounces the authority of impulse in favor of that of the moral law he catches the very phrase with which he addresses his new divinity from Milton's lips:

> Stern *daughter of the voice of God,*
> O Duty, if that name thou love.

All this brings Wordsworth very close to the spirit of Milton; it should be noted, however, that his appreciation of Milton is chiefly biographical, and gives no interpretation of *Paradise Lost,* though it points the way to one. Wordsworth shares in the tendency of his age to read Milton's works subjectively, as a personal record, ignoring the objective values which the formal eighteenth century criticism, whatever its limitations, is to be commended for having sought. Characteristically he derives his chief inspiration, not from the epics or dramas, but from the sonnets, the most personal of Milton's works.

As regards interpretation it was the emphasis given by men like Shelley and Byron rather than that of Wordsworth that was destined to survive. Though, to be sure, the excesses of Satan worship did not outlive the Byronic philosophy of life of which they were an essential part, it is not too much to say that later nineteenth century criticism has been largely dominated by the romantic point of view. For most critics Satan has remained the real, if not the technical hero of *Paradise Lost.* The earlier books of the poem have been admired at the expense of the whole, as by Macaulay, who remarked that Milton's reputation would have stood higher if he had written only the first four. The personality of the poet has been sought everywhere in his works and even his most objective utterances have been treated as expressions of his private point of view. That these values exist in *Paradise Lost* no one will for a moment deny. Considered as a whole the romantic appreciation of Milton is more vital, surely, than the Augustan and has justly enough discountenanced it. It has led, however, to the neglect of values not less vital, has distracted attention from important aspects of the poet's genius, and, above all, has stood in the way of a full acceptance of *Paradise Lost* as an embodiment of human truth, a poetic application, in Arnold's phrase, of moral ideas to life.

The fundamental difficulty in the nineteenth century approach to Milton is, after all, identical with that of the eighteenth. It lies in the fact that in either age his way of thought—not his theology only, but his general attitude and outlook—was felt to be obsolete. In the eighteenth century it encountered the general scepticism and materialism of the intellectual classes or the enervated amiability of sentimentalism; in the nineteenth it was supplanted by a new idealism, which, having just escaped the shackles of orthodoxy, reacted against the irrationality of Milton's hard and coherent system of theology and, even more violently, against the materialistic terms to which he reduces supersensuous reality. He is unfavorably contrasted in this respect with Dante, whose Heaven of light, and love, and pure spirit is set against Milton's battlemented and bejewelled city of God, which, despite its splendors, is, as Milton has taken pains to make it, analogous at all points to earth. The same indictment is drawn against the naive materialism of Milton's entire narrative, which is held to do violence even to his own best thought. When, for example, Satan affirms that "the mind is its own place" and when Gabriel holds up to Adam's contemplation "a paradise within thee happier far" Milton has seemed to be transcending the limitations of Puritanism and to be speaking the language of modern idealism, but these utterances are felt to be in contradiction with the basic assumptions of the poem. The idea of a Heaven and Hell of spirit has seemed to accord but ill with the tragedy of the fall, with the facts of Satan's revolt, and with the constitution of a material Hell. To insist on such doctrines would be "to shatter the fabric of the poem." They must not, therefore, be insisted on. From the standpoint of idealism the substance of *Paradise Lost* must be condemned and the whole poem be regarded as an absurd but glorious fiction, based on an obsolete tradition which Milton naively accepted and which he exalted by virtue of his poetic power.

This, essentially, is the view taken by Sir Walter Raleigh, whose work on Milton must rank as the most brilliant treatment of the poet's art in the history of nineteenth century criticism. The study is, indeed, too broad and rich to be confined within a formula, but despite the freshness and sympathy of its treatment and the fullness with which it voices the accumulated wisdom regarding Milton of preceding generations of critics, it is yet limited in scope by preconceptions which its author holds in common with writers like De Quincey, Masson and Pattison, not to mention others of a still earlier school. In his discussion of the scheme of *Paradise Lost* Raleigh is chiefly concerned with noting the insuperable difficulties imposed not merely upon our belief but on our imagination by the necessity Milton was under of giving "physical, geometric embodiment to a far-reaching scheme of abstract speculation and thought— parts of it very reluctant to such treatment." This undoubtedly is sound, but it assumes that the abstract speculation, namely the theology, and not the human reality which coexists with it and takes its significance partly but only partly from it, constitutes the true substance and content of the poem. For Raleigh *Paradise Lost* is neither more nor less than "an imposing monument to dead ideas." When he comes to deal with the characters of the poem Raleigh's failure to rate the moral insight of Milton at its true value leads him to judgments to which it is impossible for the present writer to subscribe. By exalting the grandeur of Satan Milton is said to have "stultified the professed moral of the poem and emptied it of all spiritual content, led by a profound poetic instinct to preserve epic truth at all costs."

In his treatment of Adam and Eve he is felt to be dealing essentially with unrealities. Raleigh, though he does not go to such lengths of ridicule as Taine, sees Adam as little better than a stupid and wooden projection of the more forbidding elements of Milton's Puritan personality. To Eve he allows a certain degree of humanity, but he makes her chiefly the vehicle of a Miltonic diatribe against woman. The concluding judgment is stated quite flatly. "While Milton deals with abstract thought or moral truth his handling is tight, pedantic, and disagreeably hard. But when he comes to describe his epic personages, and his embodied visions, all is power, and vagueness, and grandeur. His imagination, escaped from the narrow prison of his thought, rises like a vapor, and, taking shape before his eyes, proclaims itself his master."

Now all that Raleigh or any critic claims for the grandeur of Milton's imagination is undeniably true, but it is to be doubted if the poet himself would have valued an immortality of fame accorded to him only on such terms. The theme of his epic was to him no poetic fiction, and a judgment of his work based on this assumption would have outraged his deepest convictions. For him at least the fall was true, and the conviction of its truth is a condition of the entire sincerity of his treatment. The subject was dignified in his mind, not by its grandeur, but by its superior validity as an explanation of human experience. For it he had discarded the Arthurian material; into it he had thrown his heart. That readers for whom it was no longer in some sense true could by any means enter into a full understanding of his work he would never have believed.

For most modern readers the nineteenth century estimate, as embodied in Raleigh's *Milton,* is the final estimate. The poem is read, if read at all, for its art, its eloquence, its elevation. The events which it recounts and Milton's interpretation of those events are felt to belong to an order of belief which can possess, at best, but a curious historic interest. The poem remains, in Raleigh's phrase, "a monument to dead ideas." It is, of course, of little avail to attempt to restore *Paradise Lost* to its original authority by asking such readers to suspend their disbelief and adopt the convictions which underlie it simply because, without them, it is impossible to regard the work with Milton's eyes. If Milton's thought is really dead it is impossible to galvanize it into life. But it is to mistake the real drift of the newer Miltonic study to assume that it proposes any such factitious rehabiliation of *Paradise Lost*. It proposes rather, as I read it, a reinterpretation and a revaluation of the poem in terms neither of sentimentalism nor of romanticism nor of Victorian idealism but of humanism, and it seeks as a first step toward such revaluation to see Milton's philosophy as a whole by exploring his prose as well as his poetry, to set him in his right relation, not to Puritanism alone, but to the entire Renaissance, and so to realize, through a richer understanding, the significance of his work as poetic criticism of life.

For such a reinterpretation of Milton the way is paved by the fact that the Calvinistic theology is no longer a subject of controversy. It has become possible at last to approach him dispassionately, with due sympathy for whatever we may recover of permanently true and valid from the religious thought of the age. Indeed the virtues of the orthodox way of thinking are quite as apparent to us now as its defects. Thus Chesterton maintains intelligibly enough the validity of the doctrine of original sin. Certainly our reaction against the facile optimism of Victorian religious liberalism, which banished Satan to the limbo of illusion and discovered the joyous fact that all roads lead to Heaven though it were through Hell, has tended to restore to us in a marked degree the moral atmosphere in which Milton lived. Finally the tendency to find sanity and truth in the ideas of the Renaissance has infused new zeal into an Elizabethan scholarship not always so divorced from its human objectives as the critics of our Germanized research would have us believe, with the result that there has been constructed a sounder basis for Miltonic criticism than that afforded by the biographical history of Masson.

The outstanding effect of the study of Milton's philosophy

as embodied in his poetry and prose, and of the endeavor to relate him more closely to his English predecessors has been to
minimize the importance of his theology in the narrower sense,
and to exalt in its place, not merely his art and eloquence and
imagination, but those elements of insight and reflection which
he holds in common with Spenser, Hooker, Shakespeare, and
Bacon—men in whose work the northern and southern currents
of the age are fused in that richer and profounder creative humanism which is the special contribution of the English Renaissance. The essential character of that humanism is its assertion
of the spiritual dignity of man, its recognition of the degree to
which his higher destinies are in his own hands, its repudiation
of the claim of his lower nature to control his higher or of any
force or agency external to his own mind and will to achieve
for him salvation. This humanism is sharply and irreconcilably
at odds with mediaeval thought. It discards, first of all, the
ascetic principle and releases for enjoyment and use all the
agencies of self-realizing perfection. It proposes, moreover (and
this is its essential character) to achieve its goal through the
study not of God but of man and it trusts the human reason as
well as intuition and revealed truth as the instrument of its
knowledge. It turns, therefore, to Scripture for the best record
of man's nature in its relation to the God of righteousness and
love, then to the *litterae humaniores* of antiquity, where it finds
a wider revelation of man as an individual and a citizen, this
latter source constituting no denial but a completion of the
data afforded by the former.

Now Milton, throughout his life, was a humanist in both his
method and his aim. Though inheriting certain mediaeval
tendencies in thought and art, the bent of his mind, as Professor Ramsay has shown, carried him further and further away
from them. He retains to be sure certain fundamental postulates and assurances in common with mediaeval Christianity.
He is convinced of God, of the fact of evil, of the inevitableness
of retribution, and of the hope of Heaven. These postulates are
the postulates not of Puritanism alone but of the total human-

ism of the Renaissance. They are absolutely vital to Milton's thought. The intellectual scaffolding with which they are supported and which, because of the subject demanded it is given in *Paradise Lost,* though not in *Paradise Regained* or *Samson,* is not thus vital. The real "system" which Milton erects is not a theology but an interpretation of experience, based on the bed rock of human freedom, and formulated under the guiding influence of the Bible, the ancients, and the thinkers and poets of the preceding generation.

To embody such ideas as were really living in Milton's consciousness in imaginative form was in no sense a work of violence. His imagination, instead of "proclaiming itself his master," in the way in which it proclaimed itself, for example, Blake's master, because he surrendered himself wholly to it, is for Milton the powerful instrument wherewith, following methods analogous, in some ways to those of Spenser, in others to those of Shakespeare, he gives to his philosophy of life a local habitation and a name. Nor is he greatly hampered by the literalness of his acceptance of the data afforded by the Biblical tradition. For if the events connected with the fall of man were to him literal facts they were also symbols, and it is upon the rock of their symbolic or universal rather than of their literal and particular truth that his faith was based. In his treatise on Christian Doctrine Milton boldly avows the principle of Biblical interpretation which controls his treatment of the subject matter of *Paradise Lost.* The expressions of Scripture are indeed to be accepted in their literal sense, but they are to be interpreted by the individual judgment and in accord with the superior revelation of the Inner Light, which in the language of the poet's art means nothing less than the inspired imagination. In *Paradise Lost* Milton affirms that the account of the battle in Heaven is merely a way of representing spiritual truth to the human understanding. Obviously his belief is anything but naive. And as to the actual experience of Adam and Eve, not to mention the desperate plot of evil men in Hell to overthrow the reign of righteousness and law, they are richer in human truth than anything in English imaginative literature outside of Shakespeare, and Milton has been able to give them wide and permanent significance by virtue of a lifetime spent in the study of man's nature in its relation to the moral and spiritual forces by which his destiny is shaped.

In this view, therefore, Milton is no mere poetic voice speaking irrationalities, nor yet simply a transcendent imagination, but a poet of humanity, and *Paradise Lost* is primarily the epic of man's moral struggle, the record of his first defeat and the promise of his ultimate victory. Its necessary counterpart is *Paradise Regained,* in which that promise is fulfilled by the spiritual triumph of the human Christ.

Such is the emphasis toward which the Miltonic scholarship of the present day inevitably leads us. This scholarship is, in general, an outcome of the return to humanism, and contemporary humanists, whatever their special creed, should rejoice in the result. For Milton freed from the perversities of pseudo-classicism, sentimentalism, and romanticism, viewed without controversial rancor, and brought into line with his great predecessors of the Renaissance, is surely an ally. The true Milton is subject to no one of the counts in the fierce indictment which Mr. Babbitt, and Mr. More, and Mr. Sherman are directing against the literature of our own day and of our romantic past. Deeply sympathetic with the aspirations of men toward freedom of life he yet esteems freedom only as the essential condition for the functioning and self-development of the "inner check." Outward freedom and inward control or freedom with discipline is the authentic humanistic formula which Milton applies in all the domains of education, politics, morality, religion, and art. Champion of liberty though he is he yet knows that

> orders and degrees
> Jar not with liberty but well consent.

The Platonic subordination of the lower faculties of man to the higher is the central doctrine of his philosophy of life. Yet he avoids the danger of asceticism inherent in Plato's thought, condemning the Utopian politics of the *Republic* and repeatedly vindicating the free use of all the instrumentalities of man's self-realization. In the intellectual sphere, filled as he is with the zeal of knowledge and willing to toil unendingly in the search for the scattered members, even to the smallest, of the sacred body of truth, he yet affirms that

> Knowledge is as food and needs no less
> Her temperance over appetite,

and he permits the angel to warn Adam to

> Think only what concerns thee and thy being,

a sentence which, well pondered, might serve as a text for the whole humanistic indictment of the scientific preoccupations of today. In religion he does not rest with "vague intuitions of the infinite," though he is not without them, but soberly worships the God of righteousness whose dwelling is the heart of man. Finally, in art he knows what he wants and knows how to attain it. Creative and original, untrammelled in his effort to realize to the full his imaginative conception and untouched or nearly so by the formalism of the neo-classic creed, he is yet obediently loyal to the laws of a disciplined taste and he is wisely regardful of the ancients, those "models as yet unequalled of any" in excellence of literary form.

These profound convictions put Milton clearly on the side of contemporary humanism, a humanism which, however "new," is not without its essential community with the old. Such in future appreciation he will more and more be felt to be. We have insisted too long on the supposed austerity of his temper and on the narrowness of his Puritan thought; we have misinterpreted the character of the change in viewpoint of his later years and have failed to perceive that instead of passing farther from the Renaissance he had moved nearer to its central truths. Finally, adopting Arnold's hard and fast distinction of Hebraism and Hellenism, we have assumed too readily that the

Reformation and the Renaissance are in Milton contradictory and irreconcilable motives, omitting to credit him with a conscious and consistent endeavor to harmonize them, which at least challenges attention. This, indeed, is Milton's peculiar contribution to the cause and philosophy of humanism, and there is a special significance in the fact that his is the final word of the whole era. Not earlier perhaps, was even an attempt at such a conscious synthesis possible, and without the aid of poetry it could hardly even so have been accomplished. Due allowance being made for an antiquated manner of expression, Milton has given as goodly and comprehensive a formula for the aim and method of education as is to be found in the literature of the Renaissance or as any humanist could wish:

The end then of learning is to repair the ruins of our first parents by regaining to know God aright, and out of that knowledge to love him, to imitate him, to be like him, as we may the nearest by possessing our souls of true virtue, which being united to the heavenly grace of faith, makes up the highest perfection. But because our understanding cannot in this body found itself but on sensible things, nor arrive so clearly to the knowledge of God and things invisible, as by conning over the visible and inferior creature, the same method is necessarily to be followed in all discreet teaching. And seeing every nation affords not experience and tradition enough for all kinds of learning, therefore we are chiefly taught the languages of those people who have at any time been most industrious after wisdom. . . . I call therefore a complete and generous education, that which fits a man to perform justly, skilfully and magnanimously all the offices, both private and public, of peace and war.

Complementary to this is his description of the poet's function:

These abilities, wheresoever they may be found, are the gift of God, rarely bestowed, but yet to some (though most abuse) in every nation; and are of power, beside the office of a pulpit, to inbreed and cherish in a great people the seeds of virtue and public civility, to allay the perturbations of the mind, and set the affections in right tune; to celebrate in glorious and lofty hymns the throne and equipage of God's almightiness, and what he works, and what he suffers to be wrought with his providence in his church; to sing the victorious agonies of martyrs and saints, the deeds and triumphs of just and pious nations, doing valiantly through faith against the enemies of Christ; to deplore the general relapse of kingdoms and states from justice and God's true worship. Lastly, whatsoever in religion is holy and sublime, in virtue amiable and grave, whatsoever hath passion or admiration in all the changes of that which is called fortune from without, or the wily subtleties and refluxes of man's thoughts from within; all these to paint out and describe with a solid and treatable smoothness.

There is little need to quarrel with the didactic bias of Milton's theory. It imposes no necessary limitation on the scope of his art, but merely commits him to a high seriousness of purpose which is in accord with the best traditions of the age. Its practical results are *Paradise Lost, Paradise Regained,* and *Samson Agonistes,* works in which the total Renaissance is summed up and revealed as one, through a harmony of its great ideals of beauty, righteousness, and truth. Such a harmony, though made, no doubt, in the special language of the times, is valid for all times. We shall yet learn, it may be, to regard Milton as a more authentic spokesman than we had believed of three great centuries by no means silent, and we shall know him as a powerful voice of guidance amid the chaos of the present day.

DENIS SAURAT

FAITH, PHILOSOPHY, AND POETRY
IN MILTON'S WORK (1925)*

IT IS necessary to examine the purely poetical part of Milton's work to see what it adds to the results of our previous survey of his thought and character, and also to apply to his art the knowledge so far obtained of his philosophy and of his general characteristics. The two parts of his production, the abstract and the artistic, throw much light on each other.

The *De doctrina* is at once more abstract and clearer than the poems. There is in it, at bottom, very little dogma. For instance, in the treatise, Milton does not venture to risk a firm opinion on the date of the creation of the angels (relatively to that of the world) nor on the reasons of the rebellion of the angels or of the creation of the world.[1] This silence amounts to a confession of ignorance. Yet the poetry is built on most precise data on all these points, which shows that Milton looked upon dogma as a sort of myth, chiefly useful for poetical purposes. Anyhow, he always supplemented it with an inner, psychological meaning, which gives to the poetry its human, permanent value, whatever may happen to the dogma. But even so, there remain obscure points. Milton's pride and reserve kept him from giving away the whole of his thought. Although his personality is so strongly marked, the personal element in his work often escapes us. Even as he wrote on divorce in the fury

---

* From *Milton Man and Thinker*, New York, The Dial Press, copyright 1925, pp. 203-212. Reprinted by permission of The Dial Press.
[1] Cf. *Prose Works*, IV, 184, 213.

of thwarted passion and yet never mentioned his own case, so he seems to have kept back some of his most intimate beliefs from us, even in the *De doctrina,* where, as he says in the dedication, he gives mankind his "best and richest possession." One often feels, in reading him, a resistance and a reticence; and our hypotheses are not completely satisfactory. There remain in his expression gaps which so systematic a mind can hardly have left in his thought. Thus on the question of Christ's personality: perhaps Jesus was only a man for Milton; one feels obliged to give up that idea, confronted as one is by precise assertions; but doubt comes again and again as one re-reads *Paradise Regained* or *Samson Agonistes.*[2] Thus again on the question of the crucifixion, which Milton hardly mentions. Then again on the nature of God: Milton takes all attributes away from God with a zeal which must seem excessive to the right-minded. Justice seems the only attribute he leaves him, and even then he is careful to show us that justice always takes its course naturally, that it flows from the very constitution of man, without God's interference. The advanced sects in Milton's time went very far indeed. We shall see that he occasionally helped them.[3]

We know, at any rate, that he believed in a double revelation:

. . . we possess, as it were, a twofold Scripture; one external, which is the written word, and the other internal, which is the Holy Spirit; . . . that which is internal, and the peculiar possession of each believer, is far superior to all namely, the Spirit itself.[4]

But there is frequently a conflict between the two, and then

even on the authority of Scripture itself, every thing is to be finally referred to the Spirit and the unwritten word.[5]

Milton boasted his belief in the Word. With what restrictions,

---

[2] Cf. Raleigh, *Milton,* p. 168: "the central mystery of the Christian religion occupied very little space in Milton's scheme of religion and thought."

[3] See below, pp. 320-22.

[4] *Treatise of Christian Doctrine,* in *Prose Works,* IV, 447.

[5] *Ibid.,* IV, 450.

we have seen in the case of God;[6] but he knew how to explain, on occasion, that the Old Testament is full of poetical images not to be taken literally, and that in a passage of Proverbs where some have seen an allusion to the Son of God, there is only "a poetical personification of wisdom." [7] He knew, too— and this is worse—that the text of Scripture had been corrupted, in many places designedly; and he found an all too ingenious justification of God for allowing the frauds or errors to take place:

. . . the written word, I say, of the New Testament, has been liable to frequent corruption, and in some instances has been corrupted, through the number, and occasionally the bad faith of those by whom it has been handed down, the variety and discrepancy of the original manuscripts, and the additional diversity produced by subsequent transcripts and printed editions. . . .

It is difficult to conjecture the purpose of Providence in committing the writings of the New Testament to such uncertain and variable guardianship, unless it were to teach us by this very circumstance that the Spirit which is given to us is a more certain guide than Scripture, whom therefore it is our duty to follow.[8]

And especially he had discovered the terrible doctrine that the sacred writer adapted himself to the times and men for whom he wrote, and that consequently we have to translate him into our own terms of thought.[9] Lastly, and worst of all perhaps, he accounted himself directly inspired. His widow is reported to have said (and, of course, this was an echo of his own words) that "he stole from nobody but the muse that inspired him, and that was God's Holy Spirit." [10] And he certainly had very broad ideas about inspiration. "These abilities," he declared in the *Reason of Church Government*,[11] "wheresoever they be

---

[6] See above, pp. 113-15.

[7] *Treatise*, IV, 174.

[8] *Ibid.*, IV, 447-49.

[9] Cf. *Areopagitica*, in *Prose Works*, II, 98-99; *Tetrachordon*, III, 391, 420, etc.; and above, pp. 184-85.

[10] Masson, VI, 746.

[11] *Prose Works*, II, 479.

found, are the inspired gift of God, rarely bestowed, but yet to some . . . in every nation." Thus Euripides was useful to explain a point of Scripture,[12] and Spenser was a better master than Aquinas and Scot.[13]

The rationalist critic's arguments against Milton are therefore as much out of court as the orthodox theologian's. Milton has his answer ready on both sides. Neither must it be said that his faults were imposed upon him by his subject. He did exactly what he liked with his subject; he added much to it; he retrenched what he disliked. Not only did he not keep to the letter, but frequently he did not even keep to the spirit of Christianity. It is therefore exclusively the human truth of the poetry that may justify the poet. His "faults"—often they are beauties; for instance, the false situations he gets into when his sympathies are on the side he is obliged to condemn intellectually—come from his character and not from his faith. What really preoccupied Milton was the political-moral problem—this much more than the metaphysical or cosmological problem. The history of Creation has been made difficult for us by modern science. In former days, the creation of the world was not so big or so interesting an affair as in our eyes. God had created it, and there was an end of it; it was considered to be specifically God's business.

It is important also to point out that Milton needed dogma. The need of mythical thought, so strong in many poets, corresponds to a deeper tendency than the intellectual one. Certainly it helped to keep Milton in his faith—such as it was—at a time when minds less profound than his—Hobbes, Herbert of Cherbury, for example—were apparently more advanced than he. Frequently depth of mind, in men like Milton or Pascal, is an obstacle to their liberation from dogma—or, if you like, a force that keeps them in the faith. Such depth makes them find in the dogma meanings which are not there, and which satisfy them.

---

[12] *Ibid.*, IV, 270.
[13] *Ibid.*, II, 68.

But such adhesion is of doubtful value. Poets in particular need myths. Shelley re-built a mythology out of Greek fragments. Blake made up one out of the queerest materials, and possibly believed in it. For poets are always sorry when they cannot believe in their fictions. Therefore Milton believed through his poetical needs and his high need of sincerity, whereas intellectually he was very near to not believing. He insists with pride —and a certain amount of bad faith, so mixed are human motives—on the fact that his myths are truth whereas the ancients' were false. But we shall see that he used myth—or dogma— less and less in his later work. *Paradise Regained* and *Samson* are practically devoid of it.

On the whole, the only two things we can be sure he believed in are: a divine spirit, essentially unknowable, of whom we are all parts; and a moral fall, which takes place in every man, and from which every man can rise by his own strength, which is the divine spirit in him. Everything else is imagination, consciously or unconsciously. This is proved by the way he allowed himself to tamper with dogma, and by the little trouble he took to avoid contradiction. Thus the descriptions of Hell and its inhabitants in the first books of *Paradise Lost* are pure literature, even as is the allegory of Sin and Death. The dialogues between God and the Son in Book III are merely dramatic, and meant to enlighten the reader, since the course of the world is fixed from all eternity, and God can really be neither seen nor heard. The wars in Books V and VI are entirely foreign to dogma, or all but the vaguest idea of them, and the invention of gunpowder by the rebel angels has always been a scandal to true believers. Books V, VII, and VIII contain no particularly Christian dogma, and are consistent with mere deism, or even pantheism, like nearly the whole of Books XI and XII. Books IX and X contain dogma, certainly, but much addition to it, on the subject of sensuality, for instance, and always interpretation of it. Milton thus nowhere gives pure dogma, and how are we to know whether he believes more in the dogma proper than in his own poetical fancies? Lastly, on one of the most important points of his story, he obviously contradicts himself. In Book III he lays down the true doctrine:

> Thee next they sang of all Creation first,
> Begotten Son. . . .
> He Heaven of Heavens and all the powers therein
> By thee created. . . .[14]

Yet God declares in Book V:

> This day I have begot whom I declare
> My only Son, and on his holy hill
> Him have annointed. . . .
> . . . Your Head I him appoint.[15]

Milton certainly believed in the possibility of no such appointment. But he was looking for a valid poetical reason for Satan's rebellion. The appearance of the Son at a certain date was necessary to his drama. Had the Son been created first, and, as in the *Treatise of Christian Doctrine,* been really the only God the angels could possibly have known, Satan would have had no cause for rebellion on that particular day of Heaven's great year. Nor would his angels have seen any cause to follow him and call him

> Deliverer from new lords.[16]

The whole economy of Books V and VI would have been different, and dramatically inferior.

Thus it can be said that Milton did not believe in the possibility of the events of several of his cantos; and this is a warning to us not to take the rest of his mythology too seriously. Milton has warned us not to take too literally what God says of himself. What, then, of the things Milton sings of Him? Milton uses dogma as myth; his constant intrusion of Greek myth into it is a most characteristic trait. Another order of considerations

---

[14] III, 383-91.
[15] *Ibid.,* V, 603-06.
[16] *Ibid.,* VI, 451.

must also be brought forward. Blake, in a celebrated passage of
the *Marriage of Heaven and Hell,* says:

> Those who restrain Desire do so because theirs is weak enough to
> be restrained; and the restrainer or Reason usurps its place and gov-
> erns the unwilling.
>
> And, being restrained, it by degrees becomes passive till it is only
> the shadow of Desire.
>
> The history of this is written in *Paradise Lost* and the Governor,
> or Reason, is called Messiah.
>
> And the original Archangel, or possessor of the command of the
> Heavenly Host, is call'd the Devil or Satan, and his children are
> called Sin and Death.
>
> But in the Book of Job, Milton's Messiah is called Satan.
>
> For this history has been adopted by both parties.
>
> It indeed appeared to Reason as if Desire was cast out; but the
> Devil's account is that the Messiah fell, and formed a Heaven of what
> he stole from the Abyss.
>
> This is shown in the Gospel, where he prays to the Father to send
> the Comforter, or Desire, that Reason may have Ideas to build on;
> the Jehovah of the Bible being no other than he who dwells in flam-
> ing fire.
>
> Know that after Christ's death, he became Jehovah.
>
> But in Milton, the Father is Destiny, the Son a Ratio of the five
> senses and the Holy ghost Vacuum.
>
> Note.—The reason Milton wrote in fetters when he wrote of angels
> and God, and at liberty when of Devils and Hell, is because he was
> a true poet and of the Devil's party without knowing it.[17]

This passage, on the part of Blake, who did not know the
De doctrina, is sheer genius, and the proof of a fundamental
harmony of mind between him and Milton.[18]

We have seen that Christ is, in truth, Reason triumphing
over Desire. Is Satan, then, a symbol of passion, as Blake as-
serts? This raises the question of symbolism in Milton.

I do not think that Milton should be interpreted in totality,
as has been attempted with Blake, by finding for each character

---

[17] *Poetical Works,* ed. Sampson (Oxford, 1914) , pp. 248-49.

[18] See my *Blake and Milton* (Paris, Alcan, 1920) .

and each event an allegorical, hidden meaning. Milton, unlike Blake, is a clear and precise poet, perfectly in command of his ideas and art, who says what he wants to say, all he wants to say, and no more. But we are not to stop at the letter of his writing either, because, in Milton, behind the letter, there is intensity of conviction and depth of idea. Moreover, behind the ideas, there are powerful feelings, which feed them like a nutritious sap. If we do not know his ideas, we shall unduly restrict the meaning of his words. If we do not know his feelings, we shall unduly restrict the importance of his ideas.

Thus Christ is "Reason," but not through allegory: he is truly the reasonable part of each believer, each man being part of God. As for Satan, it is doubtful whether Milton did him the honor of spreading him thus into every human soul. Satan is therefore not "passion" as Christ is "reason"—that is to say, not Satan in the poems; in Milton's mind, it is quite possible that the devil is the evil element in every man, and even in God, that is to be combated severally; the conception seems to me in perfect harmony with the whole of Milton's doctrine, and gives a new depth to his art and thought. We have seen repeatedly that Satan is the prototype of all that Milton execrates—tyrants, kings, popes, priests even. They come dangerously near to being "of the devil" [19] even as the elect are "of Christ," that is to say, made of him, parts of him. This is one of the points on which Milton kept his inmost thought to himself. But it is helpful to keep the idea in mind while reading him. And anyhow, Satan is the great champion of passion in revolt against divine reason. Milton had too much poetical instinct to spoil his wonderful Satan by making an allegory of him. Yet he had diversified him and had given him all the necessary passions, that he might be, on the intellectual plane, a worthy adversary of deified reason. For it is quite true, as Blake says, that *Paradise Lost* is the struggle of passion against reason. But that is not the whole of *Paradise Lost*. It is only the general meaning, and Milton rambles at his pleasure, for he is a poet and a man of

---

[19] See above, p. 83.

letters and he believes in bringing everything that is fit subject for literature into his poem. His embroidery on the main theme is rich, and rarely inspired by philosophical ideas. The philosopher in him had ideas, but the poet it was that expressed them, and the poet had many things to express besides, on his own account.

Yet, as we have seen, in speaking of Christ Milton uses symbol in a particular way, which is warranted, as we shall see, by Augustine's authority. He believes in a physical fact, and yet that fact, real in itself, is a symbol of moral facts. The events of Scripture, the life of Jesus himself, are a sort of poetical allegory used by God, who, instead of writing in a book words that have two meanings, a literal and a figurative, causes to happen on earth events that have two senses: the plain solid fact, that Jesus lived, and the moral fact, that, concurrently, divine reason came into men. Even so, Satan is an image of passion in all men —even if he is not passion in all men—and also a reprobate angel cast down from Heaven by thunder. Thus, even when Milton did not interpret dogma so as to destroy it, as he occasionally did, he built, parallel to it, a course of psychological events that were as a sort of lining to that cloth, and were an integral part of the finished garment.

We must not, therefore, make a mere allegory of *Paradise Lost*. There is allegory in it, and myth and symbol. But at bottom Milton is a clear rationalist mind who despises "superstitions" when they correspond to no clear ideas of his own. He submitted to no symbolism, and to no dogma, further than he liked. The element of clearness, reason, culture is predominant in his mind, and his whole work is a sane and vigorous effort towards light and freedom.

E. M. W. TILLYARD

PARADISE LOST: CONSCIOUS AND UNCONSCIOUS MEANINGS (1930)*

I F THE foregoing account of the way *Paradise Lost* evolves is correct in the main, it becomes plain that everything was meant to be subordinate to the human drama. Whatever the actual result, Milton intended neither Satan nor the picture of paradisaical bliss nor the descriptions of heavenly beatitude to detract from the struggle that took place in the hearts of Adam and Eve. The thorough-going Satanists will have to sacrifice both Milton's conscious intention and the structural unity to their belief. Such a sacrifice might conceivably be necessary, but it is too drastic to be made lightly. Further, if we are to discover the main structure of Milton's conscious idea we shall best do it by examining that part of the poem round which everything else revolves.

In passing it may be pointed out that for Milton with the beliefs he professed the Fall was necessarily the most pregnant event in the history of the world. The only event that could seriously compete with it was the entrance of sin into Heaven, but the direct effect of this was limited to expulsion and irrevocable condemnation: there was no evocation of grace. But the Fall of man, occasioned by the sinful angels, instead of bringing unmitigated perdition called forth Grace in addition and was the reason of regeneration and the incarnation of the

---

* From *Milton,* London, Chatto and Windus; New York, The Macmillan Company, copyright 1930, Chaps. III and IV of Part III. Reprinted by permission of The Macmillan Company of New York.

Son. It is thus both effect and cause of the highest moment: of higher moment than the incarnation itself, which without the sin of Adam would simply not have taken place.

But the nature of the Fall is a very different problem from its comparative importance, and it is this we must examine in order to find the centre of Milton's conscious intention. Unfortunately the problem presented by the Ninth Book of *Paradise Lost* is not quite simple. There is one radical difficulty: that it is not always clear for what Adam and Eve stand. Do they stand for humanity or for man and woman? When Eve in evil hour stretches forth her rash hand for the fruit, does Milton intend her rashness to be universally human or specifically feminine? The answer may make a good deal of difference. As a matter of fact Milton seems to mix the two meanings while ultimately his old grudge against the female sex gets the upper hand of his conscious intentions, of which more presently. Let it suffice to say that this complication makes it difficult for me to accept any very simple explanation of the meaning of the Fall, like that of Addison or of Greenlaw and Saurat. Addison considers the Fall simply a matter of disobedience and is content with this rather vague explanation:

The great Moral . . . which reigns in Milton is the most universal and most useful that can be imagined: it is in short this, *that Obedience to the Will of God makes Men happy, and that Disobedience makes them miserable.* This is visibly the Moral of the principal Fable which turns upon Adam and Eve, who continued in *Paradise* while they kept the Command that was given them, and were driven out of it as soon as they had transgressed.

Milton could hardly have demurred, but mere unmotivated disobedience does not get us very far. We would know to what motive Milton consciously attributed that sin. Greenlaw[1] combines a theory of what *Paradise Lost* means with a comparison of that poem with the adventures of Guyon in the second book of *The Faerie Quene*. He opposes the Satanists and stresses the

[1] In an article, "A Better Teacher than Aquinas," in *Studies in Philology,* 1917, pp. 196-217.

Platonic rather than the Biblical influences. The theme of *Paradise Lost* is less that of obedience to God than of obedience to σωφροσύνη, to temperance, to the rational against the irrational part of human nature. There are two conflicts: one between Satan and the two intemperate vices, ambition and lust for power; the other between Adam and sensuality. These conflicts correspond to Guyon's adventures first with Mammon and then in the Bower of Bliss, and were indeed suggested by them. The Fall then will be the yielding of reason to passion, and in particular to the passion of sensuality. Saurat agrees entirely with this interpretation of the Fall. That it contains much truth I do not deny, but as a complete explanation it seems to me to disregard a large portion of Milton's text; which it may now be well to examine.

The last words of Raphael to Adam in the Eighth Book, when at sunset he departs, are prophetic of the struggle that is to come, and merit close attention.

> But I can now no more; the parting Sun
> Beyond the Earths green Cape and verdant Isles
> *Hesperean* sets, my signal to depart.
> Be strong, live happie, and love, but first of all
> Him whom to love is to obey, and keep
> His great command; take heed least Passion sway
> Thy Judgement to do aught, which else free Will
> Would not admit; thine and of all thy Sons
> The weal or woe in thee is plac't; beware.
> I in thy persevering shall rejoyce,
> And all the Blest: stand fast; to stand or fall
> Free in thine own Arbitrement it lies.
> Perfect within, no outward aid require;
> And all temptation to transgress repel.

From this it would seem that the struggle was to be between passion and reason, but it must be remembered that Raphael is speaking to Adam alone: his words need not refer to the prior temptation of Eve. Coming to the Ninth Book we find Eve leaving Adam to garden alone, fully warned and confident in her own strength to overcome any temptation, anxious even to prove her individual worth. She utters (line 335) the very Miltonic sentiment:

> And what is Faith, Love, Vertue, unassaid
> Alone, without exterior help sustaind?

But when the actual temptation occurs, her mind quite belies her apparently sober preparedness. Nor is there any need of a great wave of passion to overwhelm her resolution. Eve shows little strength of feeling: it is not so much excess of passion as triviality of mind that is her ruin. She is a prey to a variety of feelings, but it is always this triviality that allows her thus to be preyed on. First comes suspectibility to flattery. After Satan's first speech follow the lines (549-50):

> So gloz'd the Tempter, and his Proem tun'd;
> Into the Heart of *Eve* his words made way.

Then she is unwary (613-14):

> So talk'd the spirited sly Snake; and *Eve*
> Yet more amaz'd unwarie thus reply'd.

Just before following Satan to the Tree she is called 'our credulous Mother.' Confronted by the Tree for a moment she recollects herself and makes a faint resistance; but a single long speech of Satan is enough to overcome it. Well aware of Eve's shallowness he says (692-3):

> will God incense his ire
> For such a petty Trespass?

And when he ceases speaking, Milton writes (733-4):

> He ended, and his words replete with guile
> Into her heart too easie entrance won.

In other words, Eve's resistance was inexcusably trivial. The sin of greed is added next (739-44):

> Meanwhile the hour of Noon drew on, and wak'd
> An eager appetite, rais'd by the smell

> So savorie of that Fruit, which with desire,
> Inclinable now grown to touch or taste,
> Sollicited her longing eye.

But this is the only form of sensuality that sways her mind and cannot compare in power with the other motives. To say that Eve's fall expresses the struggle between reason and sensuality is to go clean contrary to the bulk of the text. Once Eve has eaten, her judgment is thoroughly upset: it is the fruit itself that is passion rather than the motives that led to eating it. Inflamed by passion she commits the *hubris* of imagined godhead and gorges herself unrestrainedly with the fruit. But mental triviality is still to the fore, for Eve imagines light-heartedly that God may not notice her act (811-16):

> And I perhaps am secret: Heav'n is high,
> High and remote to see from thence distinct
> Each thing on Earth; and other care perhaps
> May have diverted from continual watch
> Our great Forbidder, safe with all his Spies
> About him.

In sum, Eve's prime sin is a dreadful unawareness, despite all warnings, of the enormous issues involved.[2]

Adam is initially better aware. He is horrified when he hears Eve's story (888-93):

> *Adam,* soon as he heard
> The fatal Trespass done by *Eve,* amaz'd,
> Astonied stood and Blank, while horror chill
> Ran through his veins, and all his joynts relax'd;
> From his slack hand the Garland wreath'd for *Eve*
> Down drop'd, and all the faded Roses shed.

But what is his first thought? It is comradeship: to forsake Eve cannot for an instant be contemplated. Adam's speech, his first

---

[2] In his first mention of the Fall in *Paradise Regained* (i. 51) Milton speaks of "*Adam* and his facil consort *Eve*." Eve's mental triviality seems to have remained in his mind as her dominant characteristic.

comment on Eve's fall, must be momentous and had better be
quoted entire:

> O fairest of Creation, last and best
> Of all Gods Works, Creature in whom excell'd
> Whatever can to sight or thought be form'd,
> Holy, divine, good, amiable, or sweet!
> How art thou lost, how on a sudden lost,
> Defac't, deflourd, and now to Death devote?
> Rather how hast thou yeelded to transgress
> The strict forbiddance, how to violate
> The sacred Fruit forbidd'n! som cursed fraud
> Of Enemie hath beguil'd thee, yet unknown,
> And mee with thee hath ruind, for with thee
> Certain my resolution is to Die;
> How can I live without thee, how forgoe
> Thy sweet Converse and Love so dearly joyn'd
> To live again in these wilde Woods forlorn?
> Should God create another *Eve,* and I
> Another Rib afford, yet loss of thee
> Would never from my heart; no, no, I feel
> The Link of Nature draw me: Flesh of Flesh,
> Bone of my Bone thou art, and from thy State
> Mine never shall be parted, bliss or woe.[3]

This seems simple enough: the heart of any normal reader
warms with sympathy at these exquisitely tender words of
Adam refusing to forsake Eve in her extremity. And yet how
can Milton at this of all places in the poem have given Adam
his conscious approval? Unconscious approval even is difficult
to accept, for the issues at stake are so absolutely clear. Had
Milton unconsciously approved of Adam's sense of comradeship
he would have described it far less obtrusively. Now if he dis-
approves, what is Adam's sin? It is certainly not sensuality.
Adam's passions are in no wise roused: he merely voices the
natural human instinct of comradeship with his kind. Adam
cannot face solitariness, "to live again in these wilde Woods
forlorn." He does not for a moment hesitate to sacrifice the

---

[3] *Paradise Lost,* ix. 896-916.

course of action he knows to be right to his gregariousness. Ordinary man is far too weak to live alone. Milton makes the accusation with all tenderness, but I believe he meant to make it; and when we remember his own extraordinary self-sufficiency, we need not be surprised at this strange arraignment of essential human nature.

Once Adam has put gregariousness above what he fully knows to be right, he is open to every kind of weakness. He quickly falls into a mental levity similar to Eve's, arguing that perhaps God will withold his doom, and into an infatuation that dreams of Godhead. His final sin is uxoriousness. Eve has lavished praise on him for his fidelity and Milton writes (990-9) :

> So saying, she embrac'd him, and for joy
> Tenderly wept, much won that he his Love
> Had so enobl'd, as of choice to incurr
> Divine displeasure for hcr sake, or Death.
> In recompence (for such compliance bad
> Such recompence best merits) from the bough
> She gave him of that fair enticing Fruit
> With liberal hand: he scrupl'd not to eat
> Against his better knowledge, not deceav'd,
> But fondly overcome with Femal charm.

The last line is curiously inconsistent with what went before. Adam had made up his mind before Eve exercised her charms on him: her caresses were superfluous. The fruit acts on Adam as on Eve (1008-11) :

> As with new Wine intoxicated both
> They swim in mirth, and fansie that they feel
> Divinitie within them breeding wings
> Wherewith to scorn the Earth.

Adam reaches the height of criminal levity when he says

> if such pleasure be
> In things to us forbidden, it might be wish'd,
> For this one Tree had bin forbidden ten.

(Milton's grim humour never showed more dramatic power than in these lines. We can hear Eve's hectic, infatuate giggles at Adam's words.) But it is now sensuality that comes to the fore: sensuality the effect rather than the cause of the Fall. Inflamed by the fumes of the fruit the pair fall into lust, impure in itself and the more criminal as yielded to so frivolously at the most terribly fateful hour of mankind's whole history.

When the first intoxicating effect of the fruit has passed, Adam and Eve fall to quarrelling; and Milton makes it perfectly plain that he means the effect of the Fall to signify the victory of passion over reason (1121-1131):

> They sate them down to weep, nor onely Teares
> Raind at thir Eyes, but high Winds worse within
> Began to rise, high Passions, Anger, Hate,
> Mistrust, Suspicion, Discord, and shook sore
> Thir inward State of Mind, calme Region once
> And full of Peace, now tost and turbulent:
> For Understanding rul'd not, and the Will
> Heard not her lore, both in subjection now
> To sensual Appetite, who from beneath
> Usurping over sovran Reason claimd
> Superior sway.

In this strife at the end of Book Nine and in the Tenth Book the emphasis gets laid on Adam's folly in yielding to Eve's advances, on the theme of "fondly overcome with Femal charm." Adam generalises bitterly on the relations of the sexes (1182-6):

> Thus it shall befall
> Him who to worth in Women overtrusting
> Lets her Will rule; restraint she will not brook,
> And left to her self, if evil thence ensue,
> Shee first his weak indulgence will accuse.

When the Son comes to the Garden to deliver judgment, his chief ground for blaming Adam seems to be his uxorious yielding. But we must remember that Adam's defence was that Eve gave him of the tree and he did eat. The Son replies to this defence:

> Was shee thy God, that her thou didst obey
> Before his voice, or was shee made thy guide,
> Superior, or but equal, that to her
> Thou did'st resigne thy Manhood, and the Place,
> Wherein God set thee above her made of thee,
> And for thee, whose perfection farr excell'd
> Hers in all real dignitie: Adornd
> She was indeed, and lovely to attract
> Thy Love, not thy Subjection, and her Gifts
> Were such as under Government well seem'd,
> Unseemly to beare rule, which was thy part
> And person, had'st thou known thy self a right.[4]

The last line seems to show that Milton recognises a prior cause of Adam's fall, lack of self-knowledge, itself implying a kind of triviality of mind. But still Milton cannot leave alone the theme of woman's delusiveness and indulges in a heartfelt outburst before Adam and Eve become reconciled.

> O why did God,
> Creator wise, that peopl'd highest Heav'n
> With Spirits Masculine, create at last
> This noveltie on Earth, this fair defect
> Of Nature, and not fill the World at once
> With Men as Angels without Feminine,
> Or find some other way to generate
> Mankind? this mischief had not then befall'n,
> And more that shall befall, innumerable
> Disturbances on Earth through Femal snares,
> And straight conjunction with this Sex: for either
> He never shall find out fit Mate, but such
> As some misfortune brings him, or mistake,
> Or whom he wishes most shall seldom gain
> Through her perverseness, but shall see her gaind
> By a farr worse, or if she love, withheld
> By Parents, or his happiest choice too late
> Shall meet, alreadie linkt and Wedlock-bound

---

[4] *Paradise Lost*, x. 145-56.

To a fell Adversarie, his hate or shame:
Which infinite calamitie shall cause
To Humane life, and household peace confound.[5]

This prophetic outburst of Adam, so entirely uncalled for, is very illuminating. It is of course Milton's own voice, unable through the urgency of personal experience to keep silent. And it may help to explain the curious shift, mentioned above, of the motive that prompted Adam's fall: the shift from gregariousness to sensuality. The qualities that ruin most men were not shared by Milton: he has no part in their levity and their terror of standing alone. But he cannot for long keep himself out of the poem. The one occasion when he allowed passion to gain the mastery over reason was when he made his first marriage: for him personally sex was the great pitfall. And so he cannot refrain from grafting sex onto the scheme of the Fall. The story in *Genesis* is too good an excuse to be missed for uttering his ancient grievance. Even in writing of the Fall, therefore, Milton is not exempt from the sin of sacrificing reason to passion.

The question remains: how many of the motives attributed to Adam and Eve are common to humanity, how many peculiar to one sex? Mental levity is common to both Adam and Eve, but stronger in Eve. It is the besetting sin of all humanity; fear of standing alone or gregariousness is of course common to it too, but it is a sin only in the man, for it is not woman's function to stand alone. Uxoriousness is a purely masculine failing.

To sum up, Milton seems to mean by the Fall the following. There is in man a "levity and shallowness of mind," as he calls it in *The Tenure of Kings and Magistrates,* or, with varied metaphors, a "numb and chill stupidity of soul, an unactive blindness of mind," in *Reason of Church Government,* which makes him unaware of the important issues of life. Not knowing himself properly, he allows his passions to deceive and get

---

[5] *Paradise Lost,* x. 888-908.

the better of his judgment. For Milton (there is no proof that he thought it true for all men) it is through the female sex that this deception is likely to happen. Once the passions have got the upper hand, chaos ensues, all peace of mind is gone, man has fallen from true liberty to mental anarchy.

Milton connects the loss not merely of mental but of political liberty with the Fall, in a very important passage of the Twelfth Book where Michael comments on Nimrod, the first monarch. Michael says to Adam:

> Justly thou abhorr'st
> That Son, who on the quiet state of men
> Such trouble brought, affecting to subdue
> Rational Libertie; yet know withall,
> Since thy original lapse, true Libertie
> Is lost, which alwayes with right Reason dwells
> Twinn'd, and from her hath no dividual being:
> Reason in man obscur'd, or not obeyd,
> Immediately inordinate desires
> And upstart Passions catch the Government
> From Reason, and to servitude reduce
> Man till then free. Therefore since hee permits
> Within himself unworthie Powers to reign
> Over free Reason, God in Judgement just
> Subjects him from without to violent Lords;
> Who oft as undeservedly enthrall
> His outward freedom: Tyrannie must be,
> Though to the Tyrant thereby no excuse.[6]

The rest of the conscious meaning of the poem is easier to state. First may be added the doctrine of free will, without which any kind of obedience had for Milton no meaning. This he insists on so frequently and emphatically that we need not question the conscious store he set by it. Moreover the construction, by which at the end of the Eighth Book Heaven withdraws itself, leaving Adam and Eve completely free, brings the doctrine home to us more emphatically at the climax than any-

---

[6] *Paradise Lost,* xii. 79-96.

where else, and thus stresses its conscious importance in Milton's mind. No other idea is mentioned so often in the other parts of the poem also: too often according to the common view; and Pope was largely thinking of the pronouncements in Heaven on free will and foreknowledge when he accused Milton's God the Father of turning School Divine. But it is well to heed these passages if we can and try to gauge their weight in Milton's mind. I think the doctrine of free will had for him a double meaning. It was a condition of significant action and it expresses his belief in the value of the conscious will. If action was controlled beyond the power of choice by an outside force, it became separated from the mind and its value disappeared. Secondly, the kind of action or state of mind Milton felt desirable was one perfectly controlled by the conscious will. He had little belief in any deed, however seemingly great, performed instinctively or with the full significance of the issues unrealized. Part of the sin of Adam and Eve is that they fail most lamentably to realise the full issue and to make full use of the will-power that is the great weapon for good in their natures. They are not worthy of the great gift of free will. Milton's feelings about the conscious will can be well illustrated by a contrast. He would have been utterly out of sympathy with those stanzas of Wordsworth that most clearly describe the virtue of suspending completely the operations of the conscious will.

> The eye—it cannot choose but see;
> We cannot bid the ear be still;
> Our bodies feel, where'er they be,
> Against or with our will.
>
> Nor less I deem that there are Powers
> Which of themselves our minds impress;
> That we can feed this mind of ours
> In a wise passiveness.
>
> Think you, 'mid all this mighty sum
> Of things for ever speaking,
> That nothing of itself will come,
> But we must still be seeking.

> —Then ask not wherefore, here, alone
> Conversing as I may,
> I sit upon this old grey stone
> And dream my time away.

Meditation and the exercise of the imagination in calling up

> Such sights as youthfull Poets dream
> On summer eeves by haunted stream

were modes of activity Milton believed in, and the spirit that urged him to create poetry might work in a mysterious way; but the idea of cultivating a vacancy, a wise passiveness, on the assumption that all sorts of things happened without or against one's will, would have been abhorrent.

It may be surmised that if Milton belonged to the present generation he would have distrusted profoundly the idea that a good deal should be yielded to our subconscious desires. He would have felt that the danger of encouraging latent barbarity by fostering them was far greater than the dangers following their repression. Progress in evolution he would have liked to think had resulted from the creative power of the conscious will. Man said I *will* walk and he did walk. And instead of following Wordsworth he would have agreed with Shelley's words at the end of *Prometheus Unbound* to the effect that Hope may create by hoping the thing it contemplates.

Conscious control is so much a part of Milton's nature, so inseparable from the cadence of his verse, that illustration is almost superfluous. Two passages, however, are particularly illuminating. The first is from *Comus*. Comus, having heard the Lady's song, says in comment:

> But such a sacred, and home-felt delight,
> Such sober certainty of waking bliss
> I never heard till now.[7]

Waking bliss is most significant. The Lady, following not blind instinct but fully conscious of her own mind, had attained a

---

[7] 262-4.

felicity more powerful than Comus has ever dreamed of. The
other passage is the description of the fiends mustered on the
plains of Hell:

> Anon they move
> In perfect *Phalanx* to the *Dorian* mood
> Of flutes and soft Recorders; such as rais'd
> To highth of noblest temper Hero's old
> Arming to Battel, and in stead of rage
> Deliberate valour breath'd, firm and unmov'd
> With dread of death to flight or foul retreat,
> Nor wanting power to mitigate and swage
> With solemn touches, troubl'd thoughts, and chase
> Anguish and doubt and fear and sorrow and pain
> From mortal or immortal minds.[8]

Deliberate valour, the valour of the hero who knows himself
and knows what he is fighting, of Homer's Ajax praying that,
if he must die, it may be in the light, not the sudden flare-up
of ignorant recklessness, was what Milton believed in. In this
passage if anywhere Milton is on the Devils' side.

Mankind, in Milton's conscious thought, was not only perverse: it had a natural nobility and dignity. All the strength of
his conscious, traditional humanism comes out in his first description of the human pair:

> Two of far nobler shape erect and tall,
> Godlike erect, with native Honour clad,
> In naked Majestie seemd Lords of all,
> And worthie seemd, for in thir looks Divine
> The image of thir glorious Maker shon,
> Truth, Wisdom, Sanctitude severe and pure,
> Severe, but in true filial freedom plac't;
> Whence true autoritie in men.[9]

And again in his description of Adam going to meet Raphael:

---

[8] *Paradise Lost,* i. 549-59.
[9] *Paradise Lost,* iv. 288-95.

Mean while our Primitive great Sire, to meet
His god-like Guest, walks forth, without more train
Accompani'd then with his own compleat
Perfections, in himself was all his state,
More solemn then the tedious pomp that waits
On Princes.[10]

Such then is man in *Paradise Lost:* noble by nature; owing obedience to his Creator; free to choose and hence capable of action, morally good or bad, for which he alone is responsible; beset by a strange mental perverseness or levity which thwarts his native endowment and opens him to the rule of passion over reason.

That Satan and Christ in some sort represent passion and reason cannot be doubted. Such clearly was Milton's conscious intention. Satan is meant to typify those bad passions that entered man at the Fall. In the mental levity that marked the human pair he has no part. Generally he seems to express a turbulent, unreasoning energy, aiming at the impossible and dissatisfied with what it attains. His crowning folly is to imagine that he and his companions are self-created. In reply to Abdiel's opposition in the rebels' council in Book Five he says:

That we were formd then saist thou? and the work
Of secondarie hands, by task transferd
From Father to his Son? strange point and new!
Doctrin which we would know whence learnt: who saw
When this creation was? rememberst thou
Thy making, while the Maker gave thee being?
We know no time when we were not as now;
Know none before us, self-begot, self-rais'd
By our own quick'ning power, when fatal course
Had circl'd his full Orbe, the birth mature
Of this our native Heav'n, Ethereal Sons.
Our puissance is our own.[11]

---

[10] *Ibid.,* v. 350-5.
[11] *Paradise Lost,* v. 850-61.

When Satan arrives on earth with good hope of success he gets no satisfaction at the prospect of his

> dire attempt, which nigh the birth
> Now rowling, boils in his tumultuous brest,
> And like a devilish Engine back recoiles
> Upon himself; horror and doubt distract
> His troubl'd thoughts, and from the bottom stirr
> The Hell within him, for within him Hell
> He brings, and round about him, nor from Hell
> One step no more then from himself can fly
> By change of place.[12]

And when success is achieved its bitter taste is symbolised by the ashy fruit chewed by the devils in the serpentine form forced on them. There is not the slightest reason to doubt that Milton intended Satan to be a terrible warning embodiment of the unrestrained passions, inspiring horror and detestation rather than sympathy.

If Satan is unreasoning energy, Christ is intended to be energy as well as reason. He is the creator while Satan is but the destroyer. Milton means to express as much energy in his description of the world's creation in Book Seven as in any of the exploits of Satan. He does his utmost too to attribute energy to the good angels, and he sometimes succeeds. There is a fine military keenness about Gabriel and his guard in Book Four, and they have the satisfaction, rare among the celestial troops, of effecting something. But Milton seemed to connect Christ with reason above all. God the Father, praising Abdiel for his fortitude, speaks of the rebel angels,

> who reason for thir Law refuse,
> Right reason for thir Law, and for thir King
> *Messiah,* who by right of merit Reigns.[13]

This conjunction of the Messiah and reason can hardly be fortuitous. But Christ is more than an allegory of reason: he is the

---

[12] *Ibid.,* iv. 15-23.
[13] *Paradise Lost,* vi. 41-3.

divine Redeemer of mankind. (There has been no intention to imply that Milton intended either his Christ or his Satan to be purely allegorical figures. To say that they in some sort represent reason and passion does not mean that their functions stop here.) From beginning to end of *Paradise Lost* Milton adheres to the orthodox idea of guilt and redemption. It is as important to the poem as the Fall itself. God the Father states the position with the utmost clarity in the first conversation in Heaven:

> Man disobeying,
> Disloyal breaks his fealtie, and sinns
> Against the high Supremacie of Heav'n,
> Affecting God-head, and so loosing all,
> To expiate his Treason hath naught left,
> But to destruction sacred and devote,
> He with his whole posteritie must die,
> Die hee or Justice must; unless for him
> Some other able, and as willing, pay
> The rigid satisfaction, death for death.[14]

And along with the redemption of man by Christ is a professed optimism. Regenerate man, man with his reason reillumined by Christ, will rise to a more excellent state than that from which he has fallen. Thus in the end Satan's schemes have turned to good, and Adam, though himself sinning, did an ultimately beneficial act. This professed optimism is constant. We are carefully informed that Satan would never have risen from the lake of fire, had not God intended him to be the instrument of ultimate good. When at the beginning of Book Eleven Christ presents the prayers of Adam and Eve to the Father, he exalts them above anything they were capable of producing in their state of innocence. The new earth revealed to Adam by Michael near the end of the poem will be far happier than the original Eden, and Adam exclaims:

> O goodness infinite, goodness immense!
> That all this good of evil shall produce,

---

[14] *Ibid.,* iii. 203-12.

And evil turn to good; more wonderful
Then that by which creation first brought forth
Light out of darkness! full of doubt I stand,
Whether I should repent me now of sin
By mee done and occasiond, or rejoyce
Much more, that much more good thereof shall spring.[15]

Such are the main lines of the conscious plan. It may be added that *Paradise Lost* confirms the idea that matter is good. All things are created pure, the body as well as the soul of man. Milton feels this so strongly that he inserts in the long and moving speech of Adam in his despair an argument for the inseparability of soul and body and of their common mortality:

Yet one doubt
Pursues me still, least all I cannot die,
Least that pure breath of Life, the Spirit of Man
Which God inspir'd, cannot together perish
With this corporeal Clod; then in the Grave,
Or in some other dismal place, who knows
But I shall die a living Death? O thought
Horrid, if true! yet why? it was but breath
Of Life that sinn'd; what dies but what had life
And Sin? the Bodie properly hath neither.
All of me then shall die.[16]

And he delights to describe the material nature of the angels, better and airier than of men but material still.

To sum up the conscious meaning: Man was created of matter; pure, noble, but curiously fallible, having freedom of will. His mental levity and gregariousness expose him to the assaults of passion, which, while it sways reason, robs him of liberty and subjects him to slavery both within and without; but by the operation of Christ he may establish reason once again in his mind and reach a higher state than that from which he fell.

Before leaving Milton's conscious intention I should like to

---

[15] *Paradise Lost,* xii. 469-76.
[16] *Ibid.,* x. 782-92.

mention, not to discuss, one of the chief ideas in Saurat's book. After discussing Milton's idea of God, Saurat writes:

From the Absolute nothing can proceed. As Milton says, He has neither reason nor power to change into a less perfect state. How is it possible, then, to derive from the Absolute, the only necessary cause of all that is, the existence of limited individual beings? . . . Milton saw the problem. He found no solution that could be drawn from Scripture or theology. So he boldly took a passage out of the *Zohar* and made it the very centre of his metaphysics:

> . . . I uncircumscribed myself retire,
> And put not forth my goodness, which is free
> To act or not.

According to his eternal plans, God withdraws his will from certain parts of Himself, and delivers them up, so to speak, to obscure latent impulses that remain in them. Through this 'retraction' matter is created; through this retraction, individual beings are created. The parts of God thus freed from his will become persons.[17]

It has been objected that three lines provide small ground on which to found the centre of Milton's metaphysics. But they occur in a very emphatic place—God is himself explaining his own intentions in creation—they are striking in themselves, and Milton did not write lines lightly. I incline to think that Saurat is right in stressing them and in reading into them as much as he does, all the more because in the course of the poem I have felt the 'retraction' of God from Paradise, the gradual freeing of the wills of Adam and Eve till by the time of uttermost trial the process is complete.

This retraction of God has a definite object. I will quote Saurat's fascinating conjecture of what it is, but without comment, for Milton's thought is not the subject of this book. I wish merely to bring to the notice of any readers who imagine that Milton's philosophy was conventional or jejune, the daring speculations that may have occupied his mind.

---

[17] *Milton*, 123-4.

God has drawn from himself a perfectly organised society of free spirits, an expression of and a witness to his glory. . . . Evil, Sin, Suffering, end in this. There existed in the Infinite a sort of latent life which God has liberated, given over to its own forces, and which developed and expressed itself, in the good towards joy eternal, in the evil towards pain eternal. God has intensified his own existence, raising to glory the good parts of himself, casting outside of himself the evil parts of himself too, because

> Evil into the mind of God or man
> May come and go . . .

Terrible words, applied to God; and Satan confirms them with his 'The Son of God I also am.' For God is the One Being, and all is in him. This is as near as we can get to Milton's idea of God's aims: to drive out the evil latent in the Infinite, to exalt the good latent also.[18]

*   *   *

A close study of the text would reveal many instances of Milton's betraying what he will not admit or does not realize he feels. An instance was given in the last chapter: his unconscious betrayal of a personal spite against the enticements of women. To set out all the instances would be a matter of very arbitrary criticism; different people attempting the task would end with very different results: further, a whole book would be needed to record the work. So I propose to confine myself to the four chief themes in which to my thinking Milton's unconscious meaning is betrayed: Satan, Christ, Paradise, and pessimism.

There is no need to trace the growth of the Satanic school of Milton's critics: they are the best known and still, in England, the most popular. Blake perhaps made the neatest statement of their case when in the *Marriage of Heaven and Hell* he said that Milton was of the Devil's party without knowing it. Lascelles Abercrombie has put the case for Satan in its extreme form with considerable power in his short book on the Epic. Here is the gist of his idea:

---

[18] *Milton*, 132-3.

It is surely the simple fact that if *Paradise Lost* exists for any one figure, that is Satan; just as the *Iliad* exists for Achilles, and the *Odyssey* for Odysseus. It is in the figure of Satan that the imperishable significance of *Paradise Lost* is centred; his vast unyielding agony symbolises the profound antimony of the modern consciousness.

There is one very important objection to all purely Satanic explanations. The grandeur of Satan is confined to the first half of the poem; if we risk the total significance on him, the second half contributes nothing to the whole: it is an accretion, however excellent in itself. To this matter I shall return when dealing with the question of unity in the next chapter. On the other hand, I do not see how one can avoid admitting that Milton did partly ally himself with Satan, that unwittingly he was led away by the creature of his own imagination. However much the romantic critics may have been biassed in favour of passion and against reason, it is hardly likely that the strong balance of nineteenth-century feeling should be completely false. And it is not enough to say with Saurat that Satan represents a part of Milton's mind, a part of which he disapproved and of which he was quite conscious. The character of Satan expresses, as no other character or act or feature of the poem does, something in which Milton believed very strongly: heroic energy. Not that this quality is confined to Satan; how could it be, when it is the very essence of Milton's nature? It is expressed, for instance, in the technical features of Milton's verse that have been so often (and sometimes so well) described: the sustained music, the domination over words that twists them from their normal English order into a highly individual expressiveness, or any other features that go to make up his sublimity or the 'gigantic loftiness of port' praised by Johnson. For sublimity, though giving the appearance of calm, can only subsist on vast energy directed by an equally vast control. Then there is the deliberate attempt, mentioned in the last chapter, to infuse energy into the acts of Christ and of the faithful angels; and sometimes the attempt succeeds. Take, for example, the description of the Son overwhelming the rebel angels, who at the first taste of his power lose all resistance:

> Full soon
> Among them he arriv'd; in his right hand
> Grasping ten thousand Thunders, which he sent
> Before him, such as in thir Soules infix'd
> Plagues; they astonisht all resistance lost,
> All courage; down their idle weapons drop'd;
> O're Shields and Helmes, and helmed heads he rode
> Of Thrones and mighty Seraphim prostrate,
> That wish'd the Mountains now might be again
> Thrown on them as a shelter from his ire.
>
> .   .   .   .   .
>
> Yet half his strength he put not forth, but check'd
> His Thunder in mid Volie.[19]

Or take the first beginning of creation in the Seventh Book:

> On heav'nly ground they stood, and from the shore
> They view'd the vast immeasurable Abyss
> Outrageous as a Sea, dark, wasteful, wilde,
> Up from the bottom turn'd by furious windes
> And surging waves, as Mountains to assault
> Heav'ns highth, and with the Center Mix the Pole.
>   Silence, ye troubl'd waves, and thou Deep, peace,
> Said then th' Omnific Word, your discord end:
>   Nor staid, but on the Wings of Cherubim
> Uplifted, in Paternal Glorie rode
>   Farr into *Chaos*, and the World unborn;
> For *Chaos* heard his voice.[20]

Such descriptions are as impressive as descriptions of strength and energy can be without the added interest of a struggle. We certainly feel the enormous reserves of divine power: before it the angels simply fall astonished; the tumult of chaos is stilled in a moment. But there is only one figure in *Paradise Lost* whose strength is shown through conflict and endurance. This

---

[19] *Paradise Lost*, vi. 834-43, 853-4.
[20] *Ibid.*, vii. 210-21.

is Satan, and it is through him that Milton's own heroic energy is most powerfully shown. Just as *Lycidas*, the outcome of struggle, is a more powerful poem than *Comus*, which rather expresses a habit of mind, so Satan is a more powerful figure than the Son. The odds are against him, but still he struggles, and wins our profoundest sympathy and admiration. It is of no avail to retort that Satan's energies are evil. Nominally they are either evil, or only good in so far as they are a relic of his former glory. But in reading we are perfectly certain, in spite of all arguments to the contrary, that Satan showed a noble and virtuous energy in rousing himself from the fiery lake and inspiring his fellows with his own desire for action, the one thing that could make their existence tolerable. In sum it is Satan who in *Paradise Lost* best expresses that heroic energy of Milton's mind, best hitherto expressed in *Areopagitica*, which undoubtedly, though in very different form, would have been the master emotion of the projected Arthuriad.

On Milton's treatment of Christ I cannot argue, I can only dogmatise. The matter depends on the tone of Milton's verse: his professed belief presents a solid enough front. The impression I get is that Milton had no profound belief in the incarnate Christ. He happened to believe in the idea of spiritual regeneration: certain selected mortals were able to live down their innate perverseness and reach a high degree of virtue. It so happened that the story of the incarnate Christ could be made to fit this belief, and to the story Milton forced himself to give a cold, intellectual adherence. A distinction must here be made between the Son, the vicegerent of the Father, and Christ the Redeemer of mankind. In describing the first Milton could spend whole-heartedly his powers of sublime writing: in describing the second he can indeed give an impression of dignity and mercifulness, as in Christ's speech beginning "Father, thy word is past, man shall find grace," [21] but his descriptions of the Jesus of the Gospels are relatively scanty and lack the fervour of conviction. This is particularly true of the lines in

---

[21] *Paradise Lost*, iii. 227.

the Twelfth Book; lines which, had Milton felt profoundly, would necessarily have been the very height of Michael's account of the history of the world. As an example here is the account of the crucifixion:

> The Law of God exact he shall fulfill
> Both by obedience and by love, though love
> Alone fulfill the Law; thy punishment
> He shall endure by coming in the Flesh
> To a reproachful life and cursed death,
> Proclaiming Life to all who shall believe
> In his redemption, and that his obedience
> Imputed becomes theirs by Faith, his merits
> To save them, not thir own, though legal works.
> For this he shall live hated, be blasphem'd,
> Seis'd on by force, judg'd, and to death condemnd
> A shameful and accurst, naild to the Cross
> By his own Nation, slaine for bringing Life;
> But to the Cross he nailes thy Enemies,
> The Law that is against thee, and the sins
> Of all mankinde, with him there crucifi'd,
> Never to hurt them more who rightly trust
> In this his satisfaction; so he dies.[22]

It may be possible to gauge the nature of this passage better by a comparison. Take this passage from Traherne:

That Cross is a tree set on fire with invisible flame, that illuminateth all the world. The flame is Love: the Love in His bosom who died on it. In the light of which we see how to possess all the things in Heaven and Earth after His similitude. For He that suffered on it was the Son of God as you are: tho' He seemed only a mortal man. He had acquaintance and relations as you have, but He was a lover of Men and Angels. Was he not the Son of God; and Heir of the whole world? To this poor, bleeding, naked Man did all the corn and wine, and oil, and gold and silver in the world minister in an invisible manner, even as He was exposed lying and dying upon the Cross.[23]

---

[22] *Paradise Lost,* xii. 402-19.
[23] *Centuries of Meditation* (Dobell), 43.

However various the feelings aroused by this passage in different readers, it will be agreed that Traherne believed in the crucifixion very much more profoundly than Milton: the belief has entered into the intimacies of his mind. Milton could have spared it without inconvenience. Another comparison also is significant. The first council in heaven, described in the Third Book, ends with the angels' hymn to Father and Son. There is an evident contrast in the tones in which they hymn the Father Infinite and Christ the Redeemer. And the contrast is between conviction and intellectual acceptance. Although Milton was no mystic and disapproved of speculation concerning the unknowable, he was humbled and awed by that illimitable hinterland. Thus when he writes of God, the Unknowable not the School Divine, he writes with full conviction.

> Thee Father first they sung Omnipotent,
> Immutable, Immortal, Infinite,
> Eternal King; thee Author of all being,
> Fountain of Light, thy self invisible
> Amidst the glorious brightness where thou sit'st
> Thron'd inaccessible, but when thou shad'st
> The full blaze of thy beams, and through a cloud
> Drawn round about 'thee like a radiant Shrine,
> Dark with excessive bright thy skirts appeer,
> Yet dazle Heav'n, that brightest Seraphim
> Approach not, but with both wings veil thir eyes.[24]

Then, after hymning the Son as Creator, the angels sing thus of him as the Redeemer of man:

> No sooner did thy dear and onely Son
> Perceive thee purpos'd not to doom frail Man
> So strictly, but much more to pitie enclin'd,
> He to appease thy wrauth, and end the strife
> Of Mercy and Justice in thy face discern'd,
> Regardless of the Bliss wherein hee sat
> Second to thee, offerd himself to die
> For mans offence. O unexampl'd love,

---

[24] *Paradise Lost*, iii. 372-82.

> Love no where to be found less then Divine!
> Hail Son of God, Saviour of Men, thy Name
> Shall be the copious matter of my Song.[25]

This is pallid, set by the brightness of the first passage. If a contrast is admitted between Milton's beliefs in the Father and Christ, it amounts to this. He humbled himself before the unknowable, putting godhead far from his thoughts, unlike Satan and Adam and Eve in their infatuation. He admits a perverseness native to Man; he believes in free will. He would like to believe that Man, once created and set in his surroundings, has it in him to work out unaided his own salvation. But such a belief was so utterly incompatible with Christianity that it was out of the question for Milton to admit it—even to himself. We can only guess it by the reluctant tone in which he deals with what to most Christians are the central facts of their religion.

I did not mention Paradise among the themes that make up the main plan of Milton's conscious meaning, not because it is without all conscious meaning, but because much of that meaning breaks down. It is not very difficult to distinguish the two elements. The actual Paradise in Book Four consciously expresses Milton's yearning for a better state of things than this world provides: all the idealism of his youth is concentrated in that amazing description. Conscious and unconscious are at one in it. But when Milton attempts to introduce people into the picture, to present his age of innocence, he can be no more successful than any other human being in an attempt to imagine a state of existence at variance with the primal requirements of the human mind. He fails to convince us that Adam and Eve are happy, because he can find no adequate scope for their active natures.

> They sat them down, and after no more toil
> Of thir sweet Gardning labour then suffic'd
> To recommend coole *Zephyr,* and made ease

[25] *Ibid.,* 403-13.

> More easie, wholsom thirst and appetite
> More grateful, to thir Supper Fruits they fell.[26]

Milton cannot really believe in such a way of life. Reduced to
the ridiculous task of working in a garden which produces of
its own accord more than they will ever need, Adam and Eve
are in the hopeless position of Old Age Pensioners enjoying
perpetual youth. Of course Milton makes it clear that he believed a state of regeneration arrived at after the knowledge of
good and evil to be superior to a state of innocence, but he does
not convince us, as he means to do, that a state of innocence is
better than an unregenerate state of sin. On the contrary, we
feel that Milton, stranded in his own Paradise, would very soon
have eaten the apple on his own responsibility and immediately
justified the act in a polemical pamphlet. Any genuine activity
would be better than utter stagnation. I do not think these
flippant thoughts about Paradise intrude in the Ninth Book,
when Adam and Eve have turned into recognisable human beings, even before the Fall: we instinctively associate their characters with life as we know it, not with the conditions of life
that prevailed in the Garden of Eden.

Here may be mentioned an interesting essay by Paul Elmer
More[27] in which he seeks for the central significance of *Paradise Lost*. Assuming that the poem has a permanent interest,
that a successful epic must contain "some great human truth,
some appeal to universal human aspiration, decked in the garb
of symbolism," although "the poet himself may not be fully
conscious of this deeper meaning," he concludes that the essence of *Paradise Lost* is Paradise itself:

> Sin is not the innermost subject of Milton's epic, nor man's dis-
> obedience and fall; these are but the tragic shadows cast about the
> central light. Justification of the ways of God to man is not the true
> moral of the plot: this and the whole divine drama are merely the
> poet's means of raising his conception to the highest generalisation.

---

[26] *Paradise Lost*, iv. 327-31.
[27] *Shelburne Essays*, fifth series, 239-53.

The true theme is Paradise itself; not Paradise lost, but the reality of that "happy rural seat" where the errant tempter beheld

> To all delight of human sense exposed
> In narrow room nature's whole wealth, yea more,
> A heaven on earth.

Milton's paradise is his presentation of that aspiration after a Golden Age that has existed at all times among all peoples. Set between the description of Hell and the description of the world after the fall it occupies the central position of the epic and commands our highest attention.

That Milton's Paradise (I mean Paradise itself, not the life of Adam and Eve in it) is described with passion no one can possibly deny. As I said, his lifelong search for perfection, for something better than the world can give, finds its fullest expression here. But More has not really finished his essay: he omits to say by what this passionate desire for a golden age is conditioned, of what profounder feeling it is really the expression. One of his sentences might easily have supplied him with the necessary sequel. Let us not forget, he writes,

that the greatest period of our own literature, the many-tongued Elizabethan age, where the very wildernesses of verse are filled with Pentecostal eloquence and

> airy tongues that syllable men's names,

let us not forget that the dramas and tales, the epics and lyrics, of that period, from Spenser to Milton, are more concerned with this one ideal of a Golden Age wrought out in some imitation of the fields of bliss, than with any other single matter.

And the reason, he might have added, lay in the very activity of the Elizabethan age. Only an active man can create a living picture of sedentary bliss. Similarly the poignant sweetness of Milton's descriptions of Paradise and his ardent desire for perfection have less an existence of their own than express the enormous energy of Milton's mind. The description of Paradise then, without being the centre, is in harmony with the main trend of the poem. It is only in the daily life of Adam and Eve that Milton's conscious intention breaks down.

It was noted in the chapter on Milton's beliefs that he accepted in all apparent literalness the eschatology of *Revelation*. He repeats his acceptance in *Paradise Lost* and bases his optimism largely on it. The millennium and the final reception of the elect in Heaven will put right all the woes that shall have beset mankind from Adam to the second coming of Christ. There is no professed belief which Milton holds with less sincerity than this. I do not see how any honest reader can fail to detect the underlying pessimism of the poem. To enumerate all the passages where it betrays itself would take far too much space: a few examples must suffice. Pessimism betrays itself in Satan's anguished impotence at the beginning, in the warning lines at the beginning of Book Four; it is implicit in the description of Paradise, which has in it the hopeless ache for the unattainable. But it comes out strongest of all in the last four books. There is a dreadful sense of the wrongness of the order of things in the first approach of the action in the Ninth Book:

> O much deceav'd, much failing, hapless *Eve,*
> Of thy presum'd return! event perverse!
> Thou never from that houre in Paradise
> Foundst either sweet repast, or sound repose;
> Such ambush hid among sweet Flours and Shades
> Waited with hellish rancor imminent
> To intercept thy way, or send thee back
> Despoild of Innocence, of Faith, of Bliss.
> For now, and since first break of Dawne the Fiend,
> Meer Serpent in appearance, forth was come,
> And on his Quest, when likeliest he might finde
> The onely two of Mankinde, but in them
> The whole included race, his purposd prey.[28]

The woes of Adam and Eve are typical of humanity; and they never should have happened: such is, one feels, what Milton thought in the bottom of his heart. The same sense is present

---

[28] *Paradise Lost,* ix. 404-16.

even more powerfully in the incomparable description in Book
Eleven of the corruption of eternal spring and the entry of discord into the animal world. The whole is too long to quote,
but here are the last lines:

> Thus began
> Outrage from liveless things; but Discord first
> Daughter of Sin, among th' irrational,
> Death introduc'd through fierce antipathie:
> Beast now with Beast gan war, and Fowle with Fowle,
> And Fish with Fish; to graze the Herb all leaving,
> Devourd each other; nor stood much in awe
> Of Man, but fled him, or with count'nance grim
> Glar'd on him passing: these were from without
> The growing miseries, which *Adam* saw.[29]

But, it may be said, such quotations prove no more than that
Milton had a lively sense of the miseries of life. He may yet
believe that these are made more than worth while by the possibility of regeneration in Christ. Without the Fall there would
have been no special effusion of Grace, the Incarnation would
never have been required. Certainly Milton says very plainly
that in its ultimate effects the Fall was a good thing. The idea
was no new one in poetry. Here is a medieval version, which
may provide an instructive comparison:

> Adam lay ibounden
>   Bounden in a bond;
> Four thousand winter
>   Thoght he not too long;
> And all was for an appil,
>   An appil that he tok,
> As clerkes finden
>   Wreten in here book.
> Ne hadde the appil take ben,
>   The appil taken ben,
> Ne hadde never our lady
>   A ben hevene quene.

---

[29] *Ibid.*, x. 706-15.

> Blessed be the time
> > That appil take was.
> Therefore we moun singen
> > *Deo gracias.*

But such light-heartedness is for airier natures than Milton. Nor was it a joyous Mariolatry that he put in the scales: the actual effects of the Fall in Milton's poem have very little joy in them. If Christ were destined really to transform the world, we might accept Milton's assertions of hope. But in his scheme the proportion of mankind, the true elect, who are to be saved through Christ is so miserably small. From the wreck of a world corrupt to the very end a few shall be rescued but the great bulk cast out into eternal torment. The crucial passage is in the Twelfth Book where Michael describes the state of the world after Christ and the end of all things: almost the end of the poem. Let the reader judge whether the account of the world "under her own waight groaning" does not quite overshadow the vision of eternal bliss at the end.

> > What will they then
> But force the spirit of Grace it self, and bind
> His consort Libertie; what, but unbuild
> His living Temples, built by Faith to stand,
> Thir own Faith not anothers: for on Earth
> Who against Faith and Conscience can be heard
> Infallible? yet many will presume:
> Whence heavie persecution will arise
> On all who in the worship persevere
> Of Spirit and Truth; the rest, far greater part,
> Will deem in outward Rites and specious formes
> Religion satisfi'd; Truth shall retire
> Bestruck with slandrous darts, and works of Faith
> Rarely be found: so shall the world goe on,
> To good malignant, to bad men benigne,
> Under her own waight groaning, till the day
> Appeer of respiration to the just,
> And vengeance to the wicked, at return
> Of him so lately promiss'd to thy aid,

> The Womans seed, obscurely then foretold,
> Now amplier known thy Saviour and thy Lord,
> Last in the Clouds from Heav'n to be reveald
> In glory of the Father, to dissolve
> *Satan* with his perverted World, then raise
> From the conflagrant mass, purg'd and refin'd,
> New Heav'ns, new Earth, Ages of endless date
> Founded in righteousness and peace and love,
> To bring forth fruits Joy and eternal Bliss.[80]

The comfort is nominal, the fundamental pessimism unmistakable. Milton seeks to comfort himself in an imagined new order, but it is not by any such distant possibility that his wound can be healed. For from his youth on Milton had nursed the hope that mankind would improve out of its own resources. Just as he, by his will and energy, had cultivated his own mind, so could the rest of mankind, if it did but bend itself to the task, increase in mental well-being and happiness. His hopes, elated for a time by political events, were dashed far below their former lowest point, never to recover. Mankind would never in this world be any better; and Milton cannot be comforted.

This pessimism must not be misunderstood. It must not be thought that Milton blamed God for an unsatisfactory world. What he did was to blame mankind for having hopelessly thrown away their chances: they could have made the world a second paradise, and it was utterly their own fault that they failed to do so. Never for a moment does Milton disbelieve in this significance of the Fall. And in the sense that Milton believed God to be just he does not lose his faith in him. It will be remembered that in the *De Doctrina Christiana* Milton advanced two main arguments for the existence of God. This was the first:

> There can be no doubt but that every thing in the world, by the beauty of its order and the evidence of a determinate and beneficial order which pervades it, testifies that some supreme efficient

---

[80] *Paradise Lost*, xii. 524-51.

Power must have pre-existed, by which the whole was ordained for a specific end.[31]

The second argument was from conscience or right reason convincing every one 'of the existence of God . . . to whom, sooner or later, each must give an account of his own actions, whether good or bad.' The first argument he came to doubt, the second he never did. He always felt within himself a standard, and a peculiarly exacting standard, of conduct which he believed to come from outside him and which he had to obey. Some people will like to call it God, others some other name. But of Milton's belief in it—and he himself preferred to call it God—there can be no doubt. However much of the rebel in himself Milton may reveal when he created Satan, his obedience to the principle that guided his mind, to his δαίμων, is stronger still. It will be seen that only by considering this obedience and the pessimism together do we get at the meaning of *Paradise Lost*.

---

[31] Bohn, iv. 14.

ELMER EDGAR STOLL

FROM THE SUPERHUMAN TO THE HUMAN
IN PARADISE LOST (1933) *

O NE of the greatest beauties of *Paradise Lost* lies, I think,
in the gradual transition from the supernatural to the natural, in the felicitous approach and descent to the close.
I have elsewhere [1] shown the twilight scene at the last, with
its pensive mood and rhythm, the exiled pair looking forward but also backward, going hand in hand but with wandering steps and slow, to be appropriate not only to the situation—the end of Paradise, the beginning of life—but to all
the rest of the poem. I there indicated a few of the many preparations for such a quiet and consolatory ending in the avowed
purpose of God to bring good out of evil, make death not only
a penalty but a remedy, and dismiss our first parents, though
sorrowing, yet in peace. And I there hinted at the larger internal rhythm of the poem:

Twilight and dim horizons at the end—after the darkness visible and
lurid splendors of Hell, after the glories of Heaven, after the sweet
but unreal light of Paradise. At the beginning the towering passions
of the devils and the ecstasies of the saints; the naked and spotless

---

* First printed in *The University of Toronto Quarterly*, III (1933),
3-16. Reprinted in *From Shakespeare to Joyce*, Garden City, New York,
Doubleday, Company, Inc., copyright 1944 by Elmer Edgar Stoll. The essay
is here reprinted through the generous permission of the author, the editors
of *The University of Toronto Quarterly*, and Doubleday & Company, Inc.

[1] *Poets and Playwrights* (1930), chap. vii: "Was Paradise Well Lost?" and
chap. XIX above.

purity of Paradise in between; and now the shame and sorrow, and love and hope, of frail humanity.

It is on this last subject that I wish now to dwell, endeavoring to indicate how, in the conception and presentation of the scene, of the character, and of the sentiments, the poet keeps proportion and propriety, and thus leads us, also, from Hell and Heaven to Paradise and then out into the world.

2.

It is, of course, difficult to determine the purpose of an author in a long epic or novel which has taken years in the writing and has for years been borne in mind. His purpose changes, as in *Don Quixote;* his powers fail him, as in *Faust.* And this is especially the case with the expression. If Milton's purpose was, as I think, to adapt his style to the subject and scene, and gradually to approach the exquisite simplicity and chastened humanity of the close, how much of this may, in the upshot, be merely accidental, and owing to a decline in energy or a change in taste! These possibilities must be allowed for. Indeed, there is, in the later books, a drift (if ever the redoubtable Puritan drifted) to the style which prevails in *Paradise Regained.* There is something of the same dryness and conciseness, the same tendency to parenthesis, ellipsis, and a less dynamic rhythm.[2] But even in *Paradise Regained* these qualities are prominent only where Milton's imagination is not fully stimulated, and are there so frequently only because his imagination is less seldom aroused. They do not trouble us in the later *Samson Agonistes;* nor do they in the earlier epic. In the close of *Paradise Lost* there is no sign of them; and for our purposes, in this essay, they need not be considered further.

There is another rhythm in the poem than that above mentioned, still more a matter of equilibrium; I mean the paradox

---

[2] For a finely discriminating account of this and other aspects of Milton's rhythm in *Paradise Lost,* see Professor Mackail's essay on Milton in *The Springs of Helicon* (1909), to which I am here indebted.

or antinomy of good coming out of evil, of death not only a
penalty but a remedy, and even the "gate of life." This, which
has been thought to be an inconsiderate contradiction, the result of an afterthought, is really the specific problem of the
drama, and an example of that "balance or reconcilement of
opposite or discordant qualities" which Coleridge expected
in a poem. Both as art and as reality the antinomy is in the
end acceptable. The Lord does not contradict himself in that
having pronounced death as a punishment he later declares it
to be a relief. Death is both, we know. And such a reconcilement of opposites furnishes the essential structure not only of
the greatest epics but also of the greatest tragedies and lyrics.
We have only to recall great epics and tragedies of fate and free
will like the *Iliad* and the *Oedipus, Macbeth* and *Othello,* and
dramatic lyrics from Drayton's *Since there's no help, come let
us kiss and part* to Patmore's *Azalea.*

And there is still another sort of rhythm involved with this,
as the theme of woe yields to that of hope. I have elsewhere
remarked [3] upon the second and third lines,

> whose mortal taste
> Brought Death into the world, and all our woe,

as a sublime wail for the sin of the world which echoes and re-
echoes through the poem. The phrase "all our woe" is a
leitmotiv which reappears, in the same prominent position in
the meter, both when Sin takes the key of Hell from her girdle
and when the Serpent leads the woman to the tree; and in the
ninth book, that of the temptation, it recurs in changing form,
six several times. Then, once the woe has really come, the theme
subsides, and that of hope and reconciliation, touched upon
even in the following line of the Exordium, "till one greater
man restore us," replaces it. While the human pair were happy
and guiltless, woe hung over them; once fallen, it is hope in-

---

[3] Above, chap. XIX, and *Poets and Playwrights,* chap. ix: "Milton, Puritan of the Seventeenth Century." From this discussion is drawn also some
part of the subsequent description of Milton's grand style, and of the contrast between him and Dante.

stead. There is thus attained the contrasting "duplicity" of
effect, and the richness of texture, that belong to great poetry
and drama.

3.

Something of the same time-honored principle, undoubtedly, prompted the poet as at the beginning he aroused sympathy and admiration for Satan. Whether the Devil be the
hero or not (but of course he isn't) and whether or not it was
intended that he should be (but of course he wasn't) Milton,
if he was to pen a great poem on the subject and begin it at the
point in the story that he had (and rightly) chosen, did but
what must be done. Even Iago is made to win our admiration,
and though Othello both does that and wins our sympathy besides, he appears at the outset, not, like Adam, late in the story,
and is a great tragic figure, not, like him, a mere innocent.
Man and woman, until much later, are only a pair of pawns;
and Satan's true antagonist is the King of Heaven. But even
so, Milton shows flexibility and tact. Satan degenerates and
gradually loses our sympathy.[4] As he surveys the new world
and then approaches the couple in Paradise, he falls more and
more a prey to envy and hatred, jeers and sneers instead of
breathing defiance and melancholy, and stoops to flattery and
deceit. And when he returns in triumph he has recourse, in his
vainglory, to stage-acting and melodrama. Rightly his greatness
is abated and his luster beclouded as the sympathy is shifted to
the tempted and misled. In his own nature and his primal
dimensions, the demigod, though fallen, would overshadow
the human pair. So far as they know, their tempter is only the
Serpent.

But at first it is as he is—an archangel newly overthrown,
his form having not yet lost all her original brightness, matchless but with the Almighty—that he, like his followers, must
appear. They are Titans, as against the gods of Olympus; they

---

4 Sir Walter Raleigh denies this (*Milton*, 1915, p. 139) .

are spirits of evil, in keeping with the vaster imaginings in the Psalms, the Prophets, and the Revelation, and with Milton's own. For the presentation of the invisible, the seventeenth-century poet found the restricted limits and materialistic conception of Dante inadequate. He magnifies and dilates, circles about or adumbrates, where the Tuscan grapples or penetrates. To this end he has recourse to many rhetorical devices of the ancients, with a novel and mysterious effect. He employs abstraction and oxymoron, hyperbole and circumlocution, both in the speech of the beings themselves and in the description of them and their shadowy abode. Satan's

> What reenforcement we may gain from hope;
> If not, what resolution from despair. . . [5]

is a paradox or contrariety like the "darkness visible" and "if shape it might be called that shape had none," employed by the poet himself. Circumlocutions like "the sounding alchemy" for trumpets, and abstractions like "the grisly Terror" for death, abound. The fallen angels are thus and otherwise made lofty and indefinable in person and power, thought and feeling, movement and demeanor. Their deliberations are a ceremonial; their diversions a spectacle or adventure; their solace the pleasing sorcery of philosophy or a sublime concord of harp and voice (II, 527-70). And the wild and melancholy scene is a fitting background.

4.

With this the whole stylistic and metrical effect, whether in the speeches or in the poet's descriptions, is in unison. There is the true sublime, elevation without inflation. Plain and simple words are not avoided, but all common or mean associations are. The imagery is drawn from legend, history, or the large, remote, and extraordinary phenomena of nature, frequently colored or clouded by superstition. And the metrical effects have a range and volume elsewhere unexampled in Eng-

---

[5] *Paradise Lost*, I, 190-1.

lish poetry. This is the organ voice of England, and sooner
or later every stop is touched. In short, as never before in the
history of poetry, the classical and Renaissance prescription of
the "heroic" and the "marvelous" for the epic is observed;
and everything is in proportion and in harmony in this world
of shades and of woe.

It is so in Heaven, with bliss for torment, and light for darkness, though, until the schism and the battle, with rather too
much of theology and theodicy for poetry and drama. As is
well known, Milton is less at home in the ethereal regions than
with the thunderous atmosphere and bold chiaroscuro of Hell.
But there is poetry in the adoration of the saints, drama in the
combat, apocalyptic pageantry in the triumph of the Son of
God. It is the grand style, again, unmistakably. Yet not only the
art of the theater but each of the others involving time is an
"art of preparations"; and even here, amid the communings of
the dual Deity, there is a note of tenderness and of interest in
the human life that is to be which, thus remotely, prepares
us for the close. The expression of this, though still noble and
lofty, is simple, befitting the God who is to come down to earth:

> Father, thy word is past; Man shall find grace;
> And shall grace not find means, that finds her way,
> The speediest of thy winged messengers,
> To visit all thy creatures, and to all
> Comes unprevented, unimplor'd, unsought?
> Happy for Man, so coming; he her aid
> Can never seek, once dead in sins and lost;
> Atonement for himself or offering meet,
> Indebted and undone, hath none to bring:
> Behóld me then, mé for hím, life for lífe
> I óffer: on mé lèt thine ánger fáll . . .[6]

If ever there was fit wording or intonation for the divine love
and pity, it is here.

The schism and combat are, of course, previous history,
relegated to Books V and VI in the tale of Raphael. Here again

---

[6] *Ibid.*, III, 227-37.

is the organ, if not orchestral, music of Books I and II. In Book III, where stands the above passage, and the scene is Heaven, the range and volume, though appropriate, are necessarily somewhat reduced. There is no broad contrast; no strife or contention, for that is now over; and a voice tender and compassionate arises in this heroic Heaven. In Hell, for the minor key, there is only pathos, as the angels consider their own hapless fall.

5.

Satan discovers Paradise; and here there is a change. The scene is sinless and idyllic like the two inhabitants; and the height and volume of tone are reduced. This too is no such living or such country as we know of, but the proportions of either are more within our compass. It is earth and man, though before the fall. Satan, soliloquizing, still speaks in a high style, but, to fit his degenerating character and his present undertaking, a style less elevated than in Hell; and Adam and Eve, in a tone proper to their surroundings, to their worship and their love. Their imagery is drawn from nature; the poet's own, from the lovelier aspects of mythology and Greek and Latin verse. And in his contemplations and reminiscences a vein of tenderness and pathos is laid bare, with exquisitely fitting accompaniment. The organ becomes the flute, or rather, it is the same instrument played with the softer stops:

> Not that fair field
> Of Enna, where Proserpin gathering flow'rs,
> Herself a fairer flow'r, by gloomy Dis
> Was gáther'd, which còst Céres áll thàt páin
> To séek her thróugh the wórld.[7]

It is such a harmony, and cadence, as is not to be found in Books I and II, or even in Book III, but somewhat like these others: [8]

---

[7] *Ibid.*, IV, 268-72.
[8] *Ibid.*, IV, 256, 730-33.

> Flów'rs of àll húe, and withoùt thórn the róse.

> whére thy abúndance wánts
> Partákers, and ùncrópt fálls to the gróund.

For, though the scene is Paradise, the Fiend is in it. And in
the more heartfelt emotions of the human pair, though sinless
still, there is something of the seriousness or sadness of tone
that to Milton, as to most artists, is inseparable from happiness:

> to give thee being I lent
> Out of my side to thee, nearest my heart,
> Substantial life, to have thee by my side.[9]

Here already there is the throb of a mortal throat, and in Milton's Paradise there is no happiness unalloyed. At dawn they
rise, and before the curse is come upon them they work. Of
the bliss of idleness the Puritan has no conception or else no
sympathy with it; and life as we know it is not afar.

It is a felicitous arrangement that this account of our first day
on earth should include its close. Sunlight is not easily distinguishable from the light of Heaven; but twilight and the
nightingale, the moon and the stars, are neither of Heaven
above them nor of Hell under the earth; and are indissolubly
associated with the mingled emotions of our common humanity:

> Now came still evening on, and twilight gray
> Had in her sober livery all things clad;
> Silence accompanied, for beast and bird,
> They to their grassy couch, these to their nests
> Were slunk, all but the wakeful nightingale;
> She all night long her amorous descant sung;
> Silence was pleas'd; now glow'd the firmament
> With living sapphire: Hesperus, that led
> The starry host, rode brightest, till the moon,
> Rising in clouded majesty, at length
> Apparent queen, unveil'd her peerless light,
> And o'er the dark her silver mantle threw.[10]

---

[9] *Ibid.*, IV, 483-85.
[10] *Ibid.*, IV, 598-609.

With that we are nearly at home, and the expression is serene and simple as the evening itself. Three shadowy scenes in the poem linger in my memory: the "dismal situation waste and wild" at the beginning, this first sweet evening on earth near the middle, and the evening when Adam and Eve, out in the world, look back at their happy seat "wav'd over by that flaming brand." The three mark stages in the epic.

6.

Next day, with the visit of Raphael, which is prompted by the pity of the King of Heaven, comes his tremendous tale of the Rebellion and the downfall of the angels, a warning against disobedience, in the Titanic style once again. This throws the innocence that precedes and the human frailty which follows the day after, into relief. In the difference of opinion between the man and the woman before they separate in the garden, the limitations of human nature, such as have already become apparent, more clearly assert themselves—without a weakness how can one fall? And with the temptation we are in the midst of life at once, the arts and wiles of the Devil awakening the vanity and curiosity, the jealousy and willfulness of Eve. The style is not wholly simple, for Satan is the chief speaker and this is the great moment of the story; yet he is in the Serpent, and is addressing a woman. The style fluctuates, as it should do, according to speaker, mood, and occasion; but on earth it never reaches the height of that in Hell or in Heaven. The poet himself enjoys more freedom, as when he likens the Serpent, leading the way, to the will-o'-the-wisp—

> Hóvering / and bláz/ing with / delús/ive líght.[11]

For we must be reminded that he is more than bestial or human, and how he flickers and allures!

Epic grandeur must, and does, give place to drama. There is simplicity (and presently duplicity) enough in Eve, and this is fine and vivid. In Paradise, she is already fairly a woman

---

[11] *Ibid.*, IX, 639.

of this world. Having dwelt on the whole subject elsewhere,[12] I will here only point to the skill wherewith Milton avoids the danger of her now seeming a different person. In the dispute with Adam before she left him she is still irreproachable, though well-nigh a mortal female in her pique:

> But that thou shouldst my firmness therefore doubt
> To God or thee, because we have a Foe
> May tempt it, I expected not to hear.
>
> .   .   .   .   .
>
> Thoughts, which how found they harbour in thy breast,
> Adam, misthought of her to thee so dear? [13]

Yet how sweet and inveigling in wording and in rhythm! It is a sign of his love and faith that she should be permitted to "have her way!" And it is not so much her vanity and curiosity as her willfulness, and in particular her resentment against what seems to her the ungenerosity of the prohibition, that is her undoing. A very woman, she is centered in her affections and emotions: through them she falls, and once fallen she is to them a prey. Shall I tell him and share with him? Or rather not, the more to draw his love and render me more equal, and perhaps superior? But what if God have seen and death ensue, and Adam, wedded to another Eve, shall live with her enjoying, I extinct? A death to think!

> So dear I love him, that with him all deaths
> I could endure, without him live no life.[14]

And that is true, despite the blandishments and cajolery with which she approaches him and betrays him; and her feeling is sincere and unfeigned as for joy she embraces him, and

> Tenderly wept, much won that he his love
> Had so ennobl'd, as of choice to incur
> Divine displeasure for her sake, or death.[15]

---

[12] *Poets and Playwrights,* pp. 257-67 and chap. XIX above.
[13] *Paradise Lost,* IX, 279-89.
[14] *Ibid.,* IX, 832-33.
[15] *Ibid.,* IX, 991-93.

Through her vicissitudes her character is, as far as is possible, kept intact. She is still herself as, later, she retorts to the reproaches of the first of husbands for not staying at home:

> Was I to have never parted from thy side?
> As good have grown there still a lifeless rib.
> Being as I am, why didst not thou, the head,
> Command me absolutely not to go . . .[16]

But she is herself above all in her tenderness and repentance as she assumes the whole burden of fault, especially in the lines:

> Forsake me not thus, Adam; witness Heav'n
> What love sincere . . .[17]

> Between us two let there be peace; both joining,
> As joined in injuries . . .[18]

Her language is always a woman's, and this broken rhythm is that of a woman's pleading.

7.

From the moment of temptation on, the speeches of Adam and Eve are, except for some of Adam's lamentations and upbraidings, simple in expression; but now all are more complicated in matter, as befits those of a many-sided human nature. They are now the voice of pathos or affection, wisdom or fortitude, hope or fear, as at the temptation they were that of resentment and deceit, vanity and an affection beyond measure. They have the complication, but (though more of that) not the energy and elevation, or the admixture of evil, to be found in those of the fallen angels at the beginning. Even the speeches of the Lord and of the Son are less exalted than formerly, being not those of wrath and justice but of mercy and compas-

---

[16] *Ibid.*, IX, 1153-56.
[17] *Ibid.*, X, 914-15.
[18] *Ibid.*, X, 924-25.

sion. And of the Deity things are now said that were not said before:

> And thought not much[19] to clothe his enemies.[20]

> . . . yet this will prayer,
> Or one short sigh of human breath, upborne
> Ev'n to the seat of God.[21]

(The verse itself is such a sigh.)

> and in mind prepar'd, if so befal,
> For death, like that which the Redeemer died.[22]

Here, considerably before its time, is the New Dispensation, which also is to preside over the exile. Of the world under it, good being brought out of evil (though not profusely), there is a vision vouchsafed to Adam and a prophecy from the lips of Michael. And for that mingled web, good and ill together, that complex of thoughts and emotions which makes up the situation at the close and represents human experience ever since, there are now continual preparations. Of such a nature are passages like these:[23]

> but strive
> In offices of love, how we may light'n
> Each other's burden in our share of woe.

> new hope to spring
> Out of despair; joy, but with fear yet linkt.

> Thy going is not lonely, with thee goes
> Thy husband . . .

> Nor love thy life, nor hate; but what thou liv'st
> Live well; how long or short permit to Heaven.

---

[19] That is, that it was not too much to do.
[20] *Paradise Lost*, X, 219.
[21] *Ibid.*, XI, 146-48.
[22] *Ibid.*, XII, 444-45.
[23] *Ibid.*, X, 959-61; XI, 138-39, 290-91, 553-54; XII, 473-76, 614-19.

> full of doubt I stand,
> Whether I should repent me now of sin
> By me done and occasion'd, or rejoice
> Much more, that much more good thereof shall spring.

> but now lead on,
> In me is no delay; with thee to go
> Is to stay here; without thee here to stay
>   Is to go hence unwilling; thou to me
>   Art all things under Heav'n, all places thou,
>   Who for my wilful crime art banisht hence.

The last are from Eve's final words. A Romantic paradox again, yet not like Adam's, touched on in chapter XIX above. But love, the beginning, is now the end of all; and though she is not happy, still less (as has been said) "elated," in her and her mate at least good has come out of evil, strength out of weakness, sweetness out of bitterness, hope out of despair. And in those passages and others like them in the last two books, there are both the conception of life and something of the mood and utterance that we find in

> The world was all before them, where to choose
> Their place of rest, and Providence their guide:
> They hand in hand, with wan'dring steps and slow,
> Through Eden took their solitary way.[24]

8.

And hand in hand! In the preceding chapter we noticed how the poet indirectly reminds us of its being the same hand that had withdrawn and had plucked. And apart from the fine suggestion thus achieved, the simplicity, the reticence! "They left Paradise arm in arm" was once a student's version —as for a promenade!

I have elsewhere remarked [25] a fine effect, attained by Dante,

---

[24] *Ibid.*, XII, 646-49.
[25] *Poets and Playwrights*, pp. 281-89.

of continual interplay, parallelism and contrast, between life on earth and that in Hell, Purgatory, or Heaven. The earth, though not described or presented, is ever the *point de repère* of the story, and by way of the memory not only of the living men but of the shades. This, together with the impression of the spirits, human and superhuman, upon the visitor, and still more that of him upon them, is his chief and most fruitful means of presenting the spiritual world. In *Paradise Lost* no such effect of compression and volume was possible. There mortal life begins only at the end. But instead there are the effects of rhythm and equilibrium that we have noticed, and also those of progression and gradation. There are no such juxtaposition and interplay, but Hell and Heaven are intent upon the earth from the time of the fall of the angels; they there meet and contend with each other for possession of it; and though good on the whole prevails, human life, now beginning, is of their making. The last shadowy scene of exile, though another spirit informs it, recalls the first. There is, therefore, in keeping with this progress, an appropriate decrease in the magnitude, and increase in the complexity, of both the emotions and the expression, as we proceed through the great poem to its close.

JOHN CROWE RANSOM

ᐠᐠᐡᐟᐟ

A POEM NEARLY ANONYMOUS
[LYCIDAS] (1933)*

It was published in 1638, in the darkness preceding our incomparable modernity. Its origins were about as unlikely as they could be, for it was only one of the exhibits in a memorial garland, a common academic sort of volume. It appeared there without a title and signed only by a pair of initials, though now we know it both by a name and by an author. Often we choose to think of it as the work of a famous poet, which it was not; done by an apprentice of nearly thirty, who was still purifying his taste upon an astonishingly arduous diet of literary exercises; the fame which was to shine backwards upon this poem, and to be not very different from the fame which he steadily intended, being as distant as it was great. Unfortunately it is one of the poems which we think we know best. Upon it is imposed the weight of many perfect glosses, respecting its occasion, literary sources, classical and contemporary allusions, exhausting us certainly and exhausting, for a good many persons, the poem. But I am bound to consider that any triteness which comes to mind with mention of the poem is a property of our own registration, and does not affect its freshness, which is perennial. The poem is young,

---

* First printed in *The American Review*, I (1933), 179-203. Reprinted in *The World's Body*, New York, Charles Scribner's Sons, copyright 1938. The essay is here reprinted (with approximately one-third omitted) through the generous permission of the author and of Charles Scribner's Sons.

brilliant, insubordinate. In it is an artist who wrestles with an almost insuperable problem, and is kinsman to some tortured modern artists. It has something in common with, for example, *The Waste Land*. In short, the poem is *Lycidas*.

A symbol is a great convenience in discussion, and therefore I will find one in the half-way anonymity of the poem; symbolic of the poet's admirable understanding of his art, and symbolic of the tradition that governed the art on the whole in one of its flourishing periods. Anonymity, of some real if not literal sort, is a condition of poetry. A good poem, even if it is signed with a full and well-known name, intends as a work of art to lose the identity of the author; that is, it means to represent him not actualized, like an eye-witness testifying in court and held strictly by zealous counsel to the point at issue, but freed from his juridical or prose self and taking an ideal or fictitious personality. . . . Milton set out to write a poem mourning a friend and poet who had died; in order to do it he became a Greek shepherd, mourning another one. It was not that authority attached particularly to the discourse of a Greek shepherd; the Greek shepherd in his own person would have been hopeless; but Milton as a Greek shepherd was delivered from being Milton the scrivener's son, the Master of Arts from Cambridge, the handsome and finicky young man, and that was the point. In proceeding to his Master's degree he had made studies which gave him dramatic insight into many parts foreign to his own personal experience; which was precisely the technical resource he had required the moment he determined to be a poet. Such a training was almost the regular and unremarked procedure with the poets of his time. . . .

Briefly, it was Milton's intention to be always anonymous as a poet, rarely as a writer of prose. The poet must suppress the man, or the man would suppress the poet. What he wanted to say for himself, or for his principles, became eligible for poetry only when it became what the poet, the *dramatis persona* so to speak, might want to say for himself. The poet could not be directed to express faithfully and pointedly the man;

nor was it for the sake of "expression" that the man abdicated
in favor of the poet. . . .

I do not mind putting it flatly; nor drawing the conclusion
that poetry appeared to the apprentice Milton, before it could
appear anything else, and before it could come into proper
existence at all, as a sort of exercise, very difficult, and at first
sight rather beside the point. It was of course an exercise in
pure linguistic technique, or metrics; it was also an exercise
in the technique of what our critics of fiction refer to as "point
of view." And probably we shall never find a better locus than
Lycidas for exhibiting at once the poet and the man, the technique and 'the personal interest, bound up tightly and contending all but equally; the strain of contraries, the not quite
resolvable dualism, that is art.

For we must begin with a remark quite unsuitable for those
moderns to whom "expression" seems the essential quality of
poetry. *Lycidas* is a literary exercise; and so is almost any other
poem earlier than the eighteenth century; the craftsmanship,
the formal quality which is written on it, is meant to have high
visibility. Take elegy, for example. According to the gentle
and extremely masculine tradition which once governed these
matters, performance is not rated by the rending of garments,
heartbreak, verisimilitude of desolation. After all, an artist is
standing before the public, and bears the character of a qualified spokesman, and a male. Let him somewhat loudly sweep
the strings, even the tender human ones, but not without being almost military and superficial in his restraint; like the
pomp at the funeral of the king, whom everybody mourns
publicly and nobody privately. Milton made a great point of
observing the proprieties of verse. He had told Diodati, as
plainly as Latin elegiacs allowed, that "expression" was not
one of the satisfactions which they permitted to the poet: "You
want to know in verse how much I love and cherish you; believe me that you will scarcely discover this in verse, for love
like ours is not contained within cold measures, it does not
come to hobbled feet." As for memorial verse, he had already

written, in English or Latin, for the University beadle, the University carrier, the Vice-Chancellor, his niece the Fair Infant Dying of a Cough, the Marchioness of Winchester, the Bishop of Winchester, the Bishop of Ely; he was yet to write for his Diodati, and for Mrs. Katherine Thomason. All these poems are exercises, and some are very playful indeed. There is no great raw grief apparent ever, and sometimes, very likely, no great grief. For Lycidas he mourns with a very technical piety.

Let us go directly to the poem's metre—though this feature may seem a bristling technicality, and the sort of thing the tender reader may think he ought to be spared. I do not wish to be brutal, but I am afraid that metre is fundamental in the problem posed to the artist as poet. During the long apprentice-ship Milton was the experimentalist, trying nearly everything. He does not ordinarily, in the Minor Poems, repeat himself metrically; another poem means another metre, and the new metre will scarcely satisfy him any better than the last one did. Evidently Milton never found the metre in which as a highly individual poet he could feel easy, and to which he was prepared to entrust his serious work, until he had taken the ragged blank verse of contemporary drama and had done some-thing to it; tightening it up into a medium which was hard enough to exhibit form, and plastic enough to give him free-dom. In other words, it defined the poet as somebody with a clipped, sonorous, figurative manner of speaking; but it also gave a possible if indirect utterance to the natural man. Here let us ask the question always in order against a Milton poem: What was the historic metrical pattern already before him, and what are the liberties he takes with it? For he does not cut patterns out of the whole cloth, but always takes an existing pattern; stretches it dangerously close to the limits that the pattern will permit without ceasing to be a pattern; and never brings himself to the point of defying that restraint which pat-terns inflict upon him, and composing something altogether unpatterned. That is to say, he tends habitually towards the formlessness which is modern, without quite caring to arrive at that destination. It is the principle we are interested in, not the literal answer to the question, which I will try to get over briefly.

The answer given by the Milton scholars, those who know their Italian, might well be that in this poem he made a very free adaptation of the canzone. This was a stanza of indeterminate length, running it might be to twenty lines or so, marked by some intricate rhyming scheme, and by a small number of six-syllable lines inserted among the ten-syllable lines which constituted the staple. The poet was free to make up his own stanza but, once that was given, had to keep it uniform throughout the poem. Milton employs it with almost destructive freedom, as we shall see. Yet, on the other hand, the correct stanza materials are there, and we can at least say that any one of the stanzas or paragraphs might make a passable canzone. And lest his irregularities be imputed to incompetence, we must observe the loving exactitude of his line-structure, that fundamental unit of any prosody, within the stanzas. He counts his syllables, he takes no liberties there: consisting with our rather fixed impression that he scarcely knew how in all his poetry to admit an imperfect line.

The Milton scholars know their Italian, and have me at a disadvantage. Milton knew his Italian. But he also knew his Spenser, and knowing that, it seems unnecessary to inquire whether he knew his Italian too; for he had only to adapt a famous Spenserian stanza, and his acquaintance with the canzone becomes really immaterial. I imagine this point has a slight importance. It would have something to do with the problem of the English poet who wants to employ an English technique in addressing himself to an English public which can be expected to know its English formal tradition. Spenser anticipated Milton by employing the canzone effectively in at least two considerable poems; they were not elegies but at least they were marriage hymns. In 1596 he published his *Prothalamion*, upon the occasion of a noble alliance; the stanzas are exactly uniform, and they compose an admirable exercise in

Italian canzoni. But he had published in 1595 his *Epitha-lamion,* upon the occasion of his own wedding, which is much more to Milton's purpose, and ours. Here are ten eighteen-line stanzas, but here are also twelve nineteen-line stanzas, and one of seventeen lines; and one of the eighteen-line stanzas does not agree in pattern with the others. If these details escape the modern reader, it is not at all certain that they were missed by Spenser's public. I should like to think that the poetical consciousness of the aristocratic literati of that age was a state of mind having metrical form in its foreground, and Spenser intended frankly to make use of the situation. Perhaps he cal-culated that if they would go to the trouble to analyze a poem composed of intricate but regular canzoni, they might go to still great pains to analyze a poem whose canzoni were subtly irregular. . . .

The enterprising Spenser prepared the way for the daring Milton, who remarks the liberties which his celebrated exem-plar has taken and carries his own liberties further, to a point just this side of anarchy. The eleven stanzas of *Lycidas* occupy 193 lines, but are grossly unequal and unlike. Such stanzas are not in strictness stanzas at all; Milton has all but scrapped the stanza in its proper sense as a formal and binding element. But there is perhaps an even more startling lapse. Within the poem are ten lines which do not rhyme at all, and which tech-nically do not belong therefore in any stanza, nor in the poem.

Now we may well imagine that the unrhymed lines did not escape Milton's notice, and also that he did not mean nor hope that they should escape ours. The opening line of the poem is unrhymed, which is fair warning. The ten unrhymed lines should be conspicuous among the 183 rhymed ones, like so many bachelors at a picnic of fast-mated families. Let us ask what readers of *Lycidas* have detected them, and we shall see what readers are equipped with the right sensibility for an effect in form. And if the effect in this case is an effect of prose formlessness, and if nevertheless it is deliberate, we had better ask ourselves what Milton wanted with it. . . .

Milton was not enamored of the ten lines, and they stand out from their context by no peculiar quality of their own but only because they do not belong to it metrically. Therefore I would say that they constitute the gesture of his rebellion against the formalism of his art, but not the rebellion itself. They are defiances, showing the man unwilling to give way to the poet; they are not based upon a special issue but upon surliness, and general principles. It is a fateful moment. At this critical stage in the poet's career, when he has come to the end of the period of Minor Poems, and is turning over in his head the grand subjects out of which he will produce great poems, he is uneasy, sceptical, about the whole founda- tion of poetry as an art. He has a lordly contempt for its tedious formalities, and is determined to show what he can do with only half trying to attend to them. Or he thinks they are definitely bad, and proposes to see if it is not better to shove them aside.

In this uncertainty he is a modern poet. In the irregular stanzas and the rhymeless lines is registered the ravage of his modernity; it has bit into him as it never did into Spenser. And we imagine him thinking to himself, precisely like some mod- ern poets we know, that he could no longer endure the look of perfect regimentation which sat upon the poor ideas objecti- fied before him upon the page of poetry, as if that carried with it a reflection upon their sincerity. I will go further. It is not merely easy for a technician to write in smooth metres; it is perhaps easier than to write in rough ones, after he has once started; but when he has written smoothly, and contemplates his work, he is capable actually, if he is a modern poet, of go- ing over it laboriously and roughening it. I venture to think that just such a practice, speaking very broadly, obtained in the composition of *Lycidas;* that it was written smooth and re- written rough; which was treason.

I will make a summary statement which is true to the best of my knowledge. There did not at the time anywhere exist in English, among the poems done by competent technical

poets, another poem so wilful and illegal in form as this one.
. . . Milton . . . never repeated his bold experiment; and he
felt at the time that it was not an altogether successful experiment. The last stanzas become much more patterned, and in
the postscript Milton refers to the whole monody as the song
of an "uncouth Swain," who has been "with eager thought
warbling his *Dorick* lay." That is descriptive and depreca-
tory. . . .

But if the poem is a literary exercise, it does not consist only
in a game of metrical hide-and-seek, played between the long
lines and short lines, the rhymed and unrhymed. It is also
a poem in a certain literary "type," with conventions of subject-matter and style. Milton set out to make it a pastoral elegy,
and felt honor-bound to use the conventions which had developed in the pastoral elegies of the Greeks, of Virgil, of the
Italians, of Spenser; possibly of the French. The course of the
poem in outline therefore is not highly "creative," but rather
commonplace and in order, when the dead shepherd is remembered and his virtues published; when nature is made to lament him, and the streams to dry up in sympathy; when the
guardian nymphs are asked why they have not saved him;
when the untimeliness of his doom is moralized; when the corrupt church is reproached; when the flowers are gathered for
the hearse; and finally when it appears to the mourners that
they must cease, since he is not dead, but translated into a
higher region, where he lives in bliss of a not definitive sort. In
the pastoral elegy at large one of my friends distinguishes
eleven different topics of discourse, and points out that Milton,
for doubtless the first time in this literature, manages to "drag
them all into one poem"; a distinction for him, though perhaps a doubtful one. But in doing so he simply fills up the
poem; there are no other topics in it. And where is Milton
the individualist, whose metrical departures would seem to
have advertised a performance which in some to-be-unfolded
manner will be revolutionary?

When we attempt to define the poetic "quality" of this poet's performances, we are forced to confess that it consists largely in pure eclecticism; here is a poet who can simply lay more of his predecessors under tribute than another. This is not to deny that he does a good job of it. He assimilates what he receives, and adapts it infallibly to the business in hand, where scraps fuse into integer, and the awkward articulations cannot be detected. His second-hand effects are not as good as new but better; the features of pastoral elegy are not as pretty in *Lycidas* as they were in Moschus, or Virgil, or Spenser, but prettier; though generically, and even in considerable detail, the same features. We remember after all that Milton intended his effects; and among others, this one of indebtedness to models. He expected that the reader should observe his eclecticism, he was scarcely alarmed lest it be mistaken for plagiarism. It is because of something mean in our modernism, or at least in that of our critics, that we, if we had composed the poem, would have found such an expectancy tainted with such an alarm. Like all the artists of the Renaissance, Milton hankered honestly after "Fame"; but he was not infected with our gross modern concept of "originality." . . .

Of Milton's "style," in the sense of beauty of sound, imagery, syntax and dystax, idiom, I am quite unprepared to be very analytic. It is a grand style; which is to say, I suppose, that it is *the* grand style, or as much a grand style as English poets have known: the style produced out of the poet's remembrance of his classical models, chiefly Virgil. Milton has not been the only English poet to learn from Virgil, but he is doubtless the one who learned the most. Until the nineteenth century Virgil was perhaps the greatest external influence upon English literature. . . .

But Milton very nearly commanded this style. And with reason; for he had written Minor Poems in Latin as well as Minor Poems in English, and they were perhaps the more important item in his apprenticeship. This is one of the consequences:

But now my Oate proceeds,
And listens to the Herald of the Sea,
That came in *Neptune's* plea,
He ask'd the Waves, and ask'd the Fellon winds,
What hard mishap hath doom'd this gentle swain?
And question'd every gust of rugged wings
That blows from off each beaked Promontory,
They knew not of his story,
And sage *Hippotades* their answer brings,
That not a blast was from his dungeon stray'd,
That Ayr was calm, and on the level brine,
Sleek *Panope* with all her sisters play'd.
It was that fatall and perfidious Bark
Built in th'eclipse, and rigg'd with curses dark,
That sunk so low that sacred head of thine.

It is probable that no other English poet has this mastery of the Virgilian effect; it is much more Virgilian, too, than the later effect which Milton has in the lines of the *Paradise Lost,* where the great departure from the epical substance of the Virgil makes it needful to depart from the poetic tone. But Milton proves here that he had fairly mastered it. He had simply learned to know it in the Latin—learning by the long way of performance as well as by the short one of observation —and then transferred it to his native English; where it becomes a heightened effect, because this language is not accustomed at once to ease and condensation like this, and there is little competition. The great repute of the Miltonic style—or styles, variants of a style—in our literature is a consequence of the scarcity of Miltons; that is, of poets who have mastered the technique of Latin poetry before they have turned to their own.

But the author of *Lycidas,* attended into his project by so much of the baggage of tradition, cannot, by a universal way of thinking, have felt, exactly, free. I shall risk saying that he was not free. Little chance there for him to express the interests, the causes, which he personally and powerfully was developing; the poem too occasional and too formal for that. Of course the occasion was a fundamental one, it was no less than Death; and there is nobody so aggressive and self-assured but he must come to terms with that occasion. But a philosophy of death seems mostly to nullify, with its irony, the philosophy of life. Milton was yet very much alive, and in fact he regarded himself as having scarcely begun to live. The poem is almost wasted if we are seeking to determine to what extent it permitted Milton to unburden his heart.

But not quite. The passage on mortality is tense; Professor Tillyard finds the man in it. It goes into a passage on the immortality of the just man's Fame, which gives Milton's Platonic version of the ends of Puritanism. More important perhaps is the kind of expressiveness which appears in the speech of Peter. The freedom with which Milton abuses the false shepherds surpasses anything which his predecessors in this vein had indulged. He drops his Latinity for plain speech, where he can express a Milton who is angry, violent, and perhaps a little bit vulgar. It is the first time in his career that we have seen in him a taste for writing at this level. With modern readers it may be greatly to his credit as a natural man that he can feel strongly and hit hard. Later, in the period of his controversial prose, we get more of it, until we have had quite enough of this natural man. In the *Paradise Lost* we will get some "strong" passages again, but they are not Milton's response to his own immediate situation, they are dramatically appropriate, and the persons and scenes of the drama are probably remote enough to bring the passages under the precise head of artistic effect. This may be thought to hold for *Lycidas,* since it is Peter speaking in a pastoral part, and Peter still represents his villains as shepherds; but I feel that Peter sounds like another Puritan zealot, and less than apostolic.

Before I offer some generalizations about the poet and his art, I wish to refer, finally, to a feature of *Lycidas* which critics have rarely mentioned, and which most readers of my acquaintance, I believe, have never noticed, but which is technically astonishing all the same, and ought to initiate an important speculation upon the intentions of this poet. Pastoral elegies are dramatic monologues, giving the words of a single shepherd upon a single occasion; or they are dialogues giving, like so much printed drama, the speeches of several shepherds in a single scene. They may have prologues, perhaps so denominated in the text, and printed in italics, or in a body separate from the elegy proper; and likewise epilogues; the prologues and epilogues being the author's envelope of narrative within which is inserted the elegy. The composition is straightforward and explicitly logical.

Milton's elegy is otherwise. It begins without preamble as a monologue, and continues so through the former and bitterer half of the passage on Fame:

> But the fair Guerdon when we hope to find,
> And think to burst out into sudden blaze,
> Comes the blind *Fury* with th'abhorred shears,
> And slits the thin spun life. . . .

At this point comes an incredible interpolation:

> . . . But not the praise,
> *Phoebus* repli'd, and touch'd my trembling ears . . .

And Phoebus concludes the stanza; after which the shepherd apologizes to his pastoral Muses for the interruption and proceeds with his monologue. But dramatic monologue has turned for a moment into narrative. The narrative breaks the monologue several times more, presenting action sometimes in the present tense, sometimes in the past. And the final stanza gives a pure narrative conclusion in the past, without the typographical separateness of an epilogue; it is the one which contains Milton's apology for the "Dorick" quality of his performance, and promises that the author will yet appear in a serious and mature light as he has scarcely done on this occasion.

Such a breach in the logic of composition would denote, in another work, an amateurism below the level of publication. I do not know whether our failure to notice it is because we

have been intoxicated by the wine of the poetry, or dulled by
the drum-fire of the scholars' glosses, or intimidated by the
sense that the poem is Milton's. Certainly it is Milton's; therefore it was intended; and what could have been in his mind?
I have a suggestion. A feature that obeys the canon of logic
is only the mere instance of a universal convention, while the
one that violates the canon is an indestructibly private thing.
The poor "instance" would like so much to attain to the dignity of a particular. If Milton had respected the rule of composition, he must have appeared as any other author of pastoral elegy, whereas in his disrespect of it he can be the person,
the John Milton who is different, and dangerous, and very
likely to become famous. (It is ironical that the lapse in question celebrates Fame.) . . . If there is any force in this way of
reasoning, we may believe that Milton's bold play with the
forms of discourse constitutes simply one more item in his
general insubordinacy. He does not propose to be buried beneath his own elegy. Now he had done a thing somewhat on
the order of the present breach in his *L'Allegro* and *Il Penseroso.* There is a comparative simplicity to these pieces amount-
ing almost to obviousness, but they are saved in several ways.
For one thing, they are twin poems, and the parallelism or contrast is very intricate. More to our point, there is a certain
lack of definition in the substantive detail; long sentences with
difficult grammatical references, and uncertainty as to whether
the invocation has passed into the action, and as to just where
we are in the action. That trick was like the present one, indicating that the man is getting ahead of the poet, who is not
being allowed to assimilate the matter into his formal style.

More accurately, of course, *they would like to indicate it;*
the poet being really a party to the illusion. Therefore he lays
himself open to the charge of being too cunning, and of over-
reaching himself; the effect is not heroic but mock-heroic. The
excited Milton, breathless, and breaking through the logic of
composition, is charming at first; but as soon as we are forced
to reflect that he counterfeited the excitement, we are pained

and let down. The whole poem is properly an illusion, but a deliberate and honest one, to which we consent, and through which we follow the poet because it enables him to do things not possible if he were presenting actuality. At some moments we may grow excited and tempted to forget that it is illusion, as the untrained spectator may forget and hiss the villain at the theatre. But we are quickly reminded of our proper attitude. If the author tends to forget, all the more if he pretends to forget, we would recall him to the situation too. Such license we do not accord to poets and dramatists, but only to novelists, whose art is young. And even these, or the best of these, seem now determined, for the sake of their artistic integrity, to surrender it.

So *Lycidas,* for the most part a work of great art, is sometimes artful and tricky. We are disturbingly conscious of a man behind the artist. But the critic will always find too many and too perfect beauties in it ever to deal with it very harshly.

SIR HERBERT J. C. GRIERSON

PARADISE REGAINED AND
SAMSON AGONISTES (1937) *

W<small>E ARE</small> familiar with the story told by Ellwood, the Quaker, of the origin of *Paradise Regained:* "thou hast said much here of Paradise Lost; but what hast thou to say of Paradise Found?" Sir Walter Raleigh made delightful fun of the story on the just ground that *Paradise Lost* had already dealt with the theme inasmuch as the Atonement through the life and death of Christ is the main theme, the end of Michael's discourse. That is true; and yet, as I have suggested, it is what we learn from Milton's statements rather than are made to feel by the story. Ellwood felt, as we feel, some want, and Milton may have recognised this, or at any rate been glad to set over against the story of Adam's fall the steadfast resistance to temptation of the Second Adam. In doing so, moreover, he was completing the programme sketched in *The Reason of Church Government.* He had composed an epic on the "diffuse model" of Homer, Virgil and Tasso. He would now write one on the "brief model" of the Book of Job, a story told in dialogues between the tempter and the tempted, for Job's friends were also his tempters, his accusers. And for his purpose he felt the need of a style other than that of the longer poem, and he thought he had found it, for nothing can well be more different from the diction and cadences of *Par-*

---

* From *Milton and Wordsworth*, New York, The Macmillan Company, copyright 1937, Chap. VI. Reprinted with the permission of The Macmillan Company.

adise Lost than the restrained, severe language of *Paradise Regained.*

But one thing Milton did not change, his reading of human nature and history. His poem is not, as a poem on the theme by Crashaw would have been, an ecstasy over the love of Christ as revealed in his atoning death. The atonement is, indeed, foreshadowed in the opening speech of God the Father:

> But first I mean
> To exercise him in the Wilderness,
> There he shall first lay down the rudiments
> Of his great warfare, ere I send him forth
> To conquer Sin and Death the two grand foes,
> By humiliation and strong sufferance:
> His weakness shall o'ercome Satanic strength
> And all the world, and mass of sinful flesh;
> That all the Angels and Aetherial Powers,
> They now, and men hereafter may discern,
> From what consummate vertue I have chose
> This perfect Man, by merit call'd my Son,
> To earn Salvation for the Sons of men.

"Perfect Man"—Milton speaks like a Socinian, but he is quite aware that this is he who has already in Heaven been declared:

> By merit more than birthright Son of God,

and who has cast out Satan:

> him long of old
> Thou didst debel, and down from Heav'n cast
> With all his Army, now thou hast aveng'd
> Supplanted Adam, and by vanquishing
> Temptation, hast regain'd lost Paradise,
> And frustrated the conquest fraudulent.

It is in the Temptation that, by contrast with Adam, Christ shows himself perfect man. Milton's Christ is not quite the Christ of the Gospel of St. John. He is drawn on the lines on which Milton had already sketched Cromwell in the hour of Cromwell's greatest ascendancy, one who had not, like Cromwell, *learned* to subdue "the whole host of hopes, fears, and passions which infest the soul," but has done so from his mother's womb, and is able to reject at once the temptations of sense, ambition, and, if I, or Milton, understand aright the last temptation, the temptation to use miraculous power for self-glorification. *Paradise Regained* has been hardly judged, and Mr. Belloc dismisses it with contempt. I must yet confess that, not greatly caring for the picture of the hero, and acknowledging the note of hardness which has crept more and more into Milton's temper, I cannot but enjoy and admire the serene power with which the lofty sentences are woven and the dignified rhythms move:

> The city which thou seest no other deem
> Than great and glorious Rome, Queen of the Earth
> So far renown'd, and with the spoils enricht
> Of Nations; there the Capitol thou seest
> Above the rest lifting his stately head
> On the Tarpeian rock, her Citadel
> Impregnable, and there Mount Palatine
> The imperial Palace, compass huge, and high
> The Structure, skill of noblest Architects,
> With gilded battlements, conspicuous far,
> Turrets and Terraces and glittering Spires—

and so on. There is more art in the drawing out of the sense from line to line than a careless reader may at first perceive.

In *Paradise Lost* the poet and the prophet, or to put it otherwise, the poet as creator and the poet as critic, meet but fail to coalesce, come even into conflict with one another, leave on the reader's mind and imagination conflicting impressions. On the one hand the argument, as developed by Milton speaking in his own person or through the mouth of God (and Milton, as Professor Saurat has said, is the chief protagonist of Satan), aims at one effect, the justification of God's ways to men. The story itself, as the poet so vividly and dramatically presents it, leaves us with a very different impression, one not of entire acceptance of the justification. What do we see when we try to isolate the drama from the poet's contention? A war in heaven, aroused by the apparently arbitrary, almost capricious exaltation of one among many of the Sons of God; as a consequence, Satan's revenge by the seduction of Adam and Eve into a fatal breach of another apparently arbitrary tabu. If any moral springs straight out of the story itself it is, as I have said elsewhere, that the man must be the ruler in his own house:

> Therefore God's universal Law
> Gave to the man despotic power
> Over his female in due awe,
> Nor from that right to part an hour
> Smile she or lower.

In *Paradise Regained* there is less evidence of dualism, though even here, when Christ arraigns the whole of Greek philosophy and poetry, it is difficult not to suspect some inner conflict. But in the shorter epic the didactic predominates. The interest centres less in the story and characters than in the descriptions and dialogue.

With *Samson Agonistes* there is an abrupt and decisive change of tone. In no poem since *Lycidas* have the poet and the critic of life been so at one. In the early Elegy the lament for King had been sustained throughout, and twice lifted to the level of more passionate intensity:

> That strain I heard was of a higher mood,

by the poet's contemplation of his own experience, his disappointments, and hopes, and fears. In similar manner Milton in this last drama turns back on himself and, in a like strain of intense feeling, composes a dramatic vindication of his own life, and of his action and that of those whom he supported in the great historical crisis through which he had lived, and the style and verse are moulded to be the adequate investiture of his stern theme. *Lycidas* and *Samson* are the most entirely sincere and spontaneous of his quite serious poems, for *L'Allegro* and *Il Penseroso* are delightful pastimes.

To realise this fully one must recall the treatment of the story of Samson in Ecclesiastical Theology, and one must note carefully what Aristotle calls the *dianoia*, the sentiments of the poem in choral songs and in Samson's speeches. Many critics have noted the more obvious resemblances between Samson and Milton himself. He too had wedded a wife from among the Philistines and she had betrayed his fondest hopes. He too, as Masson was the first to point out, had driven from the field a boasting Harapha in the person of Salmasius. And now he too was "fallen on evil days":

> Eyeless, in Gaza, at the Mill, with slaves,

left

> to the unjust tribunals, under change of times.

An *advocatus diaboli* might justly retort that Milton had escaped the "unjust tribunals," and say with Dr. Johnson, "no sooner is he safe than he finds himself in danger, fallen on evil days and evil tongues and with danger and with darkness compassed round." But one will never be fair to Milton, supposing one wishes to be so, if one thinks of him as complaining simply of his *own* unhappy lot as a man. He is thinking of himself as identified with "the Good Old Cause" which has gone under. Thus, if even in the dramatic portrayal of Samson's bitter repentance one seems to detect a personal touch, it is not because Milton has or thinks he has anything to repent of so passionately in his own life. It is a vicarious repentance of which Samson is the mouthpiece. It is the English people, or those whom God had chosen to do a great work, who have failed, passed through the fire to perish in the smoke, laid down their heads

> in the lascivious lap
> Of a deceitful concubine, who shore me
> Like a tame wether, all my precious fleece,
> Then turn'd me out ridiculous, despoil'd,
> Shav'n, and disarm'd among my enemies.

But the radical resemblance between Samson and Milton is none of these things. To understand the significance of the story for Milton one must, as I have said, recall the reading of the story of Samson by, say, St. Augustine and St. Thomas Aquinas.

Two characters in Old Testament history caused considerable trouble to Christian moralists. They were Jephtha, who slew his own daughter,[1] and Samson, who committed suicide. "Praeterea, Samson seipsum interfecit, qui tamen connumeratur inter sanctos (ut patet Hebr. xi). Ergo licitum est alicui occidere seipsum." So Aquinas puts the question (Quaest. 64, Art. 5, Obj. 4). In his answer he follows St. Augustine, to whom the difficulty had been especially troublesome because he was busy combating the Roman and Stoical commendation of suicide. *Mors voluntaria* is, he contends, forbidden to Christians. What then of Samson? His answer is that Samson can only be excused on the ground that he acted under the direct inspiration and guidance of God. "Nec Samson aliter excusatur quod seipsum cum hostibus ruina domus oppressit, nisi quia Spiritus latenter hoc iusserat, qui per illum miracula faciebat";[2] and when later he comes to consider the case of holy women who drowned themselves to escape violation he decides that they are to be excused only if they did so "non humanitus deceptae, sed divinitus iussae, sed oboedientes, sicut de Samsone aliud nobis fas non est credere." We are bound by the Faith so to think about Samson. Donne, I may say in passing, rejects this doctrine.[3]

---

[1] Milton has considered the story of Jephtha: "What greater good to man than that revealed rule, whereby God vouchsafes to shew us how he would be worshipt? and yet that, not rightly understood, became the cause that once a famous man in Israel could not but oblige his conscience to be the sacrificer, or if not, the jailor of his innocent and only daughter" (*The Doctrine and Discipline of Divorce*, 1642). See also my "A Note upon the *Samson Agonistes* of John Milton and *Samson of Heilige Wraeck*" ("Samson, or Holy Vengeance," by Joost van den Vondel, in *Mélanges Baldensperger*, Paris, H. Champion, 1930.)

[2] *De Civitate Dei.*

[3] John Donne, *Biathanatos*, III, 5, 4: St. Augustine's view "hath no ground in history."

It is not of course Samson's suicide that is the interest of the story for Milton, though in the final Chorus he uses St. Augustine's phrase *mors voluntaria* in disclaiming any such possible accusation. The main intention of the poem is emphasized in the Argument, which was doubtless the last thing written. Samson is required to play before the Lords and People:

he at first refuses, dismissing the publick Officer with absolute denyal to come; *at length perswaded inwardly that this was from God* he yields to go along with him, who came now the second time with great threatenings to fetch him; the chorus yet remaining on the place, Manoa returns full of joyful hope, to procure ere long his Son's deliverance: in the midst of which discourse an Ebrew comes in haste; confusedly at first and afterwards more distinctly relating the Catastrophe, what Samson had done to the Philistines, and *by accident* to himself; wherewith the Tragedy ends.

The interest for Milton is the thought of God as directly inspiring men by latent impulsion to do certain things which in normal morality are forbidden. He had already touched upon this in defending the execution of the King although it was clearly not the desire of the majority of the English people.[4] He is now to make it the justification of his own actions and those of the great men with whom he co-operated. God's right to exempt chosen individuals from moral prescripts is the theme of the first choral song, the occasion being the marriages of Samson:

> Just are the ways of God,
> And justifiable to men:
> Unless there be who think not God at all,
> If any be they walk obscure;
> For of such doctrine never was there School,
> But the heart of the fool,
> And no man therein Doctor but himself.
>   Yet more there be who doubt his ways not just,
>   As to his own edicts found contradicting,

---

[4] Cromwell's election to power was "by the special direction of the Deity," "almost instructed by immediate inspiration" (*Defensio Secunda*).

> Then give the reins to wandering thought,
> Regardless of his glory's diminution;
> Till by their own perplexities involv'd
> They ravel more, still less resolv'd,
> But never find self-satisfying solution.
> As if they would confine the interminable,
> And tie him to his own prescripts,
> Who made our laws to bind us, not himself,
> And *hath full right to exempt*
> *Whomso it pleases him by choice*
> *From national obstriction, without taint*
> *Of sin, or legal debt;*
> *For with his own laws he can best dispense.*
>
> .　　.　　.　　.　　.　　.　　.　　.　　.
>
> Down Reason then, at least vain reasonings down.

To this thought he will recur as he develops the action of the play. It is a difficult kind of action to elaborate dramatically, and to this is due in the main the defect on which Johnson lays stress: "The play has a beginning and an end which Aristotle himself could not disapprove; but it must be allowed to want a middle, since nothing passes between the first act and the last that either hastens or delays the death of Samson." In this it does not differ greatly from such a play as the *Oedipus Coloneus,* which was probably in Milton's mind as he set forth the last day in the life of a great national hero. Moreover, how can an action which springs from the latent impulse of the spirit be developed with the clear logic of a drama by Racine? The Dutch poet Vondel attempted a play on the same theme, but he deprives the act of all dramatic conflict by making Samson learn in a dream exactly what he is to do and suffer.

"My locks," he tells the Chorus of Hebrew maidens, "are growing again. I am meditating vengeance on this heathen race, and that sooner than men suspect. The Spirit revealed to me this night a means to free myself from these bonds. Console yourselves! Weep no more! My departure is at hand. A triumphant death, wherewith the world shall ring, hangs over Samson's head. He shall not long, tormented and scorned by young and old, grind corn. They shall pay with the neck for the work I have done. This is my prayer, that after my death I be granted an obsequy, be buried in a grave of my fatherland.

The Chorus fears that he is meditating suicide, but he replies: "I swear to lay no hand upon my body; but I will, as becomes God's hero, give a glorious end to my life, an end that earth and sea shall talk of. You shall hear how the enemy came to *his* end." Vondel has to transfer the conflict of the drama to another theme, the legitimacy of drama on sacred subjects and in holy places. He had in mind the condemnation by the Amsterdam clergy of his own *Lucifer* (1654).

It is in a different manner that Milton's Samson dimly apprehends the approaching end of life and glimpses the possibility that he may yet be called on to do some act of service to God. When the play opens we see him repentant, admitting to the full that the fault is his own. Whatever the Chorus may say or sing of the mysteries of God's dealings with men, as is the manner of Choruses in Greek drama, Samson is quite clear on the fact that he is where he is because of his own contemptible weakness in yielding to his wife. It is a very Miltonic repentance in which there is more of wounded pride than of Christian repentance which includes forgiveness. His fault, like Adam's, had been weakness:

> of what now I suffer
> She was not the prime cause, but I myself
> Who vanquish'd with a peal of words (O weakness)
> Gave up my fort of silence to a woman.

But weakness is no excuse:

> All wickedness is weakness; that plea therefore
> With God or man will gain thee no remission.

But aware of his sin, Samson is quite sure that God will defend his own cause. When Manoa tells him of the approaching feast and what is threatened and adds:

> So Dagon shall be magnifi'd, and God
> Beside whom is no God, compar'd with idols,
> Disglorifi'd, blasphem'd and had in scorn
> By th' idolatrous rout amidst their wine;
> Which to have come to pass by means of thee,
> Samson, of all thy sufferings think the heaviest,

Samson replies calmly:

> all the contest is now
> Twixt God and Dagon; Dagon hath presum'd,
> Me overthrown, to enter lists with God,
> His Deity comparing and preferring
> Before the God of Abraham. He, be sure,
> Will not connive or linger thus provok'd,
> But will arise and his great name assert;
> Dagon must stoop, and shall ere long receive
> Such a discomfit, as shall quite despoil him
> Of all these boasted trophies won on me,
> And with confusion blank his worshippers.

Manoa accepts these words, and Milton means us to do so, as
prophetic. Nor will Samson admit reproof of his marriages.
Here again he was acting under the inspiration of God. If his
parents opposed the marriage they

> knew not
> That what I motioned was of God: I knew
> From intimate impulse, and therefore urged
> The marriage on.

Note the words "from intimate impulse," (spiritus latenter hoc
jusserat) and his claim that his youth had been "full of divine
instinct." He tells Harapha:

> I was no private, but a person rais'd
> With strength sufficient and command from Heaven
> To free my country.

When Harapha leaves he already feels that his death is certain,
but that with it may come ruin to his foes:

> Yet so it may fall out, because thir end
> Is hate, not help to me, it may with mine
> Draw their own ruin who attempt the deed.

Commanded to appear Samson refuses at first, but while stating clearly the reasons which forbid him such a deed he adds:

> Yet that he may dispense with me or thee
> Present in temples at idolatrous rites
> For some important cause, thou needst not doubt.

And even before the officer returns he feels that God is leading him:

> Be of good courage, I begin to feel
> Some rousing motions in me which dispose
> To something extraordinary my thoughts.
> I with this messenger will go along,
> Nothing to do, be sure, that may dishonour
> Our Law, or stain my vow of Nazarite.
> If there be ought of presage in the mind,
> This day will be remarkable in my life,
> By some great act, or of my days the last.

Samson is still unaware of what that great act is to be, but feels that he is led by the Spirit. When, after the display of his strength, he is conducted to the pillar to rest:

> he stood as one who pray'd,
> Or some great matter in his mind revolv'd.

And then he saw what it was. The Chorus at once emphasises the thought which has guided Milton, the thought formulated by St. Augustine. The death of Samson was not a case of *mors voluntaria* forbidden of God:

> O dearly bought revenge, yet glorious!
> Living or dying thou hast fulfill'd
> The work for which thou wast foretold
> To Israel, and now liest victorious
> Among thy slain self-kill'd
> Not willingly, but tangl'd in the fold

> Of dire necessity, whose law in death conjoin'd
> Thee with thy slaughter'd foes in number more
> Than all thy life had slain before.

So Milton reckons he is justified, and those whom he supported in the great hour of vengeance, in the eyes of God. Into no poem has he put more of his deepest feeling, his own sufferings physical and mental (but dramatised and so held at a distance), and those haunting doubts about God's ways which had looked out even in his early exultant prose: "O perfect and accomplish thy glorious acts; for men may leave their work unfinished, but thou art a God, thy nature is perfection: shouldst thou bring us thus far onwards from Egypt to destroy us in the Wilderness, though wee deserve, yet thy great name would suffer in the rejoicing of thine enemies and the deluded hope of all thy servants." So the Chorus now in more despondent terms:

> God of our Fathers, what is man!
> That thou towards him with hand so various,
> Or might I say contrarious,
> Temper'st thy providence through his short course,
> Not evenly, as thou rul'st
> The Angelic orders and inferiour creatures mute,
> Irrational and brute . . .

But in the end God vindicates himself and his servants. That is Milton's faith. Others might waver or recant, Pepys might feel much afraid that Mr. Christian "would have remembered the words that I said the day the King was beheaded that were I to preach upon him my text should be—*The memory of the wicked shall rot. . . .*" Not so Milton. "It was about this time," Bismarck said once in Sir Austen Chamberlain's presence, "that I reached that confidence in myself out of which a real belief in God's guidance of the world springs." So Milton had felt from the time he entered the fray. Wrongheaded he was perhaps, or as wicked as one may with Johnson or Mr. Belloc choose to think him, but there is sublimity in this unwavering devotion to what he believes to be a great cause, the cause of truth and justice. He will not surrender that faith in truth and justice. It gives to his work, as to Dante's, a hue at times of malevolence, less dark than in the *Divina Commedia,* but the poems are sublime if "Sublimity is the echo of a great soul." It is this reflection of his own soul in the style and verse that makes criticism of faults seem idle. "The dignity, the sanity, . . . the just subordination of detail, the due adaptation of means to ends, the high respect of the craftsman for his craft and for himself, which ennoble Virgil and the great Greeks, are all to be found in Milton, and nowhere else in English literature are they all to be found."

CHARLES WILLIAMS

AN INTRODUCTION TO
MILTON'S POEMS (1940)*

W<small>E HAVE</small> been fortunate enough to live at a time when the reputation of John Milton has been seriously attacked. The result of this attack, which has come from various sources otherwise not noticeably sympathetic with each other, has been to distract the orthodox defenders of Milton, and to compel the reconsideration everywhere of his power as a poet. This reconsideration of poetic glory has now reached everyone but Shakespeare—and, it seems, the metaphysicals and W. B. Yeats. All these, it is true, are united by one general tendency—the tendency to suggest, by one means or another, "the feeling intellect" of which Wordsworth spoke. It has been because of his supposed lack of that intellect that Milton has been chiefly repudiated. He has been supposed to be a heavy and, if resounding, yet, one might say, a comatose poet. He has been called, personally, a bad man. Mr. Middleton Murry has said so in so many words: "On the moral and spiritual side I find it easy enough to place him; he is, simply, a bad man of a very particular kind." But Mr. Murry went on to profess himself puzzled: "The difficulty is . . . that a poet so evidently great in some valid sense of the word, should have so little intimate meaning

---

* Introduction to *The English Poems of John Milton,* The World's Classics, London, Oxford University Press, 1940, pp. vii-xx. Reprinted by permission of the Oxford University Press.

for us. We cannot make him real. He does not, either in his great effects or his little ones, trouble our depths." [1]

The success of such an attack—I do not suggest that that particular demonstration was confined to Mr. Murry; I quote him because those sentences form a convenient and compact epigram of the Opposition—lay chiefly in two things: (i) the lack of power in the orthodox party; (ii) the chance that Mr. Eliot had, about the same time, defined certain weaknesses in Milton. The orthodox Chairs of Literature, it must be admitted, had for long professed the traditional view of an august, solemn, proud, and (on the whole) unintelligent and uninteresting Milton. Professor Oliver Elton had already committed himself to the hint that Milton's subject could not concern us. "What is made of the central myth? Does it in Milton's hands embody some enduring truth that speaks to the imagination? I doubt it." [2] The great academic teachers confined themselves to analyses of his diction and his rhythm. Remote from us (they, in fact, declared) was his pre-empted Eden; the pride of his Satan was his own pride, and he approved it. They argued over his Arianism or his Calvinism. They confined his instrument to the organ. They denied him cheerfulness and laughter (he who, it is said, used to sing while he had the gout!). They gloomed over him, as (they supposed) he, in his arrogant self-respect, gloomed over the world.

In the midst of this monotonous and uncritical praise, there emerged the calm voice of Mr. Eliot commenting on their subject—already admitted by them to be, to all intents and purposes, poetically alien from us. The present writer, disagreeing firmly with the effect of Mr. Eliot and indeed with some of Mr. Eliot, may admit his gratitude to Mr. Eliot for one or two critical statements. But 'the corrupt following' of Mr. Eliot went to lengths which Mr. Eliot (so far as I know) never suggested. Some writer—I have forgotten whom and I certainly

[1] *Studies in Keats,* second edition.
[2] *The English Muse.*

will not look him up—said that Mr. Eliot had 'destroyed Milton in a parenthesis.' In fact, it might be permissible to say that no critic of Milton ought to be uninformed of Mr. Eliot's article, "A Note on the Verse of John Milton." [3] I shall not discuss it here, because, frankly, I wish to discuss Milton; it is why other distinguished critics must also be ignored.

The general opposition resolved itself into four statements: (i) that Milton was a bad man; (ii) that Milton was, especially, a proud man and was continually writing approvingly about his own pride (Blake's incorrect epigram—that Milton "was of the devil's party without knowing it"—was generally used here); (iii) that Milton's verse is hard, sonorous, and insensitive; (iv) that Milton's subject was remote and uninteresting. This being almost exactly what the orthodox party had been, for centuries, saying with admiration, they were quite helpless when they found it said with contempt. The solemn rituals in praise of Milton were suddenly profaned by a change of accent, but the choruses had not altered; what then were the pious worshippers to do?

There had been, of course, another possibility all along; it may be put very briefly by saying that Milton was not a fool. The peculiar ignorance of Christian doctrine which distinguished most of the academic Chairs and of the unacademic journalists who had been hymning Milton had not prevented them from arguing about the subtle theological point of the Nature of the Divine Son in *Paradise Lost*. The peculiar opposition to high speculations on the nature of chastity felt in both academic and unacademic circles had prevented any serious appreciation of that great miracle of the transmutation of the flesh proposed in *Comus*. And the peculiar ignorance of morals also felt everywhere had enabled both circles to assume that Milton might be proud and that yet he might not at the same time believe that pride was wrong and foolish. It was never thought that, if he sinned, he might repent, and that his repentance might be written as high in his poetry as, after another manner, Dante's in his. Finally, it was not supposed, in

---

[2] *Essays and Studies*, 1937.

either of those circles, that Satan could be supposed to be Satan, and therefore a tempter; that Christ (in *Paradise Regained*) could be supposed to hold human culture a poor thing in comparison with the salvation of the soul; or that Samson, in the last great poem, could in fact reach a point of humility at which he could bring himself occasionally to protest like Job against the apparent dealings of God with the soul.

I have said nothing here against the explicit denial to Milton of any drama or of any humanity. Those denials, as well as the others, had been consecrated by custom and a false *pietas*. Yet there was no need for them. The great and sensitive poetry of that august genius had escaped his admirers. "Milton," said Landor, "wrote English like a learned language"; no one had thought it worth while to learn it as a living language. All *Paradise Lost* was supposed to be an image of pride; and yet much of *Paradise Lost* can be felt to revolve, laughingly and harmoniously, round the solemn and helpless image of pride. To discuss this in full would need a volume. All that can be done here is to dwell on a few chief points in the discussion of *Paradise Lost,* with one or two comments on the other poems. And we may begin with *Comus.*

Comus is a kind of philosophical ballet. Comus himself is, no doubt, a black enchanter, but he talks the most beautiful poetry, and he does not seriously interrupt the dance of the three young creatures opposed to him, with their heavenly attendant: there is a particular evasion of violence (when Comus is "driven in"). But what is this ritual ballet about? It is about an attempted outrage on a Mystery. The mystery which Comus desires to profane is the Mystery of Chastity. It is no use trying to deal with *Comus* and omitting chastity; *Hamlet* without the Prince would be an exciting melodrama compared to the result of that other eviction. Chastity (not only, though perhaps chiefly, that particular form of it which is Virginity; it will be observed that Sabrina, the chaste goddess, is particularly favourable to herds and shepherd life) is the means, in *Comus,* by which all evils are defeated, the flesh is transmuted, and a very high and particular Joy ensured. It may be true that we ourselves do not believe that to be so, but our disbelief is largely as habitual as our admiration of *Comus*. That is why it has been possible to admire *Comus* without any serious realization of the mystery of chastity, in spite of John Milton.

> To him that dares
> Arm his profane tongue with contemptuous words
> Against the Sun-clad power of Chastity,
> Fain would I something say, yet to what end? . . .

And that, as one may say, is that. Comus is a fool in these matters, and

> worthy that thou should'st not know
> More happiness than is thy present lot.

But the Lady and her brothers and the Attendant Spirit and Sabrina do know. They know that Chastity is the guardian and protector of fruitfulness, that Temperance is the means of intense Joy. In their eyes Comus, by refusing to admit the general principle of things and to be obedient to it, is foolishly and sinfully limiting the nature of Joy. He prefers drunkenness to the taste of wine and promiscuousness to sensitiveness. He knows nothing about that other power which can make the flesh itself immortal; he prefers to sit about in sepulchres. Let him, cries the whole lovely dance.

Obedience then and Joy are the knowledge, in their degree, of those three Youths of *Comus*. And *Paradise Lost*, following long after, did not forget its prelude. It dealt with the same subject, but differently. Obedience, in the longer poem, is no longer that of a particular devotion to a particular law; it is the proper order of the universe in relation to a universal law, the law of self-abnegation in love. This, like chastity, is a mystery, but a mystery so simple that only the two sublimely innocent figures of Adam and Eve—beautiful, august, pure, and lucid—are able to express it; they, and the glowing fires of the celestial hierarchy; they, and beyond them the passionate deity of the Divine Son. It is not only a law—something that ought to be obeyed—but a fact—something that obeys and is obeyed.

There remains, nevertheless, the possibility of disobedience to the law, of revolt against the fact. That disobedience depends on choice; and it is that choice on which the poem concentrates.

Comus had not gone so far. There is challenge there but no analysis of choice. Indeed, that is a problem which has been very rarely attacked in English verse. Generally the poets have confined themselves, sooner or later, to showing the decision; and certainly the actual motion of the will in its pure essence is inconceivable by the human imagination. Even Shakespeare, in *Macbeth*, when he reached that point, disguised it; Macbeth is half-determined; he asks if he will be safe; and when he is assured of safety he finds that he is wholly determined. But the actual decision is not there. Twice in *Paradise Lost* Milton attempted that problem: the first effort is contracted into Satan's speech on Niphates (iv. 32-113); the second is expanded into Eve's temptation, which begins with her dream (v. 8-135) and ends with the sensual degradation of her and Adam, so that the two of them, in another sense than *Comus* had foreseen, are "lingering and sitting by a new-made grave." Her temptation certainly is greater than that of her younger sister, the Lady, though it depends on the same method of flattery. To be praised and lured aside by such lines as "love-darting eyes or tresses like the morn" is well enough; but Eve needs a lordlier and more subtle, even a more metaphysical, attraction:

> Wonder not, sovran Mistress, if perchance
> Thou canst, who art sole Wonder.

This flattery is, however, of the same kind as Satan has previously, one may say, offered to himself; and, in a lesser degree, to the angels whom he persuades to follow him, in that speech (v. 769-799) which is the nearest thing in English poetry to Antony's speech in *Julius Caesar*, though Milton's lines are perhaps even more highly wrought, as they had to be, the speech being shorter. Every word echoes another; each accent is calculated—"magnific titles . . . merely titular," and so on. The aim in all three instances is the same; it is the awakening,

in Satan, in Eve, in the angels, of a sense of proper dignity, of
self-admiration, of rights withheld, of injured merit. This, it is
asserted, Milton himself felt about himself. Perhaps; but if he
did, then he certainly also thought it foolish and wrong. We
need not fall back on any exterior evidence for that nor on any
exposition of Christian morals; the evidence is in the poem itself. Satan thinks himself impaired, and what is the result?
"deep malice thence conceiving and disdain." He is full of injured merit; what is the result? "high disdain." He is the full
example of the self-loving spirit, and his effort throughout the
poem is to lure everyone, Eve, Adam, the angels, into that same
state of self-love. His description of himself in the first two
books is truthful enough—

> that fixt mind
> And high disdain from sense of injured merit
> That with the mightiest raised me to contend. . . .

But it is also ironical. Certainly Satan has this sense; only this
sense has landed him in hell—and in inaccuracy. Hell is always
inaccurate. He goes on to say of the Omnipotence that he and
his followers "shook his throne": it is only afterwards that we
discover that this is entirely untrue. Milton knew as well as we
do that Omnipotence cannot be shaken; therefore the drama
lies not in that foolish effort but in the terror of the obstinacy
that provoked it, and in the result; not in the fight but in the
fall. The irrepressible laughter of heaven at the solemn antics
of "injured merit," of the "self impair'd," breaks out. Love
laughs at anti-love.

> Nearly it now concerns us to be sure
> Of our Omnipotence . . .
> To whom the Son, with calm aspect and clear
> Lightning divine, ineffable, serene,
> Made answer: Mighty Father, thou thy foes
> Justly hast in derision.

In fact, the rebel angels only get as far through heaven as they
do because God precisely suspends their real impairment—

> What sin hath impaired, which yet hath wrought
> Insensibly, for I suspend their doom.

So much for Milton's approval of the self-loving spirit. He thought pride, egotism, and a proper sense of one's own rights the greatest of all temptations; he was, no doubt, like most people, subject to it. And he thought it led straight to inaccuracy and malice, and finally to idiocy and hell. Milton may sometimes have liked to think of himself as proud, but it is extraordinarily unlikely that he liked to think of himself as malicious and idiotic. Yet it is those two qualities he attributes to Satan as a result of his energy of self-love. When Satan sees Eve:

> Her graceful Innocence, her every air
> Of gesture or least action overawed
> His malice . . .
> That space the Evil one abstracted stood
> From his own evil, and for the time remained
> Stupidly good.

It is not, however, Eve alone who is the image of some state of being opposite to Satan's. It is all the rest of the poem, but especially it is the Divine Son. Precisely as the mark of Satan and the rebel angels is that they will not consent to be derived from anyone else; he will have it that he was like Topsy and grew by himself; so the mark of the Son, of the angels, of Adam, of Eve, is that they derive, and take delight in deriving, from someone else. Their joy is in that derivation-in-love. The Divine Son carries it into the highest state—

> this I my glory account,
> My exaltation and my whole delight,
> That thou in me well pleased declar'st thy will
> Fulfilled, which to fulfil is all my bliss.

So Eve, in a state of passionate and pure love to Adam:

> My author and disposer, what thou bid'st
> Unargued I obey.

Milton had his own views on the relation between the sexes, which (like almost any other views of the relation between the sexes) were probably wrong. But this last quotation does not spring from that only; it springs from the essential fact of things; which is everywhere this derivation-in-love. The Son is the Image of that, as Satan is the Image of personal clamour for personal independence. The casting-out of the rebel angels from heaven is the result of the conflict between the two Images —in so far as there can be any conflict between the state which is in utter union with Omnipotence and the state which is only in union with itself—if that, and the Niphates speech suggests that it is not even that. The obstinate figure of Satan does but throw up the intertwined beauty and lightness of the universe beyond him, the universe (and more than the universe) which understands, enjoys, and maintains, its continuous derivation, lordship, and obedience.

In this sense, therefore, the poem is concerned with a contrast and a conflict between two states of being. But those states are not only mythological; they are human and contemporary, and thus the poem has a great deal of interest for us. The overthrow of the rebel angels is the overthrow, spiritually, of all in whom that deriving and nourishing Love is dead. The very blaze of eyes from the chariot in which the Divine Son rides is the spectacle of a living and stupendous universe rolling on the "exhausted" rebels. There needs no battle; the exposition of the Divine Nature is enough.

> Sole Victor, from the expulsion of his foes,
> Messias his triumphal chariot turned.

It is we who are involved, one way or the other: it is not only to Adam that the Archangel's word is addressed—"Remember, and fear to transgress." [4]

---

[4] "The self-loving man," wrote Pascal about the same time as Milton wrote *Paradise Lost*, "conceives a mortal enmity against that truth which reproves him. . . . He would annihilate it, but, unable to destroy it in its essence, he destroys it as far as possible in his own knowledge and in that of others."—"Warring in heaven against heaven's *matchless* king"; *matchless* is the whole point.

Paradise Lost then is chiefly concerned with the choice between these two states of being, with the temptations which
provoke men and women to that sense of "injured merit," as
Eve and Satan are provoked, and with the terrible result of in-
dulging that sense. It is true that John Milton was not a man
for compromise. When Adam, in the fullness of his passion for
Eve, really does abandon heaven and his knowledge of God for
her, Milton denounced his act. But it was, after all, Milton who
imagined his passion so intensely as to make us almost wish
that it could be approved. There and elsewhere *Paradise Lost*
is full of the senses—even Shakespeare hardly made the human
hand more moving. This would perhaps be more obvious if we
were more attentive to the tenderness of some of the verse. It
is no doubt as a result of the long tradition of the organ-music
of Milton that the shyness of some of his verse passes unnoticed.
The famous prayer to "justify the ways of God to man" is a
prayer of humility. This is seen by considering the lines that
lead up to it. Milton, invoking the Holy Spirit, says:

> Thou from the first
> Wast present, and with mighty wings outspread
> Dovelike sat'st brooding on the vast abyss,
> And mad'st it pregnant: what in me is dark
> Illumine . . . .

And so on. Now the point is that 'Dovelike' and 'pregnant' are
words which cannot be sonorous and tremendous; it would
make nonsense of them emotionally. The passage is daring in
its hope, but shyly and modestly daring, palpitating with its
own wonder at its own audacity. Milton may have been proud
on earth (and repented of it), but he was not proud in his approach to heaven.

There is another word, at the other end of the poem, which
is another example of a certain misreading. The renewed and
repentant passion of Eve for Adam expresses itself.

> In me is no delay; with thee to go
> Is to stay here, without thee here to stay

> Is to go hence unwilling; thou to me
> Art all things under heaven, all places thou,
> Who for my wilful crime art banished hence.

This again is derivation (she from him and he from her), and
the knowledge of derivation. After which outbreak of human
love, the lines sink again into a shy softness of hope.

> This further consolation yet secure
> I carry hence; though all by me is lost,
> Such favour I unworthy am vouchsafed,
> By me the promised Seed shall all restore.

"The promised Seed" is, of course, Christ. But Milton did not
choose to use any such august title. He preferred, there, the
word Seed, and the literal meaning is not to be forgotten in the
metaphorical. The metaphorical refers back to the glorious,
devoted, self-abandoned figure—glorious because self-abandoned—which has again and again been deliberately contrasted
with Satan throughout the poem; I need name only the pause
in heaven and the pause in hell (ii. 417-29; iii. 217-26), the
two progresses through Chaos (ii. 871-1033; vii. 192-221; and
the Chaos is not only exterior; it is also the interior chaos of the
human soul); and, of course, the conflict in heaven. But the
literal meaning of "Seed" is of the new, tiny, important thing,
the actuality of the promise, the almost invisible activity upon
which all depends. So small, so intimate, so definite, is the word
that the line becomes breathless with it and with the hope of it.
That breathless audacity of purpose towards the beginning of
the poem is answered by a breathless audacity of expectation
towards the end. And at the very end humanity has its turn in
the hand again, the hand which has meant so much at certain
crises of the poem: at the separation, as if symbolically, of a
derived love from its source—

> So saying, from her husband's hand her hand
> Soft she withdrew;

and in the sin (the derived love working against its human and Divine sources) :

> So saying, her rash hand in evil hour
> Forth reaching to the fruit, she plucked, she ate;

and so now in the rejoined union of that penitence and humility which Milton knew so well:

> They hand in hand with wandering steps and slow
> Through Eden took their solitary way.

There are no linked lovers in our streets who are not more beautiful and more unfortunate because of those last lines; no reunion, of such a kind, which is not more sad and more full of hope. And then it is said that Milton is inhuman. The whole of our visibility, metaphysical, psychological, actual, has been increased by him.

It is the word "solitary," however, which looks forward to the last two poems—to *Paradise Regained* and to *Samson*. The first is completely different from *Paradise Lost*. The verse is, on the whole, less infinitely sensitive than that of the earlier poem; it is already changing to something else. There are few personages; in the earlier there had been many. They are brooding rather than active. And whereas in *Paradise Lost* everything had been exposed from the beginning, now the chief thing is hidden. The centre had previously been a spectacle; now it is a secret. The Blessed Virgin is in a state of expectation:

> his absence now
> Thus long to some great purpose he observes.

Christ himself waits:

> to what intent
> I learn not yet, perhaps I need not know.
> For what concerns my knowledge God reveals.

The urgency is in Satan, but even he is here haunted by the unknown: "who this is we must learn."

It is the discovery of this nature, which Satan does not know, and which Christ only half-knows, that is the theme of the poem. Christ's answers to Satan's efforts to find out are, in a sense, riddles, for they are given half in his own terms and half in Satan's. Food; glory; kingdoms; earthly wisdom—these are the temptations; through all of them, in Milton's phrase,

> the Son of God
> Went on and stayed not.

He goes on—or in ("into himself descended"). It is precisely into his Nature that the argument plunges to seek its discovery, but the moral trials are hardly enough; at the end Milton used something else. He came to the mysterious "standing"; moral temptation is lost in what lies behind it. "Stand or cast thyself down": be whatever you are. But the answer is still a riddle; it has precisely the lightness, almost the happiness, certainly the heavenly mockery which is always the answer to the hellish sneer. Satan is as hopelessly foolish as ever, and Jesus speaks to him, in the technique of this poem, as the Divine Son had spoken of him to the Father in the *Paradise Lost:*

> To whom the Son with calm aspect and clear
> Lightning divine, ineffable, serene,
> Made answer.

> To whom thus Jesus: Also it is written
> Tempt not the Lord thy God; he said and stood.
> But Satan, smitten with amazement, fell.

He and his had been in the same case before—

> They astonished all resistance lost,
> All courage; down their idle weapons dropped . . .
> Exhausted, spiritless, afflicted, fallen.

"So, strook with dread and anguish, fell the Fiend." Heaven is always unexpected to the self-loving spirit; he can never understand whence it derives, for he has himself renounced all derivation, as do those who follow him. It was this great and fundamental fact of human existence which Milton very well understood; it was this which his genius exerted all his tenderness and all his sublimity to express; it was this which is the cause of the continual laughter of *Paradise Lost,* and it was because of this that Milton invoked that Spirit which Itself derives from the co-equal Two.

It is not possible in the remaining space to discuss *Samson.* The verse again has changed, and I doubt if we have yet properly learnt its style. "A little onward lend thy guiding hand"—to what? To the "acquist Of true experience from this great event." What then is our true experience from the poem? Much every way; perhaps not the least is the sense of the union of Necessity and Freewill. That had been discussed in *Paradise Lost,* as an accompaniment to the spectacle and analysis of man choosing. But there the actual stress had been a little on the choice; here it is a little on "dire Necessity." Here "the cherub Contemplation" is allowed even fuller view. The persons, if they do not exactly accuse God, at least indicate to God the unanswered questions. There is no humility in refraining from asking the questions; the humility consists in believing that there may be an answer. Both asking and believing are desirable, and both are here. In the earlier poems the sense of a full comprehension had been chiefly felt in the Figure of the Divine Son—and therefore either in heaven or (if among men) then prophesied for the future. But in *Samson* there is more than a hint that the great satisfaction of all distresses is already there. It is perhaps not by a poetic accident that here and there in the poem Milton wrote like Shakespeare; in other places, like himself with a new song. The modest and appealing courage of the opening of *Paradise Lost*—'and justify the ways of God to man'—becomes an angelic beauty of victory—

> Just are the ways of God,
> And justifiable to men,
> Unless there be who think not God at all.
> If any be, they walk obscure,

> For of such doctrine never was there school
> But the heart of the fool,
> And no man therein doctor but himself.

That is precisely Satan—and men and women. But "Nothing is here for tears" is here no Stoic maxim, but something beyond—something "comely and reviving."

The phrase would cover most of Milton. So far from being granite, his verse is a continual spring of beauty, of goodness, of tenderness, of humility. The one thing he always denounced as sin and (equally) as folly was the self-closed "independent" spirit, the spirit that thinks itself of "merit," especially "of injured merit." It does not seem a moral entirely without relevance to us. All things derive in love—and beyond all things, in the only self-adequate Existence, there is the root of that fact, as of all. It is known in God; the Father speaks—

> and on his Son with rays direct
> Shone full; he all his Father manifest
> Ineffably into his face received,
> And thus the Filial Godhead answering spake.

"Filial . . . answering." Milton has been too long deprived of half his genius. He did his best to make clear what he was saying. But then, as his admirer John Dryden wrote:

> Dim as the borrowed beams of moon and stars
> To lonely, weary, wandering travellers
> Is Reason to the soul.

C. S. LEWIS

THE STYLE OF SECONDARY EPIC
AND DEFENCE OF THIS STYLE (1942)*

FORMS AND FIGURES OF SPEECH ORIGINALLY
THE OFFSPRING ,OF PASSION, BUT NOW THE
ADOPTED CHILDREN OF POWER.
COLERIDGE.

THE style of Virgil and Milton arises as the solution of a very definite problem. The Secondary epic aims at an even higher solemnity than the Primary; but it has lost all those external aids to solemnity which the Primary enjoyed. There is no robed and garlanded *aoidos*, no altar, not even a feast in a hall—only a private person reading a book in an armchair. Yet somehow or other, that private person must be made to feel that he is assisting at an august ritual, for if he does not, he will not be receptive of the true epic exhilaration. The sheer writing of the poem, therefore, must now do, of itself, what the whole occasion helped to do for Homer. The Virgilian and Miltonic style is there to compensate for—to counteract—the privacy and informality of silent reading in a man's own study. Every judgment on it which does not realize this will be inept.

---

* From *A Preface to Paradise Lost*, London, Oxford University Press, 1942, Chaps. VI-VII. Reprinted by permission of the Oxford University Press. The distinction made in earlier chapters between Primary Epic (the Homeric poems and *Beowulf*) and Secondary Epic (Virgil and Milton) is one of chronology only. Primary Epic is described as "the loftiest and gravest among the kinds of court poetry in the oral period," with the most obvious characteristic of its oral technique being "its continual use of stock words, phrases, or even whole lines."

To blame it for being ritualistic or incantatory, for lacking intimacy or the speaking voice, is to blame it for being just what it intends to be and ought to be. It is like damning an opera or an oratorio because the personages sing instead of speaking.

In a general and obvious sense this effect is achieved by what is called the "grandeur" or "elevation" of style. As far as Milton is concerned (for I am not scholar enough to analyse Virgil) this grandeur is produced mainly by three things. (1) The use of slightly unfamiliar words and constructions, including archaisms. (2) The use of proper names, not solely nor chiefly for their sound, but because they are the names of splendid, remote, terrible, voluptuous, or celebrated things. They are there to encourage a sweep of the reader's eye over the richness and variety of the world—to supply that *largior aether* which we breathe as long as the poem lasts. (3) Continued allusion to all the sources of heightened interest in our sense experience (light, darkness, storm, flowers, jewels, sexual love, and the like), but all over-topped and "managed" with an air of magnanimous austerity. Hence comes the feeling of sensual excitement *without* surrender or relaxation, the extremely tonic, yet also extremely rich, quality of our experience while we read. But all this you might have in great poems which were not epic. What I chiefly want to point out is something else—the poet's unremitting *manipulation* of his readers—how he sweeps us along as though we were attending an actual recitation and nowhere allows us to settle down and luxuriate on any one line or paragraph. It is common to speak of Milton's style as organ music. It might be more helpful to regard the reader as the organ and Milton as the organist. It is on us he plays, if we will let him.

Consider the opening paragraph. The ostensible philosophical purpose of the poem (to justify the ways of God to Man) is here of quite secondary importance. The real function of these twenty-six lines is to give us the sensation *that some great thing is now about to begin.* If the poet succeeds in doing that sufficiently, we shall be clay in his hands for the rest of Book I and perhaps longer; for be it noted that in this kind of poetry most of the poet's battles are won in advance. And as far as I am concerned, he succeeds completely, and I think I see something of how he does it. Firstly, there is the quality of weight, produced by the fact that nearly all the lines end in long, heavy monosyllables. Secondly, there is the direct suggestion of deep spiritual preparation at two points—*O spirit who dost prefer* and *What in me is dark*. But notice how cunningly this direct suggestion of great beginnings is reinforced by allusion to the creation of the world itself (*Dove-like sat'st brooding*), and then by images of rising and lifting (*With no middle flight intends to soar . . . raise and support—Highth of this great argument*) and then again how creation and rising come potently together when we are reminded that Heaven and Earth *rose out of Chaos,* and how in addition to this we have that brisk, morning promise of good things to come, borrowed from Ariosto (*things unattempted yet*), and how *till one greater Man* makes us feel we are about to read an epic that spans over the whole of history with its arch. All images that can suggest a great thing beginning have been brought together and our very muscles respond as we read. But look again and you will see that the ostensible and logical connection between these images is not exactly the same as the emotional connection which I have been tracing. The point is important. In one respect, Milton's technique is very like that of some moderns. He throws ideas together because of those emotional relations which they have in the very recesses of our consciousness. But unlike the moderns he always provides a façade of logical connections as well. The virtue of this is that it lulls our logical faculty to sleep and enables us to accept what we are given without question.

This distinction between the logical connections which the poet puts on the surface and the emotional connections whereby he really manipulates our imagination is the key to many of his similes. The Miltonic simile does not always serve to illustrate what it pretends to be illustrating. The likeness between the two things compared is often trivial, and is, indeed, required only to save the face of the logical censor. At the end of Book I the fiends are compared to elves. Smallness is the only point of resemblance. The first use of the simile is to provide contrast and relief, to refresh us by a transition from Hell to a moonlit English lane. Its second use becomes apparent when we suddenly return to where

> far within
> And in thir own dimensions like themselves
> The great Seraphic Lords and Cherubim
> In close recess and secret conclave sat,
> A thousand Demy-Gods on golden seats.
>
> (II, 796.)

It is by contrast with the fairies that these councillors have grown so huge, and by contrast with the fanciful simile that the hush before their debate becomes so intense, and it is by that intensity that we are so well prepared for the opening of Book II. It would be possible to go further and to say that this simile is simply the point at which the whole purpose of transforming the fiends to dwarfish stature is achieved, and that this transformation itself has a retrospective effect on the hugeness of Pandemonium. For the logician it may appear as something "dragged in by the heels," but in poetry it turns out to be so bound up with the whole close of the first Book and the opening of the second that if it were omitted the wound would spread over about a hundred lines. Nearly every sentence in Milton has that power which physicists sometimes think we shall have to attribute to matter—the power of action at a distance.

Examples of this subterranean virtue (so to call it) in the Miltonic simile will easily occur to every one's memory. Paradise is compared to the field of Enna—one beautiful landscape to another (IV, 268). But, of course, the deeper value of the simile lies in the resemblance which is not explicitly noted as a resemblance at all, the fact that in both these places the young and the beautiful while gathering flowers was ravished by a dark power risen up from the underworld. A moment later

Eden is compared to the *Nysician isle* and to *Mount Amara.*
Unlearned readers may reassure themselves. In order to get the
good out of this simile it is not at all necessary to look up these
places in the notes, nor has pedantry any share in the poet's
motives for selecting them. All that we need to know the poet
tells us. The one was a river island and the other a high mountain, and both were *hiding places.* If only we will read on, asking no questions, the sense of Eden's secrecy, of things infinitely
precious, guarded, locked up, and put away, will come out of
that simile and enrich what Milton is all the time trying to
evoke in each reader—the consciousness of Paradise. Sometimes,
I admit, the poet goes too far and the feint of logical connection is too outrageous to be accepted. In IV, 160-171 Milton
wants to make us feel the full obscenity of Satan's presence in
Eden by bringing a sudden stink of fish across the sweet smell
of the flowers, and alluding to one of the most unpleasant Hebrew stories. But the pretence of logical connection (that Satan
liked the flowers of Paradise *better* than Asmodeus liked the
smell of burning fish) is too strained. We feel its absurdity.

This power of manipulation is not, of course, confined to the
similes. Towards the end of Book III Milton takes Satan to
visit the sun. To keep on harping on heat and brightness would
be no use; it would end only in that bog of superlatives which
is the destination of many bad poets. But Milton makes the
next hundred lines as Solar as they could possibly be. We have
first (583) the picture of the sun *gently warming* the universe,
and a hint of the enormous distances to which this *virtue* penetrates. Then at line 588, by means of what is not much more
than a pun on the word *spot* we have Galileo's recent discovery
of the sun-spots. After that we plunge into alchemy because the
almost limitless powers attributed to gold in that science and
the connection of gold with the solar influence make a kind of
mirror in which we can view the regal, the vivifying, the *arch-
chemic* properties of the sun. Then, still working indirectly,
Milton makes us realize the marvel of a shadowless world (614-
620). After that we meet Uriel (*Fire of God*), and because the

sun (as every child knew from Spenser and Ovid, if not from Pliny and Bernardus) is the *world's eye,* we are told that Uriel is one of those spirits who are God's eyes (650) and is even, in a special sense, God's singular *eye* in this material world (660) and "the sharpest-sighted Spirit of all in Heav'n" (691). This is not, of course, the sun of modern science; but almost everything which the sun had meant to man up till Milton's day has been gathered together and the whole passage in his own phrase, "runs potable gold."

A great deal of what is mistaken for pedantry in Milton (we hear too often of his "immense learning") is in reality evocation. If Heaven and Earth are ransacked for simile and allusion, this is not done for display, but in order to guide our imaginations with unobtrusive pressure into the channels where the poet wishes them to flow; and as we have already seen, the learning which a reader requires in responding to a given allusion does not equal the learning Milton needed to find it. When we have understood this it will perhaps be possible to approach that feature of Milton's style which has been most severely criticized—the Latinism of his constructions.

Continuity is an essential of the epic style. If the mere printed page is to affect us like the voice of a bard chanting in a hall, then the chant must *go on*—smoothly, irresistibly, "upborne with indefatigable wings." We must not be allowed to settle down at the end of each sentence. Even the fuller pause at the end of a paragraph must be felt as we feel the pause in a piece of music, where the silence is part of the music, and not as we feel the pause between one item of a concert and the next. Even between one Book and the next we must not wholly wake from the enchantment nor quite put off our festal clothes. A boat will not answer to the rudder unless it is in motion; the poet can work upon us only as long as we are kept on the move.

Roughly speaking, Milton avoids discontinuity by an avoidance of what grammarians call the simple sentence. Now, if the sort of things he was saying were at all like the things that Donne or Shakespeare say, this would be intolerably tiring. He

therefore compensates for the complexity of his syntax by the
simplicity of the broad imaginative effects beneath it and the
perfect rightness of their sequence. For us readers, this means
in fact that our receptivity can be mainly laid open to the
underlying simplicity, while we have only to *play* at the complex syntax. It is not in the least necessary to go to the very
bottom of these verse sentences as you go to the bottom of
Hooker's sentences in prose. The general feeling (which will
usually be found to be correct if you insist on analysing it) that
something highly concatenated is before you, that the flow of
speech does not fall apart into separate lumps, that you are following a great unflagging voice—this is enough to keep the
"weigh" on you by means of which the poet steers. Let us take
an example:

> If thou beest he—but O how fall'n! how chang'd
> From him who in the happy Realms of Light
> Cloth'd with transcendent brightness didst outshine
> Myriads though bright: If he whom mutual league,
> United thoughts and counsels, equal hope
> And hazard in the Glorious Enterprise,
> Joynd with me once, now misery hath joynd
> In equal ruin: into what Pit thou seest
> From what highth fal'n.
>
> (I, 84.)

This is a pretty complicated sentence. On the other hand, if you
read it (and let the ghost of a chanting, not a talking, voice be
in your ear) without bothering about the syntax, you receive in
their most natural order all the required impressions—the lost
glories of heaven, the first plotting and planning, the hopes and
hazards of the actual war, and then the misery, the ruin, and
the pit. But the complex syntax has not been useless. It has preserved the *cantabile,* it has enabled you to feel, even within
these few lines, the enormous onward pressure of the great
stream on which you are embarked. And almost any sentence
in the poem will illustrate the same point.

The extremely Latin connections between the sentences serve

the same purposes, and involve, like the similes, a fair amount of illusion. A good example is *nor sometimes forget,* in III, 32. In this passage Milton is directly calling up what he indirectly suggests throughout, the figure of the great blind bard. It will, of course, be greatly enriched if the mythical blind bards of antiquity are brought to bear on us. A poet like Spenser would simply begin a new stanza with *Likewise dan Homer* or something of the sort. But that will not quite serve Milton's purpose: it is a little too like rambling, it might suggest the garrulity of an old gentleman in his chair. *Nor sometimes forget* get him across from *Sion and the flowery brooks* to *Blind Thamyris* with an appearance of continuity, like the stylized movement by which a dancer passes from one position to another. *Yet not the more* in line 26 is another example. So are *sad task Yet argument* (IX, 13) and *Since first this subject* (IX, 25). These expressions do not represent real connections of thought, any more than the prolonged syllables in Handel represent real pronunciation.

It must also be noticed that while Milton's Latin constructions in one way tighten up our language, in another way they make it more fluid. A fixed order of words is the price—an all but ruinous price—which English pays for being uninflected. The Miltonic constructions enable the poet to depart, in some degree, from this fixed order and thus to drop the ideas into his sentence in any order he chooses. Thus, for example,

> soft oppression seis'd
> My droused sense, untroubl'd though I thought
> I then was passing to my former state
> Insensible, and forthwith to dissolve.
>
> (VIII, 291.)

The syntax is so artificial that it is ambiguous. I do not know whether *untroubled* qualifies *me* understood, or *sense,* and similar doubts arise about *insensible* and the construction of *to dissolve.* But then I don't need to know. The sequence *drowsed —untroubled—my former state—insensible—dissolve* is exactly right; the very crumbling of consciousness is before us and the fringe of syntactical mystery helps rather than hinders the effect. Thus, in another passage, I read

> Heav'n op'nd wide
> Her ever-during Gates, Harmonious sound
> On golden Hinges moving.
>
> (VII, 205.)

Moving might be a transitive participle agreeing with *gates* and governing *sound;* or again the whole phrase from *harmonious* to *moving* might be an ablative absolute. The effect of the passage, however, is the same whichever we choose. An extreme modern might have attempted to reach it with

> Gates open wide. Glide
> On golden hinges . . .
> Moving . . .
> Harmonious sound.

This melting down of the ordinary units of speech, this plunge back into something more like the indivisible, flowing quality of immediate experience, Milton also achieves. But by his appearance of an extremely carpentered structure he avoids the suggestion of fever, preserves the sense of dignity, and does not irritate the mind to ask questions.

Finally, it remains to judge this style not merely as an epic style, but as a style for that particular story which Milton has chosen. I must ask the reader to bear with me while I examine it at its actual work of narration. Milton's theme leads him to deal with certain very basic images in the human mind—with the archetypal patterns, as Miss Bodkin would call them, of Heaven, Hell, Paradise, God, Devil, the Winged Warrior, the Naked Bride, the Outer Void. Whether these images come to us from real spiritual perception or from pre-natal and infantile experience confusedly remembered, is not here in question; how the poet arouses them, perfects them, and then makes them re-act on one another in our minds is the critic's concern. I use the word "arouses" advisedly. The naif reader thinks Milton is going to *describe* Paradise as Milton imagines it; in reality the poet knows (or behaves as if he knew) that this is useless. His own private image of the happy garden, like yours and mine, is full of irrelevant particularities—notably, of memories from the first garden he ever played in as a child. And the more thoroughly he describes those particularities the further we are getting away from the Paradisal idea as it exists in our minds, or even in his own. For it is something coming *through* the particularities, some light which transfigures them, that really counts, and if you concentrate on them you will find them turning dead and cold under your hands. The more elaborately, in *that* way, we build the temple, the more certainly we shall find, on completing it, that the god has flown. Yet Milton must *seem* to describe—you cannot just say nothing about Paradise in *Paradise Lost*. While seeming to describe his own imagination he must actually arouse ours, and arouse it not to make definite pictures, but to find again in our own depth the Paradisal light of which all explicit images are only the momentary reflection. We are his organ: when he appears to be describing Paradise he is in fact drawing out the Paradisal Stop in us. The place where he chiefly does so (IV, 131-286) is worth examination in detail.

It begins (131) *so on he fares. On* is the operative word. He is going on and on. Paradise is a long way off. At present we are approaching only its *border*. Distance means gradualness of approach. It is *now nearer* (133). Then come the obstacles; a *steep wilderness* with *hairy sides* (135). Do not overlook *hairy*. The Freudian idea that the happy garden is an image of the human body would not have frightened Milton in the least, though, of course, the main point is that the ascent was *grotesque and wild* (136) and *access denied* (137). But we want something more than obstacle. Remember that in this kind of poetry the poet's battles are mainly won in advance. If he can give us the idea of increasing expectancy, the idea of the Paradisal light coming but not yet come, then, when at last he has to make a show of describing the garden itself, we shall be already conquered. He is doing his work *now* so that when the climax comes we shall actually do the work for ourselves. Therefore, at line 137, he begins playing on the note of progression—upward progression, a vertical serialism. *Overhead* is *insuperable height* of trees (138). But that is not enough. The trees are ladder-like or serial trees (cedar, pine, and fir) with one traditionally eastern and triumphal tree (the palm) thrown in (139). They stand up like a stage set (140) where Milton is thinking of *silvis scaena coruscis*. They go up in tiers like a theatre (140-142). Already, while I read, I feel as if my neck ached with looking higher and higher. Then quite unexpectedly, as in dream landscapes, we find that what seemed the top is not the top. Above all these trees, *yet higher* (142) springs up the green, living wall of Paradise. And now a moment's rest from our looking upward; at a wave of the wand we are seeing the whole thing reversed—we are Adam, King of Earth, looking *down* from that green rampart into this lower world (144-145)—and, of course, when we return it seems loftier still. For even that wall was not the real top. Above the wall—yes, at last, almost beyond belief, we see for once with mortal eyes the trees of Paradise itself. In lines 147-149 we get the first bit of direct description. *Of course,* the trees have golden fruit. We always knew they would. Every myth has told us so; to ask for "originality" at this point is stark insensibility. But we are not allowed to go on looking at them. The simile of the rainbow (150-152) is introduced and at once our glimpse of Paradise recedes to the rainbow's end. Then the theme of serialism is picked up again—the air is growing purer every minute (153); and this idea (*Quan la douss aura venta*) at once passes into a nineteen-line exploitation of the most evocative of the senses, suddenly countered by the stench of Satan (167). Then a pause, as if after a crashing piece of orchestration, and we go back to the images of gradual approach, Satan still journeying *on* (172). Now the obstacles grow more formidable and it presently turns out (as the Trojans had found on sighting Italy) that the real entrance is *on the other side* (179).

What follows is concerned with the main theme of the story and may be omitted here. We return to Paradise at 205. We are in at last, and now the poet has to do something in the way of description; well for him that the Paradise-complex in us is now thoroughly awake and that almost any particular image he gives us will be caught up and assimilated. But he does not begin with a particular image, rather with an idea—*in narrow room Nature's whole wealth*. The "narrow room," the sense of a small guarded place, of sweetness rolled into a ball, is essential. God had *planted* it all (210). Not created it, but planted it—an anthropomorphic God out of Ezekiel XXXI, the God of our childhood and man's, making a toy garden as *we* made them when we were children. The earliest and lowest levels are being uncovered. And all this realm was studded once with rich and ancient cities; a *pleasant soil* (214), but the mountain of Paradise, like a jewel set in gold, *far more pleasant* (215) so that an emotion stolen from the splendour of the cities now flows into our feeling of Paradise. Then come the trees, the mythical and numinous trees, and *vegetable gold* from the garden of Hesperus (217-222). Then the rivers, which like Alph plunge into darkness and rise from it through *pores* at the bidding of *kindly thirst* (228), and Paradise again reminds us of a human body; and in contrast with this organic dark we have *crisped brooks* above (237) and the hard, bright suggestions of *pearl* and *gold* (238). Finally, from line 246 to 265, we get actual description. It is all, most rightly, generalized, and it is short. A reader who dislikes this kind of poetry would possibly express his objection to Milton's Paradise by saying it contained "all the right things"—odorous gums, golden fruit, thornless roses, murmuring falls—and would prefer something he had not expected. But the unexpected has here no place. These references to the obvious and the immemorial are there not to give us new ideas about the lost garden but to make us know that the garden is found, that we have come home at last and reached the centre of the maze—our centre, humanity's centre, not some private centre of the poet's. And they last only long enough to do so. The representation begins swelling and trembling at 264 with the nervous reiteration of *airs* in order that it may *burst* in the following lines—may flow over into a riot of mythology where we are so to speak, drenched. That is the real climax; and then, having been emparadised, we are ready at line 288 to meet at last the white, erect, severe, voluptuous forms of our first parents.

*   *   *

I believe I am right in saying that the reaction of many readers to the chapter I have just finished might be expressed in the following words. "You have described exactly what we do *not* call poetry. This manipulation of the audience which you attribute to Milton is just what distinguishes the vile art of the rhetorician and the propagandist from the disinterested activity of the poet. This evocation of stock responses to conventional situations, which you choose to call Archetypal Patterns, is the very mark of the cheap writer. This calculated pomp and grandiosity is the sheer antithesis of true poetic sincerity—a miserable attempt to appear high by mounting on stilts. In brief, we always suspected that Milton was bogus, and you have confirmed our suspicion. *Habemus confitentem reum.*" I hardly expect to convert many of those who take such a view; but it would be a mistake not to make clear that the difference between us is essential. If these are my errors they are not errors into which I have fallen inadvertently, but the very lie in the soul. If these are my truths, then they are basic truths the loss of which means imaginative death.

First, as to Manipulation. I do not think (and no great civilization has ever thought) that the art of the rhetorician is necessarily vile. It is in itself noble, though of course, like most arts, it can be wickedly used. I do not think that Rhetoric and Poetry are distinguished by manipulation of an audience in the one and, in the other, a pure self expression, regarded as its own end, and indifferent to any audience. But these arts, in my opinion, definitely aim at doing something to an audience. And both do it by using language to control what already exists in our minds. The differentia of Rhetoric is that it wishes to produce in our minds some practical resolve (to condemn Warren Hastings or to declare war on Philip) and it does this by calling the passions to the aid of reason. It is honestly practised when the orator honestly believes that the thing which he calls the passions to support *is* reason, and usefully practised when this belief of his is in fact correct. It is mischievously practised when that which he summons the passions to aid is, in fact, unreason, and dishonestly practised when he himself knows that it is unreason. The proper use is lawful and necessary because, as Aristotle points out, intellect of itself "moves nothing": the transition from thinking to doing, in nearly all men at nearly all moments, needs to be assisted by appropriate states of feeling. Because the end of rhetoric is in the world of action, the objects it deals with appear foreshortened and much of their reality is omitted. Thus the ambitions of Philip are shown only in so far as they are wicked and dangerous, because indignation and moderate fear are emotional channels through which men pass from thinking to doing. Now good poetry, if it dealt with the ambitions of Philip, would give you something much more like their total reality—what it felt like to be Philip and Philip's place in the whole system of things. Its Philip would, in fact, be more *concrete* than the Philip of the orator. That is because poetry aims at producing something more like vision than it is like action. But vision, in this sense, includes passions. Certain things, if not seen as lovely or detestable, are not being correctly seen at all. When we try to rouse some one's hate of toothache in order to persuade him to ring up the dentist, this is rhetoric; but even if there were no practical issue involved, even if we only wanted to convey the reality of toothache for some speculative purpose or for its own sake, we should still have failed if the idea produced in our friend's mind did not include the hatefulness of toothache. Toothache, with that left out, is an abstraction. Hence the awakening and moulding of the reader's or hearer's emotions is a necessary element in that vision of concrete reality which poetry hopes to produce. Very roughly, we might almost say that in Rhetoric imagination is present for the sake of passion (and, therefore, in the long run, for the sake of action), while in poetry passion is present for the sake of imagination, and therefore, in the long run, for the sake of wisdom or spiritual health—the rightness and richness of a man's total response to the world. Such rightness, of course, has a tendency to contribute indirectly to right action, besides being in itself exhilarating and tranquillizing; that is why the old critics were right enough when they said that Poetry taught by delighting, or delighted by teaching. The rival theories of Dr. Richards and Professor D. G. James are therefore perhaps not so different that we cannot recognize a point of contact. Poetry, for Dr. Richards, produces a wholesome equilibrium of our psychological attitudes. For Professor James, it presents an object of "secondary imagination," gives us a view of the world. But a concrete (as opposed to a purely conceptual) view of reality would in fact involve right attitudes; and the totality of right attitudes, if man is a creature at all adapted to the world he inhabits, would presumably be in wholesome equilibrium. But however this may be, Poetry certainly aims at making the reader's mind what it was not before. The idea of a poetry which exists only for the poet—a poetry which the public rather overhears than hears—is a foolish novelty in criticism. There is nothing specially admirable in talking to oneself. Indeed, it is arguable that Himself is the very audience before whom a man postures most and on whom he practises the most elaborate deceptions.

Next comes the question of Stock Responses. By a Stock Response Dr. I. A. Richards means a deliberately organized attitude which is substituted for "the direct free play of experience." In my opinion such deliberate organization is one of the first necessities of human life, and one of the main functions of art is to assist it. All that we describe as constancy in love or friendship, as loyalty in political life, or, in general, as perseverance—all solid virtue and stable pleasure—depends on organizing chosen attitudes and maintaining them against the eternal flux (or "direct free play") of mere immediate experience. This Dr. Richards would not perhaps deny. But his school puts the emphasis the other way. They talk as if improvement of our responses were always required in the direction of finer discrimination and greater particularity; never as if men needed responses more normal and more traditional than they now have. To me, on the other hand, it seems that most people's responses are not "stock" enough, and that the play of experience is too free and too direct in most of us for safety or happiness or human dignity. A number of causes may be assigned for the opposite belief. (1) The decay of Logic, resulting in an untroubled assumption that the particular is real and the universal is not. (2) A Romantic Primitivism (not shared by Dr. Richards himself) which prefers the merely natural to the elaborated, the un-willed to the willed. Hence a loss of the old conviction (once shared by Hindoo, Platonist, Stoic, Christian, and "humanist" alike) that simple "experience," so far from being something venerable, is in itself mere raw material, to be mastered, shaped, and worked up by the will. (3) A confusion (arising from the fact that both are voluntary) between the organization of a response and the pretence of a response. Von Hügel says somewhere, "I kiss my son not only because I love him, but in order that I may love him." That is organization, and good. But you may also kiss children in order to make it *appear* that you love them. That is pretence, and bad. The distinction must not be overlooked. Sensitive critics are so tired of seeing good Stock responses aped by bad writers that when at last they meet the reality they mistake it for one more instance of posturing. They are rather like a man I knew who had seen so many bad pictures of moonlight on water that he criticized a real weir under a real moon as "conventional." (4) A belief (not unconnected with the doctrine of the Unchanging Human Heart which I shall discuss later) that a certain elementary rectitude of human response is "given" by nature herself, and may be taken for granted, so that poets, secure of this basis are free to devote themselves to the more advanced work of teaching us ever finer and finer discrimination. I believe this to be a dangerous delusion. Children like dabbling in dirt; they have to be *taught* the stock response to it. Normal sexuality, far from being a *datum,* is achieved by a long and delicate process of suggestion and adjustment which proves too difficult for some individuals and, at times, for whole societies. The Stock response to Pride, which Milton reckoned on when he delineated his Satan, has been decaying ever since the Romantic Movement began—that is one of the reasons why I am composing these lectures. The Stock response to treachery has become uncertain; only the other day I heard a respectable working man defend Lord Haw-Haw by remarking coolly (and with no hint of anger or of irony), "You've got to remember that's how he earns his pay." The Stock response to death has become uncertain. I have heard a man say that the only "amusing" thing that happened while he was in hospital was the death of a patient in the same ward. The Stock response to pain has become uncertain; I have heard Mr. Eliot's comparison of evening to a patient on an operating table praised, nay gloated over, not as a striking picture of sensibility in decay, but because it was so "pleasantly unpleasant." Even the Stock response to pleasure cannot be depended on; I have heard a man (and a young man, too) condemn Donne's more erotic poetry because "sex," as he called it, always "made him think of lysol and rubber goods." That elementary rectitude of human response, at which we are so ready to fling the unkind epithets of "stock," "crude," "bourgeois" and "conventional," so far from being "given" is a delicate balance of trained habits, laboriously acquired and easily lost, on the maintenance of which depend both our virtues and our pleasures and even, perhaps, the survival of our species. For though the human heart is not unchanging (nay, changes almost out of recognition in the twinkling of an eye) the laws of causation are. When poisons become fashionable they do not cease to kill.

The examples I have cited warn us that those Stock responses which we need in order to be even human are already in danger. In the light of that alarming discovery there is no need to apologize for Milton or for any other pre-Romantic poet. The older poetry, by continually insisting on certain Stock themes—as that love is sweet, death bitter, virtue lovely, and children or gardens delightful—was performing a service not only of moral and civil, but even of biological, importance. Once again, the old critics were quite right when they said that poetry "instructed by delighting," for poetry was formerly one of the chief means whereby each new generation learned, not to copy, but by copying to make,[1] the good Stock responses. Since poetry has abandoned that office the world has not bettered. While the moderns have been pressing forward to conquer new territories of consciousness, the old territory, in which alone man can live, has been left unguarded, and we are in danger of finding the enemy in our rear. We need most urgently to recover the lost poetic art of enriching a response without making it eccentric, and of being normal without being vulgar. Meanwhile—until that recovery is made—such poetry as Milton's is more than ever necessary to us.

There is, furthermore, a special reason why mythical poetry ought not to attempt novelty in respect of its ingredients. What it does with the ingredients may be as novel as you please. But giants, dragons, paradises, gods, and the like are themselves the expression of certain basic elements in man's spiritual experience. In that sense they are more like words—the words of a language which speaks the else unspeakable—than they are like the people and places in a novel. To give them radically new characters is not so much original as ungrammatical. That strange blend of genius and vulgarity, the film of *Snow-White*, will illustrate the point. There was good unoriginality in the drawing of the queen. She was the very archetype of all beautiful, cruel queens: the thing one expected to see, save that it was truer to type than one had dared to hope for. There was

---

[1] "We learn how to do things by doing the things we are learning how to do," as Aristotle observes (*Ethics*, II, i).

bad originality in the bloated, drunken, low comedy faces of the dwarfs. Neither the wisdom, the avarice, nor the earthiness of true dwarfs were there, but an imbecility of arbitrary invention. But in the scene where Snow-White wakes in the woods both the right originality and the right unoriginality were used together. The good unoriginality lay in the use of small, delicate animals as comforters, in the true *märchen* style. The good originality lay in letting us at first mistake their eyes for the eyes of monsters. The whole art consists not in evoking the unexpected, but in evoking with a perfection and accuracy beyond expectation the very image that has haunted us all our lives. The marvel about Milton's Paradise or Milton's Hell is simply that they are there—that the thing has at last been done—that our dream stands before us and does not melt. Not many poets can thus draw out leviathan with a hook. Compared with this the short-lived pleasure of any novelty the poet might have inserted would be a mere kickshaw.

The charge of calculated grandiosity, of "stilts" remains. The difficulty here is that the modern critic tends to think Milton is somehow trying to deceive. We feel the pressure of the poet on every word—the *builded* quality of the verse—and since this is the last effect most poets wish to produce to-day, we are in danger of supposing that Milton also would have concealed it if he could, that it is a tell-tale indication of his failure to achieve spontaneity. But does Milton want to sound spontaneous? He tells us that his verse was unpremeditated in fact and attributes this to the Muse. Perhaps it was. Perhaps by that time his own epic style had become "a language which thinks and poetizes of itself." But that is hardly the point. The real question is whether an *air* of spontaneity—an impression that this is the direct outcome of immediate personal emotion— would be in the least proper to this kind of work. I believe it would not. We should miss the all-important sense that *something out of the ordinary is being done.* Bad poets in the tradition of Donne write artfully and try to make it sound colloquial. If Milton were to practise deception, it would be the other way round. A man performing a rite is not trying to make you think that this is his natural way of walking, these the unpremeditated gestures of his own domestic life. If long usage has in fact made the ritual unconscious, he must labour to make it look deliberate, in order that we, the assistants, may feel the weight of the solemnity pressing on his shoulders as well as on our own. Anything casual or familiar in his manner is not "sincerity" or "spontaneity," but impertinence. Even if his robes were not heavy in fact, they ought to *look* heavy. But there is no need to suppose any deception. Habit and devout concentration of mind, or something else for which the Muse is as good a name as any other, may well have brought it to pass that the verse of *Paradise Lost* flowed into his mind without labour; but what flowed was something stylized, remote from conversation, hierophantic. The style is not pretending to be "natural" any more than a singer is pretending to talk.

Even the poet, when he appears in the first person within his own poem, is not to be taken as the private individual John Milton. If he were that, he would be an irrelevance. He also becomes an image—the image of the Blind Bard—and we are told about him nothing that does not help that archetypal pattern. It is his office, not his person, that is sung. It would be a gross error to regard the opening of *Samson* and the opening of Book III as giving us respectively what Milton really felt, and what he would be thought to feel, about his blindness. The real man, of course, being a man, felt many more things, and less interesting things, about it than are expressed in either. From that total experience the poet selects, for his epic and for his tragedy, what is proper to each. The impatience, the humiliation, the questionings of Providence go into *Samson* because the business of tragedy is "by raising pity and fear, or terror, to purge the mind of those and such-like passions . . . with a kind of delight stirred up by reading or seeing those passions well imitated." If he had not been blind himself, he would still (though with less knowledge to guide him) have put just those elements of a blind man's experience into the mouth of Samson: for the "disposition of his fable" so as to "stand best with verisimilitude and decorum" requires them. On the other hand, whatever is calm and great, whatever associations make blindness venerable—all this he selects for the opening of Book III. Sincerity and insincerity are words that have no application to either case. We want a great blind poet in the one, we want a suffering and questioning prisoner in the other. "Decorum is the grand masterpiece."

The grandeur which the poet assumes in his poetic capacity should not arouse hostile reactions. It is for our benefit. He makes his epic a rite so that we may share it; the more ritual it becomes, the more we are elevated to the rank of participants. Precisely because the poet appears not as a private person, but as a Hierophant or Choregus, we are summoned not to hear what one particular man thought and felt about the Fall, but to take part, under his leadership, in a great mimetic dance of all Christendom, ourselves soaring and ruining from Heaven, ourselves enacting Hell and Paradise, the Fall and the repentance.

Thus far of Milton's style on the assumption that it is in fact as remote and artificial as is thought. No part of my defence depends on questioning that assumption, for I think it ought to be remote and artificial. But it would not be honest to suppress my conviction that the degree to which it possesses these qualities has been exaggerated. Much that we think typically "Poetic Diction" in *Paradise Lost* was nothing of the sort, and has since become Poetic Diction only because Milton used it. When he writes of an *optic glass* (I, 288) we think this a poetical periphrasis because we are remembering Thomson or Akenside; but it seems to have been an ordinary expression in Milton's time. When we read *ruin and combustion* (I, 46) we naturally exclaim *aut Miltonus aut diabolus!* Yet the identical words are said to occur in a document of the Long Parliament. *Alchymy* (II, 517) sounds like the Miltonic vague: it is really almost a trade name. *Numerous* as applied to verse (V, 150) sounds "poetic," but was not. If we could read *Paradise Lost* as it really was we should see more play of muscles than we see now. But only a little more. I am defending Milton's style as a ritual style.

I think the older critics may have misled us by saying that "admiration" or "astonishment" is the proper response to such poetry. Certainly if "admiration" is taken in its modern sense, the misunderstanding becomes disastrous. I should say rather that joy or exhilaration was what it produced—an overplus of robust and tranquil well-being in a total experience which contains both rapturous and painful elements. In the *Dry Salvages* Mr. Eliot speaks of "music heard so deeply that it is not heard at all." Only as we emerge from the mode of consciousness induced by the symphony do we begin once more to attend explicitly to the sounds which induced it. In the same way, when we are caught up into the experience which a "grand" style communicates, we are, in a sense, no longer conscious of the style. Incense is consumed by being used. The poem kindles admirations which leave us no leisure to admire the poem. When our participation in a rite becomes perfect we think no more of ritual, but are engrossed by that *about which* the rite is performed; but afterwards we recognize that ritual was the sole method by which this concentration could be achieved. Those who in reading *Paradise Lost* find themselves forced to attend throughout to the sound and the manner have simply not discovered what this sound and this manner were intended to do. A schoolboy who reads a page of Milton by chance, for the first time, and then looks up and says, "By gum!" not in the least knowing how the thing has worked, but only that new strength and width and brightness and zest have transformed his world, is nearer to the truth than they.

DOUGLAS BUSH

MILTON (1945)*

W HOEVER the third of English poets may be, Milton's
place has been next to the throne, and for most of us he still
stands there, "Like Teneriff or Atlas unremov'd." But to the
defeatism of the "Armistice" period, 1918-39, the naturalistic
passion and irresponsibility of Donne appealed much more
than a passion for order and righteousness, and devotion to one
kind of writing necessitated a zealous dislike of all other kinds.
The supreme English artist, the only one to be matched with
Virgil and Dante in what Arnold called "the sure and flawless
perfection of his rhythm and diction," became the rhetorician
who had crushed the fruitful metaphysical movement, divorced
thought and feeling, and imposed an artificial style and prosody upon English poetry for over two hundred years, until it
was freed from bondage by the "metaphysical" poets of our
time. In addition to such recent detractors Milton has always
had dubious friends. The admiration for the great rebel felt
by men like Blake and Shelley was mixed with antipathy for
the theological system to which he was supposedly committed,
and nineteenth-century critics in general were inclined to save
his "poetry" by casting his ideas overboard. In our day, while
a few critics were reacting violently against him, Milton's
thought began to be seriously explored and appreciated by
scholars; they invoked a broader formula to unify and save the

---

* From *English Literature in the Earlier Seventeenth Century*, Oxford
History of English Literature, Oxford, the Clarendon Press, 1945. This
selection, reprinted by permission of the Clarendon Press, includes the
introduction and Secs. 4-6 and 9 of Chap. XII, "Milton."

artist and thinker, and the rigid son of the Reformation became the bold son of the Renaissance. This conception, however, gained ground just as its ideological parent, Burckhardt's
popular theory of the Renaissance, was being abandoned, and
the new Milton, though he embodied some significant and
amiable features which had been lacking in the grim Puritan,
looked decidedly too much like a nineteenth-century liberal.
This brief and unqualified summary indicates at least that Milton's poetic and philosophic character is less simple and obvious than friends as well as foes have often assumed it to be.
Our present view of Milton is not unanimous or final but, with
a better understanding of his background, roots, and evolution,
we have perhaps struck a juster balance between the Renaissance humanist and the Puritan. Milton may be called the last
great exponent of Christian humanism in its historical continuity, the tradition of classical reason and culture fused with
Christian faith which had been the main line of European
development. His Christian humanism, intensified and somewhat altered by the conditions of his age and country and by
his own temperament, becomes as he grows old a noble anach-
ronism in an increasingly modern and mundane world.

*   *   *

4.

The central articles of Milton's ethical and religious creed
were developed in his prose, and we may here take both a backward and a forward glance, remembering that the creed was
always growing under the pressure of thought and experience,
and that some of the most significant developments, at least in
tone and emphasis, appeared only in the late poems.

If the first article was liberty, it was the liberty achieved
through religious discipline, through education in the fullest
sense of the word. In his letter (1644) to Hartlib, the Baconian
and Comenian reformer, Milton showed, as he had in his pro-
lusions, some affinity with Baconian critics of the prescribed
methods and materials of education, both scholastic and lin-

guistic, and—partly perhaps because of the demands of war—
he gave a larger importance to the study of science than many
of the older humanists had given. In the main, however, he
wrote in the orthodox tradition of Renaissance and medieval
humanism. His view is aristocratic (later he was to feel more
strongly the need of popular education) ; he aims at the production of useful and cultivated citizens and leaders, not scholars; and he assumes that the classics are the fundamental literature of knowledge as well as of power. In stressing religion and
virtue, the training of the moral judgement and the will, he
only adds 'a personal earnestness to what had been the chief
object of Christian humanism in all ages and countries. Of the
two definitions of education in the tract, what might be called
the "modern" one is constantly quoted, but the "medieval" one
is even more truly Miltonic:

The end then of learning is to repair the ruins of our first parents by
regaining to know God aright, and out of that knowledge to love him,
to imitate him, to be like him, as we may the neerest by possessing our
souls of true vertue, which being united to the heavenly grace of faith
makes up the highest perfection.

That is the substance of the last words between Michael and
Adam, and by that time the author had gained a fuller comprehension of their meaning.

It was inevitable that Milton should break with Calvinism
as Erasmus had broken with Luther. A humanist believing in
human and divine reason could not uphold the depravity of
man and the arbitrary will of an inscrutable God. No ordi-
nance, human or from heaven, Milton declared in *Tetrachordon,* can bind against the good of man. And in the tracts on
divorce, in *Areopagitica,* and most fully and explicitly in the
Christian Doctrine, Milton evolved that enlarged conception
of Christian liberty of which he was in his day the great exponent. That conception of the self-directing independence of
the regenerate man, of his freedom from external prescription,
could be both aristocratic and revolutionary; it was, of course,

far removed from the licence of the unregenerate and irresponsible. Man's guide is not the letter of civil or biblical law but the law of the Spirit written in the hearts of believers; for Milton as for Hooker and Taylor and other Christian humanists the law of God is the law of right reason and of nature. With Christian values and motives are fused ancient, aristocratic, and rational ideals of private and republican freedom. Both the right reason of the individual and the saving remnant of the regenerate are, like the created universe, worlds of divine order in the midst of chaos.

A good deal, though not all, of the purpose and substance of Milton's chief works is crystallized in some eloquent and familiar sentences of *Areopagitica:*

I cannot praise a fugitive and cloister'd vertue, unexercis'd & unbreath'd, that never sallies out and sees her adversary, but slinks out of the race, where that immortall garland is to be run for, not without dust and heat. Assuredly we bring not innocence into the world, we bring impurity much rather: that which purifies us is triall, and triall is by what is contrary. That vertue therefore which is but a youngling in the contemplation of evill, and knows not the utmost that vice promises to her followers, and rejects it, is but a blank vertue, not a pure; her whitenesse is but an excrementall whitenesse; Which was the reason why our sage and serious Poet Spencer, whom I dare be known to think a better teacher then Scotus or Aquinas, describing true temperance under the person of Guion, brings him in with his palmer through the cave of Mammon, and the bowr of earthly blisse that he might see and know, and yet abstain. . . .

Many there be that complain of divin Providence for suffering Adam to transgresse, foolish tongues! when God gave him reason, he gave him freedom to choose, for reason is but choosing; he had bin else a meer artificiall Adam, such an Adam as he is in the motions. We our selves esteem not of that obedience, or love, or gift, which is of force: God therefore left him free, set before him a provoking object, ever almost in his eyes; herein consisted his merit, herein the right of his reward, the praise of his abstinence. Wherefore did he creat passions within us, pleasures round about us, but that these rightly temper'd are the very ingredients of vertu? . . .

This justifies the high providence of God, who though he command us temperance, justice, continence, yet powrs out before us ev'n to a profusenes all desirable things, and gives us minds that can wander beyond all limit and satiety.

This last sentence, with its verbal anticipations of *Paradise Lost,* is a particular reminder of Milton's method of justifying God's ways to men, his emphasis on human freedom of choice and human responsibility. The unwary Eve falls through "pride And wandring vanitie," the credulous and mistaken desire for an apparent good, which mislead her reason, and Adam, whose reason is not deceived, allows uxorious passion to sway his will and break his higher tie with God. In putting the simple biblical story on a partly humanistic and rational basis, in making it a many-sided conflict between reason and unreason, "knowledge" and "ignorance," temperance and excess, hierarchic order and anarchic disorder, Milton had behind him the whole tradition of Christian humanism; two contemporary examples are the first chapter of Browne's *Pseudodoxia Epidemica* and Henry More's *Conjectura Cabbalistica.* But Milton has also risen above—some might say he had fallen below—the bold confidence of *Areopagitica* and *Tetrachordon.* If the zealous pamphleteer had not quite fully realized that reason and rectitude could partake of self-sufficient human pride, the ageing poet has had the lesson proved on his pulses. He has not abandoned the principles of Christian liberty and right reason, for these are religious and fundamental, but he has a new understanding of the prime need of humility and obedience. Irreligious pride and religious humility are indeed the one great theme of his major poems.

In *Paradise Lost,* even in exalting human reason and freedom, Milton stresses human weakness and the dangers of pride, which ruin Eve and Adam as well as Satan. The fallen angels lose themselves in the mazes of philosophic debate. The whole temptation of Eve is an appeal to the desire for godlike knowledge and power. In the long astronomical discussion of the eighth book, and with reiterated emphasis at the end of the poem, Adam is warned to check his roving fancy and to learn that the sum of wisdom is not scientific learning but everyday Christian goodness. We may be surprised at such "obscurantism" in the man who had been kindled by Baconian ideas, who had given science a large place in his educational scheme, and who had written the great defense of free inquiry. But Milton is not condemning science in itself (he pays tribute to Galileo in the epic as well as in *Areopagitica*), he is only taking scientific knowledge and speculation as a cardinal example of the pride and presumption which obscure the true ends and values of life. Like all Christian humanists from Petrarch to Matthew Arnold, he feared the confusing of wisdom and knowledge, law for man and the law for thing. In the *Reason of Church Government* (1642) he had distinguished between the lower wisdom of natural science and the only high valuable wisdom of religion, and in the following decades it might well seem that the rising tide of scientific thought threatened to sweep away religious and ethical values altogether. For Milton as for the Cambridge Platonists, the physical and metaphysical worlds were a divine order with a divine purpose, and man was made in the image of God, with a spark of divine reason and divine will.

We may notice here a parallel case in *Paradise Regained*. Many readers, knowing Milton's lifelong devotion and infinite debt to classical literature and thought, feel a shock when they come upon Christ's repudiation of the philosophy, poetry, and oratory of Greece, which has just received through Satan the poet's beautiful and heart-felt praise. The shock is unwarranted. Like other Christian humanists, Milton had always set the Bible above all other writings, and he gave still higher authority to "the Spirit and the unwritten word." It is only in comparison with the divine light of humble Christian faith and virtue that Greek philosophy, like science, appears as the product of arrogant human pride. In itself, so far as it goes, it is good; Christ Himself, earlier in the poem, had ranked Socrates next to Job. Milton's favourite secular authors up to the end were ancients, and this very poem—not to mention its companion, *Samson Agonistes*—owes much to them. His condemnation is relative rather than absolute. At the same time his vehemence here is a mark of the growing inwardness of his thought; in his age he turns more and more from a degenerate world and secondary aids to cling to ultimate truth. He is saying, as his old opponent Bishop Hall, the Christian Stoic, had said, that true light and peace of mind are to be won not at Athens but at Jerusalem.

The briefest survey of Milton's religious thought and feeling makes sufficiently absurd the romantic idea that he was of the devil's party without knowing it, that Satan was the real hero of *Paradise Lost*. But the idea is not yet dead in the popular or sometimes in the scholarly mind. The magnificent vitality of Satan has occasioned much idle discussion as well as wrongheaded eulogy. It is a matter of course that Shakespeare, though not a villain, could create heroic villains; why it should be a wonder and a problem that Milton could is not clear. The Satanist fallacy starts from complete misunderstanding of Satan's first speech. Here no less than later he shows himself in every word as a mighty outlaw, a great embodiment of pride and passion and a false ideal of liberty, and the intelligent reader, who does not need the poet's guiding comments, reacts as he reacts to the lawless speeches of Iago, Edmund, or Macbeth. Milton was of course a doctrinal poet as Shakespeare was not (though he often uses the technique of dramatic objectivity), but his beliefs and principles, however much philosophized by learning and heightened by Puritan fervour, were in the same tradition as Shakespeare's—and Hooker's and many other men's. It is not altogether his fault if readers debauched by sentimental and romantic liberalism and naturalism are incapable of either intellectual or emotional response to the classical, Christian, medieval, and Renaissance doctrines of law and order in the soul, in society, and in the cosmos.

Those moderns who cannot comprehend or feel Milton's religious and ethical thought have no better understanding of a poetic method based also on law and order, so that the self-imposed limitations of all classical art become in him a simple-minded ignorance of the complexities of human nature and life. But Milton is at least no more naïve than Aeschylus and Sophocles, and the complexities and passions of mankind are the stuff of his major poems. Adam and Eve are condemned, as they must be; but the poet's acceptance of God's just punishment carries with it an enlarged charity towards His erring creatures. We follow with dramatic fullness the process by which the regal pair, created perfect, become Everyman and Everywoman, and we see them on the way to regeneration. The compassion that Milton feels for them culminates in the marvellously simple and suggestive close, the picture of two human beings alone in the world, with "Providence thir guide." Whether or not Milton justified the ways of God, his belief in a divinely ordered world did not impose a superficial unity and harmony upon his profoundly human and poetical sense of division and conflict, evil strength and evil weakness.

5.

To speak briefly, as we must, of Milton's theological thought is to recognize his essential orthodoxy and to slight particular heresies. The explicit statement of his views, ethical and social as well as theological, is the *De Doctrina Christiana* (first printed in 1825) which, however early it originated, had reached virtually final form by about 1658-60 and was later amplified only in some details. Starting from such models as Ames and Wollebius, Milton was at great pains, with much discussion of the commentators, to systematize his own beliefs, and he sought also, apparently, to draw up a body of biblical teaching which all Protestants might accept. In such a biblical compilation the humanistic ethic so important in Milton's thought is not conspicuous, much less the imaginative action of his poetic fable. But the *Christian Doctrine* provides chapter and verse for the theological concepts of *Paradise Lost* and, since seventeenth-century theology was seldom flaccid, something of the hardness of the treatise is carried over into parts of the poem. At least Milton's metaphysical theology seems hard to those who consider egocentric emotionalism the highest level of religious experience.

Christ, God's executive agent in the heavenly war and in the creation and judgement of man, is the Logos, the Creative Word, and, in contrast with Satan, the incarnation of supreme love and right reason. He is also the Redeemer and the Mediator through whom man becomes regenerate. Milton not only accepts but glorifies the Atonement in both verse and prose, though his more instinctive emphasis seems to be, like that of the Cambridge Platonists, on the imitation of Christ, the divine life. The Arian or anti-Trinitarian view of the inferiority of Christ and the Holy Spirit to the Father, while clearly set forth in the treatise, is less distinct and obvious in the poem (which did not disturb generations of orthodox readers), but no doctrinal passage in the poem is inconsistent with the Arianism of Milton's formal theology.

Like Christ, God is Divine Love and much more. If at times He seems to resemble an almighty cat watching a human mouse, the trouble lies in the somewhat legal character of Christian theology itself and in the inevitable effects of dramatization. God suffers, paradoxically, through being the mouthpiece for the very doctrines which clear Him of arbitrary cruelty and justify His ways to men, the Arminian and Miltonic doctrines of free grace extended to all believers and of the right reason, free will, and responsibility of man. Against the Absolute Will of Calvinism Milton sets up Absolute Reason, the ultimate source and guarantee of life, order, justice, all the values comprehended by the spark of divine reason in man. There may be artistic defects in Milton's presentation, but there is nothing thin or cold in the conception. In the great words of Hooker,

of lawe there can be no lesse acknowledged, then that her seate is the bosome of God, her voyce the harmony of the world, all thinges in heaven and earth doe her homage, the very least as feeling her care, and the greatest as not exempted from her power, but Angels and men and creatures of what condition so ever, though ech in different sort and maner, yet all with uniforme consent, admiring her as the mother of their peace and joy.

That is the divine and natural harmony, the hierarchical order, which Satan seeks to overthrow in the universe and in the soul of man.

To enlarge a little upon Milton's metaphysics, his conception of the infinity, omnipresence, and omnipotence of God lies behind some ideas which may seem to approach pantheism, though Milton is no pantheist; he does not confound the Creator with Creation. God includes all causes, even the material. God did not create the world out of nothing, as orthodox tradition maintained, but out of the eternal substance which is a part of Himself. Uncircumscribed by necessity or chance, God communicates His goodness by manifesting Himself throughout the great scale of being which descends from Christ and the angels through the creatures and things of earth. All things proceed from God and, unless depraved by evil, return to Him. Chaos is Chaos because He has not chosen to put forth His creative virtue upon it. (The germ of this idea is perhaps what in the *Timaeus* is called "the absence of God.") Milton affirms the reality and the goodness of matter; matter is not distinct from spirit but is for ever passing into it. The optimism inherent in such metaphysical monism receives characteristic expression from the poet-musician in half-mystical celebrations of cosmic harmony. It is obviously related to the ethical optimism that Milton shared also with the Cambridge Platonists, and for him it is a partial bulwark against the pessimism of experience. This metaphysical monism is not incompatible with the ethical dualism that is Christian and Platonic. What God is in the universe the divine faculty of reason is in man, and when man's reason is not in active control his nature becomes a chaos of passions. An ethical corollary of Milton's belief in the essential oneness of matter and spirit is his mature conception of human love, a conception which retains his early Christian and Platonic idealism without his early asceticism. Another logical consequence is the belief that man dies wholly until the day of resurrection; in this Milton is allied with contemporary "mortalists."

If this outline of some of Milton's central ideas has taken space which should have been given to "the poetry," it is still the merest sketch of the creed he devoted his life and art to proclaiming. If the fundamental part of the creed be dismissed as elementary and commonplace, it was for Milton as for other great men and great writers the armour of a Christian soldier. And, it may be added, there is very little of the specifically Puritan in *Paradise Lost,* or indeed in the whole body of Milton's poetry. Finally, what we think of as Milton's theology belongs mainly to the *Christian Doctrine* and *Paradise Lost,* and his particular and changing beliefs are much less significant than his progress towards belief, in a deeper sense of the word. His earlier Christian humanism had been largely directed towards militant action; the decline and collapse of that external hope left him feeling the need of a closer walk with God. In his late poems, in place of the old ardent confidence in public reform, we find an "un-Miltonic" emphasis on private experience, on humility, obedience, faith, and divine help.

6.

We have had incidental hints of the epic ambitions which no Renaissance poet cherished more ardently than Milton. He had long contemplated the British theme which critical theory and poetic example prescribed, and his final choice was evidently determined by various causes, the scepticism induced by his own and others' study of early history, the cleavage in sentiment between "Saxon" parliamentarians and "British" royalists, the general European reaction in favour of biblical subjects, and chiefly, no doubt, his desire for a fable which would carry all that he now wished to say about God and man. The British and biblical subjects listed in the Cambridge manuscript (*c.* 1639-42) were planned as dramas, and Milton made four dramatic outlines of Adam's fall; indeed, the tale of Adam and Eve is in its very nature the pattern of a morality play. However, Milton did not give up his original and more satisfying project of an heroic poem. Having elected his subject and form, he still faced a problem which had existed in a smaller degree for Virgil and not at all for Homer, that is, the treatment of abstract spiritual ideas in the concrete terms of the heroic epic. As occasional apologies in the text indicate, Milton was conscious of the problem, if less fully conscious than the modern reader who feels that he has outgrown the epic tradition. The battles in heaven, the account of Creation, and the survey of Hebrew history, to mention three cardinal examples, remain more or less potent symbols of the contrast between chaotic passion and divine order, between destruction and the creative works of peace, between man's sinfulness and God's providence, yet the protracted and realistic treatment of such material, which early readers could enjoy for its own sake, means for us, in spite of many fine passages, an obscuring of symbolic values. Above all, the anthropomorphic and "royalist" presentation of God, which was almost unavoidable in a heroic poem, has misled many readers and critics into seeing only the trappings of a tyrant and not the religious and metaphysical ideas He embodies.

In the elaboration of his narrative and drama Milton had two main resources, the plastic materials of classical story and, more directly, the whole Bible and the body of extra-biblical lore accumulated in Jewish and Christian commentary and in imaginative treatments of the Creation and the fall of Lucifer and of man. How many works of this last kind Milton had read we do not know; the *Adamus Exul* (1601) of Grotius and the *Adamo* (1613) of Andreini are perhaps the closest to *Paradise Lost*. Milton's poem is the great surviving monument of the immense mass of Renaissance writing, exegetical and poetical, which dealt with the matter of Genesis. God Himself hardly knew more about the beginnings of the world than the Du Bartas whom the young Milton had admired in Sylvester's popular translation and whose Protestant epic his own superseded. Imaginative versions of religious "history" were bound to keep within the limits of orthodoxy (a flexible orthodoxy, to be sure), so that they all have a degree of family resemblance, and very many items, large and small, in Milton's fable are inevitably conventional. A Renaissance poet, like a Greek dramatist, was expected to show his originality in the reworking of traditional themes, and to appreciate Milton's re-creative power we have only to think of Satan.

On the classical side Milton followed especially Virgil, the supreme model of epic decorum, and, like Virgil, he gave a new meaning to the devices he imitated—celestial machinery, the roll-call and council of leaders, epic games, the recapitulatory narrative after the plunge *in medias res,* and the unfolding of future events. To mention a few items from various sources, the revolt of the angels blends theological tradition with the wars of giants and Titans and gods; the rebel army in hell marches like the Spartans in Plutarch's *Lycurgus;* Satan and Gabriel confront each other like Turnus and Aeneas in their last combat; Eve gives the first hint of her "facile" nature by admiring her reflection in a pool, like Narcissus; the biblical description of the flood invites expansion from Ovid and Du Bartas; and so on. But with all his diverse means of amplification Milton remains so close to the original fable that many readers cannot feel certain where the Bible leaves off and the poet begins.

When various cosmological theories were current it was natural for a layman and a poet to follow what is called the Ptolemaic system. Milton knew enough science to discuss the old and familiar notions of the diurnal rotation of the earth and the plurality of worlds, and to treat Copernican ideas with respect, but the actual universe of *Paradise Lost* was a Miltonic mixture of the traditional and the imaginative, and was modern chiefly in its immensity. He was, as we have seen, too much of a Christian humanist to let scientific speculation divert him from the problems of direct importance to man and society. It has been said that Shakespeare lived in a world of time, Milton in a world of space, but for Milton space is not parallel to the spectre of devouring Time which haunted so many minds of the Renaissance. In his medieval scale of values, science, so far as it is a description of God's works, is a branch of theology and as such he, like Du Bartas, can make use of it. Hence too, unlike some men of his century, Milton was apparently at no time bewildered and dismayed by a consciousness of the silence of infinite space. The axis of his faith rested on God and the soul of man, and if that faith was sometimes shaken, the cause was not any trepidation of the spheres. Without misgiving he accepts the universe as his scene and his imagination triumphantly expands to fill it. No other English poet has such a God-like vision of the world, a vision revealed in the great pictures of boundless chaos and warring elements and in the constant suggestion of vast distances. Such imperial command of space doubtless belongs to the age of the telescope, yet we may remember that no poet of the same age rivals the blind Milton and, further, that a sense of space was not wholly lacking in earlier men, among them such ancients as Lucretius, Ovid, and Manilius.

If Milton's "unhuman" fable and unlocalized setting invite austere grandeur of treatment, he achieves passionate warmth and organic unity through his profound concern with "man, the heart of man, and human life"; all his epic machinery and decoration are subservient to that. But there are, apart from the general interrelations of plot and character, various special devices by which his story is integrated and linked with the human and familiar. The action in heaven and hell is knit together by such contrasted parallels as the infernal and celestial assemblies and the "merit" of Satan and Christ and details like the march of the angels and the opening of the gates. A more subtle kind of symbolism, already conspicuous in Spenser, involves a continual antithesis between natural simplicity, goodness, love, light, and life on the one hand and artificial luxury, evil, hate, darkness, and death on the other. While Homeric similes in the main keep us aware of a normal pastoral life beyond the roar of battle and the waves, Milton's allusiveness takes of course a much wider range, from Galileo to "the

Sons Of Belial" and the burglar. His geographical names are not merely incantation but an economical as well as sonorous way of calling up great events and great tracts of space and time. In becoming less familiar—since it takes a world war to stir the modern reader out of his geographical illiteracy—Milton's allusions have become less realistic than they were in his own age. The investing of Satan with oriental pomp and power was not glamorous tinsel for men whose grandfathers had feared the mighty Turk and coveted "the wealth of Ormus and of Ind." But if Milton's references are commonly prompted by substantial reasons, they may also be vague enough to sustain and heighten our sense of remoteness or mystery or grandeur or horror. And that is in keeping with his fable and purpose. His vast stage and superhuman action demand, not the minute realism of Dante, but the constant use of the general and suggestive, whether in the pictures of hell or of the "enormous bliss" of Eden. But that goes with and is controlled by a fundamental concreteness of thought and vision. Keats observed Milton's habit of "stationing" characters in relation to solid objects; we see Adam "under a Platan" and Satan disfigured "on th' Assyrian mount." Unlike the true romantic, Milton never surrenders to the vague and unearthly. One remarkable instance is that .magnificently romantic island salt and bare, "The haunt of Seales and Orcs, and Sea-mews clang," which disproves the special sanctity of what George Fox called steeple-houses.

Classical generality and romantic suggestion are never more perfectly fused than in Milton's images from ancient myth. They are the culmination of Renaissance art. They are, too, an index to Milton's own artistic and spiritual evolution; his successive allusions to Orpheus, for instance, reflect the lyrical serenity of *L'Allegro* and *Il Penseroso,* the troubled disenchantment of *Lycidas,* the noble fortitude of the invocation to light, and the bitterness of the strident outburst against Bacchus and his revellers. While Milton's classical mythology shared in his general evolution from Elizabethan luxuriance through a chastened splendour to bare severity, and while the later books of

Paradise Lost and the two last poems largely forbade the use of myth, this more than any other element in his writing retained the old sensuous warmth. In Milton generally, as in the Renaissance tradition, the unique value of the mythological symbol is its ideal beauty. Like such moderns as Arnold and T. S. Eliot, Milton instinctively turns away from the ugly present to the freshness and fecundity of the early world. The finest of all his similes, "Not that faire field Of Enna," owes its complex magic to the musical and structural pattern, to the pathos of familiarity in the phrase "all that pain," and to the implication that another innocent and lovely—and motherless—Proserpine is about to be gathered by the prince of darkness. Both the myth and the image of the flower are recalled, with a mixture of tragic irony and pity, in the description of Eve just before the temptation, when she goes forth like Ceres in her prime and when she is tying up the drooping stalks,

> Her self, though fairest unsupported Flour,
> From her best prop so farr, and storm so nigh.

The various pictures of the "Silvan Scene," in which Milton lets himself go, though not beyond control, in the evocation of an earthly paradise, are not merely a gorgeous exercise in a Renaissance convention (still less an attempt to render the sensation of being in a garden), they spring from the poet's half-unconscious desire to believe in some ideal perfection unmarred by evil. Yet Milton is no poet of escape and he never loses his hold upon reality; over the idyllic beauty of Eden lies the ironic shadow of the tempter.

Milton's classical mythology may, in his most solemn moods, be blended with Hebraic or Christian feeling, as in the allusion to Proserpine and the prayers into which he transformed addresses to the epic Muse, or in the sonnet on his dead wife. But although tradition had reconciled classical and Hebrew story, and although the mature Milton could still link myth with religious and moral truth, he always claimed Christian superiority to "th' Orphean Lyre" and he could feel, as Spenser did not, a conflict. His anti-pagan scruples, so often incorporated in the text of *Paradise Lost,* illustrate the dilemma of a sacred poet and a Puritan bred in the congenial air of Renaissance classicism. For one example, the lines about Mulciber's fall from heaven—which are, incidentally, a romantic transmutation of Homeric humour and embody an un-Homeric sense of space—begin and end with expressions of hostile disbelief, yet they contain a richness of detail and of sound notable even in Milton.

The use of blank verse for an heroic poem was a great innovation, and Milton's handling of it added, not a new province, but a new world, to English prosody. But we cannot touch upon technicalities or even go very far into generalities. Milton's versification is of course inseparable from his diction and tone, and in recent years the organ-voice of England has been charged with an inorganically monotonous elevation of style and movement remote from the language and rhythms of common speech. There are always people who complain that Poussin is not Picasso or that Bach is not Prokofiev. Milton's poetic and critical heritage and his own purpose prescribed a long poem, and in a long poem the reader must be made to feel the continuity, "the enormous onward pressure of the great stream" on which he is embarked. It is rather idle to compare bits of *Paradise Lost* with the short pieces of the metaphysical poets or with the dramatic texture of Shakespeare, or with such a totally different kind of epic as Dante's. Standing before the altar, as Milton habitually stood, he would have been profane if he had not worn his singing robes. A ritualistic elevation of style and movement may be as essential to an heroic subject as colloquial realism to realistic subjects and, on the Miltonic level, is a much rarer phenomenon. We can hardly imagine the gap there would be in English poetry, or in our own experience, if *Paradise Lost* were not there.

Critics who dismiss Milton on these grounds must also dismiss his models and peers, almost the whole array of Greek and Roman poets. Those poets in general created a dominant but not a simple impression by eliminating or subordinating peripheral detail; otherwise they would have been reproducing the disorder of nature and evading the artist's proper task. Their complexity of texture and reference is an ordered not a tangential complexity. Not feeling the need to tell all they know, and not believing that all the facts of experience are born free and equal, they would not have understood that their method betrayed a limitation, or a divorce, of thought and sensibility. Poetry, Milton conceived, should be "lesse suttle and fine, but more simple, sensuous and passionate" than logic and rhetoric. For one example of sensuous and passionate writing which is far from "simple" in the derogatory sense, an example of the purest classical art and one of the most moving things in English poetry, there is the invocation to light:

> Thus with the Year
> Seasons return, but not to me returns
> Day, or the sweet approach of Ev'n or Morn,
> Or sight of vernal bloom, or Summers Rose,
> Or flocks, or heards, or human face divine. . . .

Then the ancient poets commonly used an artificial "poetical" style which, like Milton's, raised the mind above everyday things. Milton's style is no more remote from popular English than Virgil's is from popular Latin, or Homer's from popular Greek. Besides, much of what in Milton is loosely condemned as classical idiom is rather an effect of condensation. If "Adam the goodliest man of men since borne" is an odious Miltonic classicism, what shall we say of Dekker's apostrophe to London, "Thou art the goodliest of thy neighbors, but the prowdest?" Milton may, in the interest of logical and emotional design and emphasis, place words and phrases with something of the freedom of an inflected language, but the attentive reading to which he is entitled—and seldom receives from counsel for the prosecution—will reveal the continual gain in fullness of texture and communication. As for his syntax, it never troubles those who leave it alone.

Granted an inevitable and fitting stylization in *Paradise Lost,* the poem has far more variety of manner and movement than is commonly appreciated. Its length and general clarity encourage the vague assumption that Milton splashes at a ten-league canvas with brushes of comets' hair, that his smallest unit is the paragraph with its planetary wheel, that his art is too simply rhetorical for the subtler effects of phrase and rhythm. The sensitive and unprejudiced reader may discover for himself what there is no space to illustrate, the perpetual and significant variations, both broad and minute, in narrative of action, in description, in exposition, in oratory; and, within these categories, the further variations in manner between, say, the descriptions of chaos and of Eden, the speeches of Moloch and of Belial. One large contrast, exemplified in count-less details as well as in the prevailing tone, separates the epic narrative and drama of the opening books from the intimate drama of the garden. The great archangel who had opposed the Almighty becomes a sardonic Richard III or malignant Iago; the mother of mankind becomes a very feminine woman, much more concerned about Adam's reactions than about God's. In accordance with Milton's view of the fall as comprehending many sins, Adam and Eve pass through the phases of disobedi-ence and levity, sensual passion, shame, fear, mutual recrimi-nation, despair, reunited love and loyalty to each other, and finally true penitence. And the stately speech which had been appropriate to regal innocence gives place to the broken, real-istic accents of human experience. Readers spoiled by the heroic energy, spaciousness, and colour of the epic books neglect the story of the fall, the centre around which all other events and characters are so greatly ordered, yet the one achievement is hardly less remarkable in its way than the other, and reveals a dramatic power and depth of pity that Milton is seldom al-lowed. Nor is there in English poetry a more suggestive com-plexity of feeling, conveyed as much by rhythm as by words, than in the last lines of the poem—an indescribable blend of sadness and hope, frailty and trust.

* * *

9.

To survey Milton's work from the beginning to *Samson* is

to be impressed by both the uniformity and the variety of style. Always sensitively aware of critical theory and poetic practice, he was a disciple of Ovid, of the Elizabethans, of Jonson, and in those early stages he showed himself a more and more independent master of his craft. *Comus* looked both backward and forward. In *Lycidas* and the heroic sonnets began the forging of the grand style, which was to be the medium of *Paradise Lost*. That grandeur, however uncommon, is not un-English. In Milton as in Bacon, Browne, and other representatives of ornate sublimity, the main texture is pure English. It would be odd if it were not, since in all the essential features of his personality and work Milton was one of the most thoroughly English of English authors. What is more important is that he was a man, and "So far from being granite, his verse is a continual spring of beauty, of goodness, of tenderness, of humility." The word "Miltonic," commonly applied to *Paradise Lost* or to the three major works of the poet's last phase, really includes three very different styles, and within *Paradise Lost* itself there are large variations. Those several styles were dictated by the principle of decorum, which was for Milton the artist what religious and philosophic principles were for the man and the thinker, and the principle of decorum, like the others, united liberty and discipline. But in Milton's general movement away from epic grandeur towards plain, undecorated, dramatic speech it is not altogether fanciful—after we have given decorum its large due —to see a parallel to his inward evolution, his arrival at a deeper and more personal understanding of God and human experience.

Milton's style was the natural accompaniment of his view of the function of poetry. He was the last English poet whose unified mastery of learning might fairly justify the claim of the *vates* to be a teacher of his age. For him as for Spenser poetry embraced learning on the one side and action on the other. But Milton's knowledge, though much greater than Spenser's, was essentially of the same kind. During his lifetime the mere widening of knowledge, especially in science, had gone beyond the grasp of any one man, and through the division of labour the unacknowledged legislators of mankind were losing their leadership. Milton was a poet; Dryden was a man of letters. The inspiration and purposes of knowledge had changed also. While the humanistic values of the classical tradition were united with the religious and ethical force of medieval and reformed Christianity, Milton was still possible. But the philosophy of the seventeenth century had been steadily undermining the ground on which Milton stood, had been destroying the soul of Christian humanism and of poetry. Milton's partial consciousness of that movement only fortified his religious and ethical faith. In spite of his public career, his immersion in the problems of his time, he became more and more an isolated figure, like Abdiel, Christ, and Samson.

The militant prophet of the revolution rallied from defeat

> With plain Heroic magnitude of mind
> And celestial vigour arm'd,

with a purer and humbler need of God. If the spirit of the revolutionary Milton partook of Constantine's vision, "τούτῳ νίκα," the theme of his major poems is "E la sua volontate è nostra pace." Unless our faculties have been vitiated by gross and violent stimulants, or by ultra-sophisticated negations, we cannot open Milton without an access of both strength and humility, a feeling that we are greater, and weaker, than we know. And that tonic power comes not merely from beauty of phrase and rhythm but from Milton's magnanimous concern with the highest issues and values in life, from his recognition of the intellectual and irreligious pride which, as of late we have more clearly realized, has been the undoing of modern man, and from his positive and passionate faith in God and goodness. In the twentieth century many men have undergone a kind of Miltonic disillusionment; Milton himself did not stop there.

T. S. ELIOT

MILTON (1947)*

Samuel Johnson, addressing himself to examine Milton's versification, in the *Rambler* of Saturday, 12 January 1751, thought it necessary to excuse his temerity in writing upon a subject already so fully discussed. In justification of his essay this great critic and poet remarked: "There are, in every age, new errors to be rectified, and new prejudices to be opposed." I am obliged to phrase my own apology rather differently. The errors of our own times have been rectified by vigorous hands, and the prejudices opposed by commanding voices. Some of the errors and prejudices have been associated with my own name, and of these in particular I shall find myself impelled to speak; it will, I hope, be attributed to me for modesty rather than for conceit if I maintain that no one can correct an error with better authority than the person who has been held responsible for it. And there is, I think, another justification for my speaking about Milton, besides the singular one which I have just given. The champions of Milton in our time, with one notable exception, have been scholars and teachers. I have no claim to be either: I am aware that my only claim upon your attention, in speaking of Milton or of any other great poet, is by appeal to your curiosity, in the hope that you may care to know what a contemporary writer of verse thinks of one of his predecessors.

I believe that the scholar and the practitioner in the field of

* Annual Lecture on a Master Mind, Henriette Hertz Trust, read March 26, 1947 before the British Academy. Reprinted from *The Proceedings of the British Academy*, Vol. XXXIII, by the generous permission of the author and the British Academy, and by arrangement with the Oxford University Press.

literary criticism should supplement each other's work. The criticism of the practitioner will be all the better, certainly, if he is not wholly destitute of scholarship; and the criticism of the scholar will be all the better if he has some experience of the difficulties of writing verse. But the orientation of the two critics is different. The scholar is more concerned with the understanding of the masterpiece in the environment of its author: with the world in which that author lived, the temper of his age, his intellectual formation, the books which he had read, and the influences which had moulded him. The practitioner is concerned less with the author than with the poem; and with the poem in relation to his own age. He asks: Of what *use* is the poetry of this poet to poets writing to-day? Is it, or can it become, a living force in English poetry still unwritten? So we may say that the scholar's interest is in the permanent, the practitioner's in the immediate. The scholar can teach us where we should bestow our *admiration* and *respect:* the practitioner should be able, when he is the right poet talking about the right poet, to make an old masterpiece actual, give it contemporary importance, and persuade his audience that it is interesting, exciting, enjoyable, and *active.* I can give only one example of contemporary criticism of Milton, by a critic of the type to which I belong if I have any critical pretensions at all: that is the Introduction to Milton's *English Poems* in the "World's Classics" series, by the late Charles Williams. It is not a comprehensive essay; it is notable primarily because it provides the best prolegomenon to *Comus* which any modern reader could have; but what distinguishes it throughout (and the same is true of most of Williams's critical writing) is the author's warmth of feeling and his success in communicating it to the reader. In this, so far as I am aware, the essay of Williams is a solitary example.

I think it is useful, in such an examination as I propose to make, to keep in mind some critic of the past, of one's own type, by whom to measure one's opinions: a critic sufficiently remote in time, for his local errors and prejudices to be not identical with one's own. That is why I began by quoting Samuel Johnson. It will hardly be contested that as a critic of poetry Johnson wrote as a practitioner and not as a scholar. Because he was a poet himself, and a good poet, what he wrote about poetry must be read with respect. And unless we know and appreciate Johnson's poetry we cannot judge either the merits or the limitations of his criticism. It is a pity that what the common reader to-day has read, or has remembered, or has seen quoted, are mostly those few statements of Johnson's from which later critics have vehemently dissented. But when Johnson held an opinion which seems to us wrong, we are never safe in dismissing it without inquiring why he was wrong; he had his own "errors and prejudices," certainly, but for lack of examining them sympathetically we are always in danger of merely countering error with error and prejudice with prejudice. Now Johnson was, in his day, very much a modern: he was concerned with how poetry should be written in his own time. The fact that he came towards the end, rather than the beginning of a style, the fact that his time was rapidly passing away, and that the canons of taste which he observed were about to fall into desuetude, does not diminish the interest of his criticism. Nor does the likelihood that the development of poetry in the next fifty years will take quite different directions from those which to me seem desirable to explore, deter me from asking the questions that Johnson implied: How should poetry be written now? and what place does the answer to this question give to Milton? And I think that the answers to these questions may be different now from the answers that were correct twenty-five years ago.

There is one prejudice against Milton, apparent on almost every page of Johnson's *Life of Milton,* which I imagine is still general: we, however, with a longer historical perspective, are in a better position than was Johnson to recognize it and to make allowance for it. This is a prejudice which I share myself: an antipathy towards Milton the man. Of this in itself I have nothing further to say: all that is necessary is to record one's

awareness of it. But this prejudice is often involved with another, more obscure: and I do not think that Johnson had dis-
engaged the two in his own mind. The fact is simply that the
Civil War of the seventeenth century, in which Milton is a
symbolic figure, has never been concluded. The Civil War is not
ended: I question whether any serious civil war ever does end.
Throughout that period English society was so convulsed and
divided that the effects are still felt. Reading Johnson's essay
one is always aware that Johnson was obstinately and passionately of another party. No other English poet, not Wordsworth,
or Shelley, lived through or took sides in such momentous
events as did Milton; of no other poet is it so difficult to consider the poetry simply as poetry, without our theological and
political dispositions, conscious and unconscious, inherited or
acquired, making an unlawful entry. And the danger is all the
greater because these emotions now take different vestures. It
is now considered grotesque, on political grounds, to be of the
party of King Charles; it is now, I believe, considered equally
grotesque, on moral grounds, to be of the party of the Puritans;
and to most persons to-day the religious views of both parties
may seem equally remote. Nevertheless, the passions are un-
quenched, and if we are not very wide awake their smoke will
obscure the glass through which we examine Milton's poetry.
Something has been done, certainly, to persuade us that Milton
was never really of any party, but disagreed with everyone.
Mr. Wilson Knight, in *Chariot of Wrath*, has argued that Milton was more a monarchist than a republican, and not in any
modern sense a "democrat." And Professor Saurat has produced
evidence to show that Milton's theology was highly eccentric,
and as scandalous to Protestants as to Catholics—that he was,
in fact, a sort of Christadelphian, and perhaps not a very orthodox Christadelphian at that; while on the other hand Mr. C. S.
Lewis has opposed Professor Saurat by skilfully arguing that
Milton, at least in *Paradise Lost*, can be acquitted of heresy
even from a point of view so orthodox as that of Mr. Lewis
himself. On these questions I hold no opinion: it is probably

beneficial to question the assumption that Milton was a sound Free Churchman and member of the Liberal Party; but I think that we still have to be on guard against an unconscious partisanship if we aim to attend to the poetry for the poetry's sake.

So much for our prejudices. I come next to the positive objection to Milton which has been raised in our own time, that is to say, the charge that he is an unwholesome influence. And from this I shall proceed to the permanent strictures of reproof (to employ a phrase of Johnson's) and, finally, to the grounds on which I consider him a great poet and one whom poets to-day might study with profit.

For a statement of the *generalized* belief in the unwholesomeness of Milton's influence I turn to Mr. Middleton Murry's critique of Milton in his *Heaven and Earth*—a book which contains chapters of profound insight, interrupted by passages which seem to me intemperate. Mr. Murry approaches Milton after his long and patient study of Keats; and it is through the eyes of Keats that he sees Milton.

Keats [Mr. Murry writes] as a poetic artist, second to none since Shakespeare, and Blake, as a prophet of spiritual values unique in our history, both passed substantially the same judgment on Milton: 'Life to him would be death to me.' And whatever may be our verdict on the development of English poetry since Milton, we must admit the justice of Keats's opinion that Milton's magnificence led nowhere. 'English must be kept up,' said Keats. To be influenced beyond a certain point by Milton's art, he felt, dammed the creative flow of the English genius in and through itself. In saying this, I think, Keats voiced the very inmost of the English genius. To pass under the spell of Milton is to be condemned to imitate him. It is quite different with Shakespeare. Shakespeare baffles and liberates; Milton is perspicuous and constricts.

This is a very confident affirmation, and I criticize it with some diffidence because I cannot pretend to have devoted as much study to Keats, or to have as intimate an understanding of his difficulties, as Mr. Murry. But Mr. Murry seems to me here to be trying to transform the predicament of a particular poet with a particular aim at a particular moment in time into a censure of timeless validity. He appears to assert that the liberative function of Shakespeare and the constrictive menace of Milton are permanent characteristics of these two poets. "To be influenced beyond a certain point" by any one master is bad for any poet; and it does not matter whether that influence is Milton's or another's; and as we cannot anticipate where that point will come, we might be better advised to call it an *un*certain point. If it is not good to remain under the spell of Milton, is it good to remain under the spell of Shakespeare? It depends partly upon what genre of poetry you are trying to develop. Keats wanted to write an epic, and he found, as might be expected, that the time had not arrived at which another English epic, comparable in grandeur to *Paradise Lost,* could be written. He also tried his hand at writing plays: and one might argue that *King Stephen* was more blighted by Shakespeare than *Hyperion* by Milton. Certainly, *Hyperion* remains a magnificent fragment which one re-reads; and *King Stephen* is a play which we may have read once, but to which we never return for enjoyment. Milton made a great epic impossible for succeeding generations; Shakespeare made a great poetic drama impossible; such a situation is inevitable, and it persists until the language has so altered that there is no danger, because no possibility, of imitation. Anyone who tries to write poetic drama, even to-day, should know that half of his energy must be exhausted in the effort to escape from the constricting toils of Shakespeare: the moment his attention is relaxed, or his mind fatigued, he will lapse into bad Shakespearian verse. For a long time after an epic poet like Milton, or a dramatic poet like Shakespeare, nothing can be done. Yet the effort must be repeatedly made; for we can never know in advance when the moment is approaching at which a new epic, or a new drama, will be possible; and when the moment does draw near it may be that the genius of an individual poet will perform the last mutation of idiom and versification which will bring that new poetry into being.

I have referred to Mr. Murry's view of the bad influence of Milton as generalized, because it is implicitly the whole personality of Milton that is in question: not specifically his beliefs, or his language or versification, but the beliefs as realized in that particular personality, and his poetry as the expression of it. By the *particular* view of Milton's influence as bad, I mean that view which attends to the language, the syntax, the versification, the imagery. I do not suggest that there is here a complete difference of subject-matter: it is the difference of approach, the difference of the focus of interest, between the philosophical critic and the literary critic. An incapacity for the abstruse, and an interest in poetry which is primarily a technical interest, dispose my mind towards the more limited and perhaps more superficial task. Let us proceed to look at Milton's influence from this point of view, that of the writer of poetry in our own time.

The reproach against Milton, that his technical influence has been bad, appears to have been made by no one more positively than by myself. I find myself saying, as recently as 1936, that this charge against Milton

appears a good deal more serious if we affirm that Milton's poetry could *only* be an influence for the worse, upon any poet whatever. It is more serious, also, if we affirm that Milton's bad influence may be traced much farther than the eighteenth century, and much farther than upon bad poets: if we say that it was an influence against which we still have to struggle.

In writing these sentences I failed to draw a threefold distinction, which now seems to me of some importance. There are three separate assertions implied. The first is, that an influence has been bad in the past: this is to assert that good poets, in the eighteenth or nineteenth century, would have written better if they had not submitted themselves to the influence of Milton. The second assertion is, that the contemporary situation is such that Milton is a master whom we should avoid. The third is, that the influence of Milton, or of any particular poet, can be *always* bad, and that we can predict that wherever it is found, at any time in the future, however remote, it will be a bad influence. Now, the first and third of these assertions I am no longer prepared to make, because, detached from the second, they do not appear to me to have any meaning.

For the first, when we consider one great poet of the past, and one or more other poets, upon whom we say he has exerted a bad influence, we must admit that the responsibility, if there be any, is rather with the poets who were influenced than with the poet whose work exerted the influence. We can, of course, show that certain tricks or mannerisms which the imitators display are due to conscious or unconscious imitation and emulation, but that is a reproach against their injudicious choice of a model and not against their model itself. And we can never prove that any particular poet would have written better poetry if he had escaped that influence. Even if we assert, what can only be a matter of faith, that Keats would have written a very great epic poem if Milton had not preceded him, is it sensible to repine for an unwritten masterpiece, in exchange for one which we possess and acknowledge? And as for the remote future, what can we affirm about the poetry that will be written then, except that we should probably be unable to understand or to enjoy it, and that therefore we can hold no opinion as to what "good" and "bad" influences will *mean* in that future? The only relation in which the question of influence, good and bad, is significant, is the relation to the immediate future. With that question I shall engage at the end. I wish first to mention another reproach against Milton, that represented by the phrase "dissociation of sensibility."

I remarked many years ago, in an essay on Dryden, that

In the seventeenth century a dissociation of sensibility set in, from which we have never recovered; and this dissociation, as is natural, was due to the influence of the two most powerful poets of the century, Milton and Dryden.

The longer passage from which this sentence is taken is quoted by Dr. Tillyard in his *Milton*. Dr. Tillyard makes the following comment:

> Speaking only of what in this passage concerns Milton, I would say that there is here a mixture of truth and falsehood. Some sort of dissociation of sensibility in Milton, not necessarily undesirable, has to be admitted; but that he was responsible for any such dissociation in others (at least till this general dissociation had inevitably set in) is untrue.

I believe that the general affirmation represented by the phrase "dissociation of sensibility" (one of the two or three phrases of my coinage—like "objective correlative"—which have had a success in the world astonishing to their author) retains some validity; but I now incline to agree with Dr. Tillyard that to lay the burden on the shoulders of Milton and Dryden was a mistake. If such a dissociation did take place, I suspect that the causes are too complex and too profound to justify our accounting for the change in terms of literary criticism. All we can say is, that something like this did happen; that it had something to do with the Civil War; that it would even be unwise to say it was caused by the Civil War, but that it is a consequence of the same causes which brought about the Civil War; that we must seek the causes in Europe, not in England alone; and for what these causes were, we may dig and dig until we get to a depth at which words and concepts fail us.[1]

Before proceeding to take up the case against Milton, as it stood for poets twenty-five years ago—the second, and only significant meaning of "bad influence"—I think it would be

---

[1] On one point I should take issue with Dr. Tillyard. A little further on he quotes another phrase of mine, of earlier date: "The Chinese Wall of Milton's blank verse." He comments: "It must have been an ineffective wall, for *Venice Preserved, All for Love* and similar plays in blank verse were not confined by it; they owe nothing to Milton's versification." Of course not— these were *plays*, and I have long maintained that dramatic blank verse and non-dramatic blank verse are not the same thing. The Chinese Wall there, if it existed, was erected by Shakespeare.

best to consider what permanent strictures of reproof may be drawn: those censures which, when we make them, we must assume to be made by enduring laws of taste. The essence of the permanent censure of Milton is, I believe, to be found in Johnson's essay. This is not the place in which to examine certain particular and erroneous judgements of Johnson; to explain his condemnation of *Comus* and *Samson* by his applying dramatic canons which to us seem inapplicable; or to condone his dismissal of the versification of *Lycidas* by the specialization, rather than the absence, of his sense of rhythm. Johnson's most important censure of Milton is contained in three paragraphs, which I must ask leave to quote in full.

Throughout all his greater works [says Johnson] there prevails an uniform peculiarity of *diction,* a mode and cast of expression which bears little resemblance to that of any former writer; and which is so far removed from common use, that an unlearned reader, when he first opens the book, finds himself surprised by a new language.

This novelty has been, by those who can find nothing wrong with Milton, imputed to his laborious endeavours after words suited to the grandeur of his ideas. *Our language,* says Addison, *sunk under him.* But the truth is, that both in prose and in verse, he had formed his style by a perverse and pedantic principle. He was desirous to use English words with a foreign idiom. This in all his prose is discovered and condemned; for there judgment operates freely, neither softened by the beauty, nor awed by the dignity of his thoughts; but such is the power of his poetry, that his call is obeyed without resistance, the reader feels himself in captivity to a higher and nobler mind, and criticism sinks in admiration.

Milton's style was not modified by his subject; what is shown with greater extent in 'Paradise Lost' may be found in 'Comus.' One source of his peculiarity was his familiarity with the Tuscan poets; the disposition of his words is, I think, frequently Italian; perhaps sometimes combined with other tongues. Of him at last, may be said what Jonson said of Spenser, that he *wrote no language,* but has formed what Butler called a *Babylonish dialect,* in itself harsh and barbarous, but made by exalted genius and extensive learning the vehicle of so much instruction and so much pleasure, that, like other lovers, we find grace in its deformity.

This criticism seems to me substantially true: indeed, unless we accept it, I do not think we are in the way to appreciate the peculiar greatness of Milton. His style is not a *classic* style, in that it is not the elevation of a *common* style, by the final touch of genius, to greatness. It is, from the foundation, and in every particular, a personal style, not based upon common speech, or common prose, or direct communication of meaning. Of some great poetry one has difficulty in pronouncing just what it is, what infinitesimal touch, that has made all the difference from a plain statement which anyone could make; the slight transformation which, while it leaves a plain statement a plain statement, has made it at the same time great poetry. In Milton there is always the maximal, never the minimal, alteration of ordinary language. Every distortion of construction, the foreign idiom, the use of a word in a foreign way or with the meaning of the foreign word from which it is derived rather than the accepted meaning in English, every idiosyncrasy is a particular act of violence which Milton has been the first to commit. There is no cliché, no poetic diction in the derogatory sense, but a perpetual sequence of original acts of lawlessness. Of all modern writers of verse, the nearest analogy seems to me to be Mallarmé, a much smaller poet, though still a great one. The personalities, the poetic theories of the two men could not have been more different; but in respect of the violence which they could do to language, and justify, there is a remote similarity. Milton's poetry is poetry at the farthest possible remove from prose; his prose seems to me too near to half-formed poetry to be good prose.

To say that the work of a poet is at the farthest possible remove from prose would once have struck me as condemnatory: it now seems to me simply, when we have to do with a Milton, the precision of its peculiar greatness. As a poet, Milton seems to me probably the greatest of all eccentrics. His work illustrates no general principles of good writing; the only principles of writing that it illustrates are such as are valid only for Milton himself to observe. There are two kinds of poet who can ordinarily be of use to other poets. There are those who suggest, to one or another of their successors, something which they have not done themselves, or who provoke a different way of doing the same thing: these are likely to be not the greatest, but smaller, imperfect poets with whom later poets discover an affinity. And there are the great poets from whom we can learn negative rules: no poet can teach another to write well, but some great poets can teach others some of the things to avoid. They teach us what to avoid, by showing us what great poetry can do without—how *bare* it can be. Of these are Dante and Racine. But if we are ever to make use of Milton we must do so in quite a different way. Even a small poet can learn something from the study of Dante, or from the study of Chaucer: we must perhaps wait for a great poet before we find one who can profit from the study of Milton.

I repeat that the remoteness of Milton's verse from ordinary speech, his invention of his own poetic language, seems to me one of the marks of his greatness. Other marks are his sense of structure, both in the general design of *Paradise Lost* and *Samson,* and in his syntax; and finally, and not least, his inerrancy, conscious or unconscious, in writing so as to make the best display of his talents, and the best concealment of his weaknesses.

The appropriateness of the subject of *Samson* is too obvious to expatiate upon: it was probably the one dramatic story out of which Milton could have made a masterpiece. But the complete suitability of *Paradise Lost* has not, I think, been so often remarked. It was surely an intuitive perception of what he could not do, that arrested Milton's project of an epic on King Arthur. For one thing, he had little interest in, or understanding of, individual human beings. In *Paradise Lost* he was not called upon for any of that understanding which comes from an affectionate observation of men and women. But such an interest in human beings was not required—indeed its *absence* was a necessary condition—for the creation of his figures of Adam and Eve. These are not a man and woman such as any we know: if they were, they would not be Adam and

Eve. They are the original *Man* and *Woman*, not types, but prototypes: if they were not set apart from ordinary humanity they would not be Adam and Eve. They have the general characteristics of men and women, such that we can recognize, in the temptation and the fall, the first motions of the faults and virtues, the abjection and the nobility, of all their descendants. They have ordinary humanity to the right degree, and yet are not, and should not be, ordinary mortals. Were they more particularized they would be false, and if Milton had been more interested in humanity, he could not have created them. Other critics have remarked upon the exactness, without defect or exaggeration, with which Moloch, Belial, and Mammon, in the second book, speak according to the particular sin which each represents. It would not be suitable that the infernal powers should have, in the human sense, characters, for a character is always mixed; but in the hands of an inferior manipulator, they might easily have been reduced to *humours*.

The appropriateness of the material of *Paradise Lost* to the genius and the limitations of Milton, is still more evident when we consider the visual imagery. I have already remarked, in a paper written some years ago,[2] on Milton's weakness of visual observation, a weakness which I think was always present—the effect of his blindness may have been rather to strengthen the compensatory qualities than to increase a fault which was already present. Mr. Wilson Knight, who has devoted close study to recurrent imagery in poetry, has called attention to Milton's propensity towards images of engineering and mechanics; to me it seems that Milton is at his best in imagery suggestive of vast size, limitless space, abysmal depth, and light and darkness. No theme and no setting, other than that which he chose in *Paradise Lost*, could have given him such scope for the kind of imagery in which he excelled, or made less demand upon those powers of visual imagination which were in him defective.

Most of the absurdities and inconsistencies to which John-

---

[2] In *Essays and Studies by Members of the English Association*, vol. xxi, 1936, pp. 32 ff.

son calls attention, and which, so far as they can justly be isolated in this way, he properly condemns, will I think appear in a more correct proportion if we consider them in relation to this general judgement. I do not think that we should attempt to *see* very clearly any scene that Milton depicts: it should be accepted as a shifting phantasmagory. To complain, because we first find the arch-fiend "chain'd on the burning lake," and in a minute or two see him making his way to the shore, is to expect a kind of consistency which the world to which Milton has introduced us does not require.

This limitation of visual power, like Milton's limited interest in human beings, turns out to be not merely a negligible defect, but a positive virtue, when we visit Adam and Eve in Eden. Just as a higher degree of characterization of Adam and Eve would have been unsuitable, so a more vivid picture of the earthly Paradise would have been less paradisiacal. For a greater definiteness, a more detailed account of flora and fauna, could only have assimilated Eden to the landscapes of earth with which we are familiar. As it is, the impression of Eden which we retain, is the most suitable, and is that which Milton was most qualified to give: the impression of *light*—a daylight and a starlight, a light of dawn and of dusk, the light which, remembered by a man in his blindness, has a supernatural glory unexperienced by men of normal vision.

We must, then, in reading *Paradise Lost*, not expect to see clearly; our sense of sight must be blurred, so that our *hearing* may become more acute. *Paradise Lost*, like *Finnegans Wake* (for I can think of no work which provides a more interesting parallel: two great books by blind musicians, each writing a language of his own based upon English) makes this peculiar demand for a readjustment of the reader's mode of apprehension. The emphasis is on the sound, not the vision, upon the word, not the idea; and in the end it is the unique versification that is the most certain sign of Milton's intellectual mastership.

On the subject of Milton's versification, so far as I am aware, little enough has been written. We have Johnson's essay in the

Rambler, which deserves more study than it has received, and we have a short treatise by Robert Bridges on *Milton's Prosody.* I speak of Bridges with respect, for no poet of our time has given such close attention to prosody as he. Bridges catalogues the systematic irregularities which give perpetual variety to Milton's verse, and I can find no fault with his analysis.[3] But however interesting these analyses are, I do not think that it is by such means that we gain an appreciation of the peculiar rhythm of a poet. It seems to me also that Milton's verse is especially refractory to yielding up its secrets to examination of the single line. For his verse is not formed in this way. It is the period, the sentence and still more the paragraph, that is the unit of Milton's verse; and emphasis on the line structure is the minimum necessary to provide a counter-pattern to the period structure. It is only in the period that the wave-length of Milton's verse is to be found: it is his ability to give a perfect and unique pattern to every paragraph, such that the full beauty of the line is found in its context, and his ability to work in larger musical units than any other poet—that is to me the most conclusive evidence of Milton's supreme mastery. The peculiar feeling, almost a physical sensation of a breathless leap, communicated by Milton's long periods, and by his alone, is impossible to procure from rhymed verse. Indeed, this mastery is more conclusive evidence of his intellectual power, than is his grasp of any *ideas* that he borrowed or invented. To be able to control so many words at once is the token of a mind of most exceptional energy.

It is interesting at this point to recall the general observations upon blank verse, which a consideration of *Paradise*

---

[3] Beyond raising one question, in connexion with Bridge's account of Milton's use of recessive accent. It does not seem to me that such recession, as of *obscéne* to *óbscene* in the line

Next Chemos, the obscene dread of Moab's sons

simply reverses the value of the two syllables: I should say that the second syllable retains something of its length, and the first something of its shortness, and that the surprise and variety are due to each syllable becoming *both* long and short. The effect is like that of a tide-rip, in which a peculiar type of wave is produced by the conflict of two opposing forces.

Lost prompted Johnson to make towards the end of his essay.

The music of the English heroic lines strikes the ear so faintly, that it is easily lost, unless all the syllables of every line co-operate together; this co-operation can only be obtained by the preservation of every verse unmingled with another as a distinct system of sounds; and this distinctness is obtained and preserved by the artifice of rhyme. The variety of pauses, so much boasted by the lovers of blank verse, changes the measures of an English poet to the periods of a declaimer; and there are only a few skilful and happy readers of Milton, who enable their audience to perceive where the lines end or begin. *Blank verse,* said an ingenious critic, *seems to be verse only to the eye.*

Some of my audience may recall that this last remark, in almost the same words, was often made, a literary generation ago, about the "free verse" of the period: and even without this encouragement from Johnson it would have occurred to my mind to declare Milton to be the greatest master of free verse in our language. What is interesting about Johnson's paragraph, however, is that it represents the judgement of a man who had by no means a deaf ear, but simply a *specialized* ear, for verbal music. Within the limits of the poetry of his own period, Johnson is a very good judge of the relative merits of several poets as writers of blank verse. But on the whole, the blank verse of his age might more properly be called unrhymed verse; and nowhere is this difference more evident than in the verse of his own tragedy *Irene:* the phrasing is admirable, the style elevated and correct, but each line cries out for a companion to rhyme with it. Indeed, it is only with labour, or by occasional inspiration, or by submission to the influence of the older dramatists, that the blank verse of the *nineteenth* century succeeds in making the absence of rhyme inevitable and right, with the rightness of Milton. Even Johnson admitted that he could not wish that Milton had been a rhymer. Nor did the nineteenth century succeed in giving to blank verse the flexibility which it needs if the tone of common speech, talking of the topics of common intercourse, is to be employed; so that when our more modern practitioners of blank verse do not touch the sublime, they frequently approach the ridiculous. Milton perfected non-dramatic blank verse and at the same time imposed limitations, very hard to break, upon the use to which it may be put if its greatest musical possibilities are to be exploited.

I now come to the point at which it is desirable to quote passages in illustration of what I have been saying about Milton's versification. It is best, I think, to take familiar passages, rather than to seek originality by choosing those which have been less often drawn to our attention. The first is the Invocation which opens Book III of *Paradise Lost.*

> Hail holy light, offspring of Heaven first-borne,
> Or of th' Eternal Coeternal beam
> May I express thee unblam'd? Since God is light,
> And never but in unapproached light
> Dwelt from Eternitie, dwelt then in thee,
> Bright effluence of bright essence increate.
> Or hear'st thou rather pure Ethereal stream,
> Whose Fountain who shall tell? before the Sun,
> Before the Heavens thou wert, and at the voice
> Of God, as with a Mantle didst invest
> The rising world of waters dark and deep,
> Won from the void and formless infinite.

This passage is compact of Miltonic philosophy, but for that I must refer you to such critics as Professor Saurat and Mr. Lewis. For my purpose, it illustrates, first, Milton's power in the use of imagery of light. Second, it illustrates the closeness of the structure. If we were to attempt to analyse the Miltonic music line by line, that music would be lost: the individual line is right, not merely in itself, not merely in relation to the lines immediately preceding and following, but in relation to every other line in the passage. To extract this passage of twelve lines is to mutilate it. I contrast with this passage the following. In what I have just read there is no divagation from the point; the next passage is chosen to show Milton's skill in extending a period by introducing imagery which tends to distract us from the real subject.

Thus Satan talking to his neerest Mate
With Head uplift above the wave, and Eyes
That sparkling blaz'd, his other Parts besides
Prone on the Flood, extended long and large
Lay floating many a rood, in bulk as huge
As whom the Fables name of monstrous size,
Titanian or *Earth-born,* that warr'd on *Jove,*
Briarios or *Typhon,* whom the Den
By ancient *Tarsus* held, or that Sea-beast
Leviathan, whom God of all his works
Created hugest that swim th' Ocean stream:
Him haply slumbring on the *Norway* foam
The pilot of some small night-founder'd Skiff,[4]
Deeming some Island, oft, as Sea-men tell,
With fixed Anchor in his scaly rind
Moors by his side under the Lee, while Night
Invests the Sea, and wished Morn delayes:
So stretcht out huge in length the Arch-fiend lay
Chain'd on the burning Lake. . . .

There are, as often with Milton, criticisms of detail which could be made. I am not too happy about eyes that both blaze and sparkle, unless Milton meant us to imagine a roaring fire ejecting sparks: and that is *too* fiery an image for even supernatural eyes. The fact that the lake was burning somewhat diminishes the effect of the fiery eyes; and it is difficult to imagine a burning lake in a scene where there was only darkness visible. But with this kind of inconsistency we are familiar in Milton. What I wish to call to your attention is the happy introduction of so much extraneous matter. Any

---

[4] The term *night-foundered,* which I presume to be of Milton's invention, seems unsuitable here. Dr. Tillyard has called my attention to the use of the same adjective in *Comus,* i. 483:

Either som one like us night-foundered here

where, although extravagant, it draws a permissible comparison between travellers lost in the night, and seafarers in extremity. But when, as here in *Paradise Lost,* it is transferred from the travellers on land to adventurers by sea, and not to the men but to their *skiff,* the literal meaning of *founder* immediately presents itself. A *foundered* skiff could not be *moored,* to a whale or to anything else.

writer, straining for images of hugeness, might have thought
of the whale, but only Milton could have included the anec-
dote of the deluded seamen without our wanting to put a
blue pencil through it. We *nearly* forget Satan in attending
to the story of the whale; Milton recalls us just in time. Therefore the diversion strengthens, instead of weakening, the passage. Milton plays exactly the same trick a few lines further on,
when he speaks of Satan's shield:

> the broad circumference
> Hung on his shoulders like the Moon, whose Orb
> Through Optic Glass the *Tuscan* Artist views
> At Ev'ning from the top of *Fesole,*
> Or in *Valdarno,* to descry new Lands,
> Rivers or Mountains in her spotty Globe.
> His Spear, to equal which the tallest pine
> Hewn on *Norwegian* hills, to be the Mast
> Of some great Ammiral, were but a wand. . . .

Here I think that the two sudden transitions, to the Tuscan
astronomer and thence to the Norwegian pine, followed by the
concentrated astonishing image of sea-power, are most felicitous. If I may put it in this way without being misunderstood, I find in such passages a kind of inspired *frivolity,* an enjoyment by the author in the exercise of his own virtuosity,
which is a mark of the first rank of genius. Addison, whose
opinion is quoted and confirmed by Johnson, said that *Para-
·dise Lost* is "universally and perpetually interesting"; the two
critics found the source of this perpetual interest in the subject
matter; but the assertion of Johnson that "all mankind will,
through all ages, bear the same relation to Adam and Eve,
and must partake of that good and evil which extend to themselves," even when it commands the assent of the Christian
believer, will not wholly account for the absorbed attention
which I think any poetry lover to-day ought to be able to give
to the poem from end to end. I find the reason more certainly
in the extraordinary style which because of its perpetual variety compels us to curiosity to know what is coming next, and

in the perpetual surprises of reference such as those I have just quoted.

It may be observed also, that Milton employs devices of eloquence and of the word-play in which poets of his time were practised, which perpetually relieve the mind, and facilitate the declamation. Frequently the same word is happily repeated.

> My sentence is for open Warr: Of Wiles,
> More unexpert, I boast not: then let those
> *Contrive* who *need*, or when they *need*, not now.
> For while they *sit contriving*, shall the rest,
> Millions that stand in Arms, and longing wait
> The Signal to ascend, *sit* lingring here
> Heav'ns fugitives . . .[5]

To give another instance:

> *Receive* him coming, to *receive* from us
> Knee-tribute still unpaid, prostration vile,
> Too much *to one*, but double how endur'd,
> *To one* and to his image now proclaim'd?

He also uses alliteration, and most effectively:

> Of midnight march, and hurried meeting here.

Of such devices, none is quite original; Milton's blank verse would not have been possible without developments which had taken place in the two generations preceding; but what Milton made from what he learned is unique. Some of these devices appear in the late plays in which Shakespeare returned to realize surprising possibilities of his earliest manner:

> 'Tis still a dream; or else such stuff as madmen
> Tongue, and brain not; either both, or nothing;
> Or senseless speaking, or a speaking such
> As sense cannot untie . . .

---

[5] It might, of course, be objected that "millions that *stand* in arms" could not at the same time "*sit* lingring."

Nobly he yokes
A smiling with a sigh, as if the sigh
Was that it was, for not being such a smile;
The smile mocking the sigh, that it would fly
From so divine a temple to commix
With winds that sailors rail at.

The long and involved sentence structure is conspicuously
developed by Massinger, from whom Milton may have taken
a hint. I quote again a passage from Massinger which I quoted
long ago in an essay on that dramatist:

What though my father
Writ man before he was so, and confirm'd it,
By numbering that day no part of his life
In which he did not service to his country;
Was he to be free therefore from the laws
And ceremonious forms in your decrees?
Or else because he did as much as man
In those three memorable overthrows,
At Granson, Morat, Nancy, where his master,
The warlike Charalois, with whose misfortunes
I bear his name, lost treasure, men and life,
To be excused from payment of those sums
Which (his own patrimony spent) his zeal
To serve his country forced him to take up?

The talent expended upon such a construction was, of course,
ill-applied to the theatre. The verse has got out of hand, for
dramatic purposes; and its only possible future was through the
genius of Milton.

I come at last to compare my own attitude, as that of a poetical practitioner perhaps typical of a generation twenty-five
years ago, with my attitude to-day. I have thought it well to
take matters in the order in which I have taken them: to discuss
first the censures and detractions which I believe to have permanent validity, and which were best made by Johnson, in
order to make clearer the causes, and the justification, for hos-
tility to Milton on the part of poets at a particular juncture.
And I wished to make clear those excellences of Milton which

particularly impress me, before explaining why I think that the study of his verse might at last be of benefit to poets.

I have on several occasions suggested, that the important changes in the idiom of English verse which are represented by the names of Dryden and Wordsworth, may be characterized as successful attempts to escape from a poetic idiom which had ceased to have a relation to contemporary speech. This is the sense of Wordsworth's Prefaces. By the beginning of the present century another revolution in idiom—and such revolutions bring with them an alteration of metric, a new appeal to the ear—was due. It inevitably happens that the young poets engaged in such a revolution will exalt the merits of those poets of the past who offer them example and stimulation, and depreciate the merits of poets who do not stand for the qualities which they are zealous to realize. This is not only inevitable, it is right. It is even right, and certainly inevitable, that their practice, still more influential than their critical pronouncements, should attract their own readers to the poets by whose work they have been influenced. Such influence has certainly contributed to the taste, if we can distinguish the *taste* from the *fashion*, for Donne. I do not think that any modern poet, unless in a fit of irresponsible peevishness, has ever denied Milton's consummate powers. And it must be said that Milton's diction is not a poetic diction in the sense of being a debased currency: when he violates the English language he is imitating nobody, and he is inimitable. But Milton does, as I have said, represent poetry at the extreme limit from prose; and it was one of our tenets that verse should have the virtues of prose, that diction should become assimilated to cultivated contemporary speech, before aspiring to the elevation of poetry. Another tenet was that the subject-matter and the imagery of poetry should be extended to topics and objects related to the life of a modern man or woman; that we were to seek the non-poetic, to seek even material refractory to transmutation into poetry, and words and phrases which had not been used in poetry before. And the study of Milton could be of no help: it was only a hindrance.

We cannot, in literature, any more than in the rest of life, live in a perpetual state of revolution. If every generation of poets made it their task to bring poetic diction up to date with the spoken language, poetry would fail in one of its most important obligations. For poetry should help, not only to refine the language of the time, but to prevent it from changing too rapidly: a development of language at too great a speed would be a development in the sense of a progressive deterioration, and that is our danger to-day. If the poetry of the rest of this century takes the line of development which seems to me, reviewing the progress of poetry through the last three centuries, the right course, it will discover new and more elaborate patterns of a diction now established. In this search it might have much to learn from Milton's extended verse structure; it might also avoid the danger of a *servitude* to colloquial speech and to current jargon. It might also learn that the music of verse is strongest in poetry which has a definite meaning expressed in the properest words. Poets might be led to admit that a knowledge of the literature of their own language, with a knowledge of the literature and the grammatical construction of other languages, is a very valuable part of the poet's equipment. And they might, as I have already hinted, devote some study to Milton as, outside the theatre, the greatest master in our language of freedom within form. A study of *Samson* should sharpen anyone's appreciation of the justified irregularity, and put him on guard against the pointless irregularity. In studying *Paradise Lost* we come to perceive that the verse is continuously animated by the departure from, and return to, the regular measure; and that, in comparison with Milton, hardly any subsequent writer of blank verse appears to exercise any freedom at all. We can also be led to the reflection that a monotony of unscannable verse fatigues the attention even more quickly than a monotony of exact feet. In short, it now seems to me that poets are sufficiently removed from Milton, and sufficiently liberated from his reputation, to approach the study of his work without danger, and with profit to their poetry and to the English language.

PART TWO
EXCERPTS AND BRIEF COMMENT

ANDREW MARVELL

ON PARADISE LOST (1674)

When I beheld the Poet blind, yet bold,
In slender Book his vast Design unfold,
Messiah Crown'd, God's Reconcil'd Decree,
Rebelling Angels, the Forbidden Tree,
Heav'n, Hell, Earth, Chaos, All; the Argument
Held me a while misdoubting his Intent,
That he would ruin (for I saw him strong)
The sacred Truths to Fable and old Song
(So *Sampson* grop'd the Temple's Posts in spite)
The World o'erwhelming to revenge his sight.
    Yet as I read, soon growing less severe,
I lik'd his Project, the success did fear;
Through that wide Field how he his way should find
O'er which lame Faith leads Understanding blind;
Lest he perplex'd the things he would explain,
And what was easy he should render vain.
    Or if a Work so infinite he spann'd,
Jealous I was that some less skilful hand
(Such as disquiet always what is well,
And by ill imitating would excel)
Might hence presume the whole Creation's day
To change in Scenes, and show it in a Play.
    Pardon me, Mighty Poet, nor despise
My causeless, yet not impious, surmise.
But I am now convinc'd, and none will dare
Within thy Labours to pretend a share.

Thou hast not miss'd one thought that could be fit,
And all that was improper dost omit:
So that no room is here for Writers left,
But to detect their Ignorance or Theft.
    That Majesty which through thy Work doth Reign
Draws the Devout, deterring the Profane.
And things divine thou treat'st of in such state
As them preserves, and thee, inviolate.
At once delight and horror on us seize,
Thou sing'st with so much gravity and ease;
And above human flight dost soar aloft
With Plume so strong, so equal, and so soft.
The Bird nam'd from that Paradise you sing
So never flags, but always keeps on Wing.
    Where couldst thou words of such a compass find?
Whence furnish such a vast expense of mind?
Just Heav'n thee like *Tiresias* to requite
Rewards with Prophecy thy loss of sight.
    Well mightst thou scorn thy Readers to allure
With tinkling Rime, of thy own sense secure;
While the *Town-Bayes* writes all the while and spells,
And like a Pack-horse tires without his Bells:
Their Fancies like our Bushy-points appear,
The Poets tag them, we for fashion wear.
I too transported by the Mode offend,
And while I meant to Praise thee must Commend.
Thy Verse created like thy Theme sublime,
In Number, Weight, and Measure, needs not Rime.

JOHN DRYDEN

EPIGRAM ON MILTON (1688)

THREE poets, in three distant ages born,
Greece, Italy, and England did adorn.
The first in loftiness of thought surpass'd,
The next in majesty, in both the last:
The force of Nature could no farther go;
To make a third, she join'd the former two.

ESSAY ON SATIRE (1693)

* * *

As FOR Mr. Milton, whom we all admire with so much justice, his subject is not that of an heroic poem, properly so called. His design is the losing of our happiness; his event is not prosperous, like that of all other epic works; his heavenly machines are many, and his human persons are but two. But I will not take Mr. Rymer's work out of his hands: he has promised the world a critique on that author; wherein, though he will not allow his poem for heroic, I hope he will grant us, that his thoughts are elevated, his words sounding, and that no man has so happily copied the manner of Homer, or so copiously translated his Grecisms, and the Latin elegances of Virgil. It is true, he runs into a flat of thought, sometimes for a hundred lines together, but it is when he is got into a track of Scripture. His antiquated words were his choice, not his necessity; for therein he imitated Spenser, as Spenser did Chaucer. And though, perhaps, the love of their masters may have transported both too far, in the frequent use of them, yet, in my opinion, obsolete words may then be laudably revived, when either they are more sounding, or more significant, than those in practice; and when their obscurity is taken away, by joining other words to them, which clear the sense; according to the new rule of Horace, for the admission of new words. But in both cases a moderation is to be observed in the use of them: for unnecessary coinage, as well as unnecessary revival, runs into affectation; a fault to be avoided on either hand. Neither will I justify Milton for his blank verse, though I may excuse him, by the example of Hannibal Caro, and other Italians, who have used it; for whatever causes he alleges for the abolishing of rhyme, (which I have not now the leisure to examine), his own particular reason is plainly this, that rhyme was not his talent; he had neither the ease of doing it, nor the graces of it; which is manifest in his *Juvenilia,* or verses written in his youth, where his rhyme is always constrained and forced, and comes hardly from him, at an age when the soul is most pliant, and the passion of love makes almost every man a rhymer, though not a poet.

*　　*　　*

JOHN TOLAND

𝄢𝄢

THE LIFE OF JOHN MILTON (1698)

---

*   *   *

Aᶠᵗᵉʳ the twelfth Year of his Age, such was his insatiable thirst for Learning, he seldom went to bed before midnight. This was the first undoing of his Eys, to whose natural debility were added frequent Headachs, which could not retard or extinguish his laudable Passion for Letters. Being thus initiated in several Tongues, and having not slightly tasted the inexpressible Sweets of Philosophy, he was sent at 15 to *Christ's College* in *Cambridg* to pursue more arduous and solid Studies. This same Year he gave several Proofs of his early Genius for Poetry, wherein he afterwards succeded so happily, that to all Ages he'l continue no less the Ornament and Glory of *England,* than *Homer* is own'd to be that of *Greece,* and *Virgil* of *Italy.* He first translated som Psalms into English Verse. . . . In his seventeenth Year he wrote a handsom Copy of English Verses on the Death of a Sister's Child that dy'd of a Cough; and the same Year a Latin Elegy on the Death of the Bishop of *Winchester,* with another on that of *Ely.* 'Twas then also that he compos'd his fine Poem on the Gunpouder-Treason; concerning all which and the rest of his Juvenil pieces, the judicious *Morhof,* in his *Polyhistor Literarius,* says, that *Milton's* Writings shew him to have bin a Man in his very Childhood; and that these Poems are excedingly above the ordinary Capacity of that Age. He continu'd in *Cambridg* seven years, where he liv'd with great Reputation, and generally belov'd, till taking the degree of Master of Arts, and performing his Exercises with much applause, he left the University; for he aim'd at none of those Professions that require a longer stay in that place. Som of his Academic Performances are still extant among his occasional Poems, and at the end of his familiar Letters. The five succeding years he liv'd with his Father in his Country Retirement at *Horton* near *Colebrook* in *Barkshire,* where at full leisure he perus'd all the *Greec* and *Latin* Writers; but was not so much in love with his Solitude, as not to make an excursion now and then to *London,* somtimes to buy Books, or to meet Friends from *Cambridg;* and at other times to learn som new thing in the Mathematics or in Music, with which he was extraordinarily delighted. It was about this time he wrote from *London* a Latin Elegy to his intimat Friend *Charles Diodati,* wherein som Verses reflecting on the University, and preferring the Pleasures of the Town, gave a handle afterwards to certain Persons no less ignorant than malitious to report that either he was expel'd for som Misdemeanor from *Cambridg,* or left it in discontent that he obtain'd no Preferment: and that at *London* he spent his time with Leud Women, or at Playhouses. But the falsity of this story we shall in due place demonstrat. . . . He wrote another Latin Elegy to *Charles Diodati;* and in his twentieth year he made one on the approach of the Spring: but the following year he describes his falling in love with a Lady (whom he accidentally met, and never afterwards saw) in such tender Expressions, with those lively Passions, and Images so natural, that you would think Love himself had directed his Pen, or inspir'd your own Breast when you peruse them. . . . He attain'd that perfection himself in the *Italian* Language, as to make som Songs on a real or feign'd Mistress, in one of which he gives a handsom account of his writing in this Tongue. . . .

What imploy'd a good part of his Thoughts for many years before, and was at first only design'd to be a Tragedy, I mean his incomparable Epic Poem, intitul'd *Paradise Lost,* he now had sufficient leisure to prosecute and finish. . . . As to the choice of his Subject, or the Particulars of his Story, I shall say nothing in defence of them against those People who brand 'em with Heresy and Impiety: for to incur the Displeasure of certain ignorant and supercilious Critics, argues free thinking, accurat Writing, and a generous Profession of Truth. I'm sure if *Hesiod,* or such other fabulous Authors in the rude ages of the World, had given so intelligible, coherent, and delightful an account of the Creation of the Universe, and the Origin of Mankind their System had past for Divine Inspiration; and the Unbelievers of it would appear to be so few, that any of 'em might well be shewn for a Monster rather than be thought worthy of Punishment or Confutation. As to the regularity of the Poem, I never knew it question'd by any but such as would build themselves a Reputation on the flaws and mistakes they discover in other Mens Labors. But the unparallel'd Sublimity and Force of the Expression, with the delicacy of his Thoughts, and the copiousness of his Invention, are unanimously own'd by all ranks of Writers. He has incontestably exceded the fecundity of *Homer,* whose two Poems he could almost repeat without book: nor did he com much short of the correctness of *Virgil;* which is affirm'd by one whose judgment in this Province will be acknowledg'd by every man that is not willing to expose the defect of his own. I mean the famous *John Dryden,* the best *English* Poet alive, the present Glory of our Stage, and the Model of the same to future Ages; for he (having absolutely master'd these three Originals by framing a Tragedy out of *Paradise Lost,* making the Charms of *Virgil* appear in the *English* Tongue, and studying *Homer* for the same purpose) pronounces his Judgment in favor of Milton by this incomparable and envy'd Epigram.

> Three Poets in three distant Ages born,
> *Greece, Italy,* and *England* did adorn:
> The first in Loftiness of Thought surpast;
> The next in Majesty; in both the last.
> The Force of Nature could no further go:
> To make a Third, she join'd the other Two. . . .

An Epic Poem is not a bare History delightfully related in harmonious Numbers, and artfully dispos'd; but it always contains, besides a general representation of Passions and Affections, Virtues and Vices, som peculiar Allegory or Moral. *Homer* therfore, according to *Dionysius Halicarnassaeus,* expresses strength of Body in his *Iliad* by the Wars of the *Greecs* and *Trojans,* but particularly by the valiant Deeds of *Achilles:* and in his *Odysseus* he describes generosity of Mind by the Adventures and Wandrings of *Ulysses* in his return from *Troy.* Thus *Torquato Tasso* has prefixt an Explication to his *Gierusalemme Liberata:* Nor was *Milton* behind any body in the choice or dignity of his Instruction; for to display the different Effects of Liberty and Tyranny, is the chief design of his *Paradise Lost.* . . .

In the year 1670 he publish'd his *Paradise Regain'd,* consisting of four Books; but generally esteem'd much inferior to *Paradise Lost,* which he could not endure to hear, being quite of another mind: yet this occasion'd som body to say wittily enough that *Milton* might be seen in *Paradise Lost,* but not in *Paradise Regain'd.* With this last Book he publisht his *Samson Agonistes,* an admirable Tragedy, not a ridiculous mixture of Gravity and Farce according to most of the Modern, but after the Example of the yet unequal'd Antients, as they are justly cal'd, *Aeschylus, Sophocles,* and *Euripides.* . . .

Our Author's Juvenil and Occasional Poems, both in *English* and *Latin,* were printed in one small Volume. I took notice of the best of 'em in many places of this Discourse; but the Monody wherin he bewails his Learned Friend Mr. *King* drown'd in the *Irish* Seas, is one of the finest he ever wrote. . . .

Thus liv'd and dy'd *JOHN MILTON,* a Person of the best Accomplishments, the happiest Genius, and the vastest Learning which this Nation, so renown'd for producing excellent Writers, could ever yet shew: esteem'd indeed at home, but much more honor'd abroad, where almost in his very Childhood he made a considerable figure, and continues to be still reputed as one of the brightest Luminaries of the Sciences. . . .

I shall now conclude this Discourse with a Character given of him by a Man of unparallel'd Diligence and Industry, who has disoblig'd all sides merely for telling the Truth either intirely, or without disguise; and who, since most Men have the frailty of ingaging in Factions, cannot be suspected of Partiality in favor of *Milton*. He was a Person, says *Anthony Wood* in the first Volume of his *Athenae Oxonienses,* of wonderful Parts, of a very sharp, biting, and satyrical Wit: he was a good Philosopher and Historian; an excellent Poet, Latinist, Grecian, and Hebrician; a good Mathematician and Musician; and so rarely endow'd by Nature, that had he bin but honestly principled, he might have bin highly useful to that Party, against which he all along appear'd with much Malice and Bitterness.

* * *

JOHN DENNIS

THE PASSION OF BYBLIS (1692)

---

*   *   *

Ⅰ AM not so miserably mistaken, as to think rhiming essential
to our *English* Poetry. I am far better acquainted with *Milton,*
than that comes to. Who without the assistance of Rhime, is
one of the most sublime of our *English* Poets. Nay, there is
something so transcendently sublime in his first, second, and
sixth Books, that were the Language as pure as the Images are
vast and daring, I do not believe it could be equall'd, no, not
in all Antiquity.

*   *   *

THE GROUNDS OF CRITICISM
IN POETRY (1704)

*   *   *

SPECIMEN

*Being the Substance of what will be said in the Beginning
of the* Criticism *upon* Milton.

Ⅱ HE next Poet of whom we shall treat is *Milton,* one of the
greatest and most daring Genius's that has appear'd in the
World, and who has made his Country a glorious present of
the most lofty, but most irregular Poem, that has been produc'd
by the Mind of Man. That great Man had a desire to give the
World something like an Epick Poem; but he resolv'd at the

same time to break thro' the Rules of *Aristotle*. Not that he was ignorant of them, or contemn'd them. On the contrary, no Man knew them better, or esteemed them more, because no Man had an Understanding that was more able to comprehend the necessity of them; and therefore when he mention'd them in the little Treatise which he wrote to Mr. *Hartlib,* he calls the Art which treats of them, a sublime Art. But at the same time he had discernment enough to see, that if he wrote a Poem which was within the compass of them, he should be subjected to the same Fate which has attended all who have wrote Epick Poems ever since the time of *Homer;* and that is to be a Copyist instead of an Original. Tis true, the Epick Poets who have liv'd since *Homer,* have most of them been Originals in their Fables, which are the very Souls of their Poems; but in their manner of treating those Fables, they have too frequently been Copyists. They have Copyed the Spirit and the Images of *Homer;* even the great *Virgil* himself is not to be excepted. *Milton* was the first, who in the space of almost 4000 Years, resolved, for his Country's Honour and his own, to present the World with an Original Poem; that is to say, a Poem that should have his own Thoughts, his own Images, and his own Spirit. In order to this he was resolved to write a Poem, that, by vertue of its extraordinary Subject, cannot so properly be said to be against the Rules, as it may be affirmed to be above them all. He had observ'd, that *Aristotle* had drawn his Rules which he has given us for Epick Poetry from the Reflections which he had made upon *Homer.* Now he knew very well, that in *Homer* the Action lay chiefly between Man and Man: For *Achilles* and *Hector* are properly the Principals, and the Gods are but Seconds. He was resolved therefore, that his Principals should be the Devil on one side and Man on the other: and the Devil is properly his Hero, because he gets the better. All the persons in his Poem, excepting two, are either Divine or Infernal. So that most of the Persons and particularly one of the Principals, being so very different from what *Homer* or *Aristotle* ever thought of, could not possibly be subjected to their

Rules, either for the Characters or the Incidents. We shall now shew for what Reasons the choice of *Milton*'s Subject, as it set him free from the Obligation which he lay under to the Poetical Laws, so it necessarily threw him upon new Thoughts, new Images, and an Original Spirit. In the next place we shall shew, that his Thoughts, his Images, and by consequence too his Spirit, are actually new, and different from those of *Homer* and *Virgil*. Thirdly, We shall shew, that besides their Newness, they have vastly the Advantage of those of *Homer* and *Virgil*. And we shall make this appear from several things, but principally from the Description of Hell, which has been describ'd by those three great Poets with all their Force and with all their Art. After that, we shall proceed to say something of *Milton's* Expression and his Harmony; and then we shall come to mark his Defects with so much the more exactness, because some of them ought to be avoided with the utmost Caution, as being so great, that they would be Insupportable in any one who had not his extraordinary Distinguishing Qualities.

*   *   *

LETTERS ON MILTON & WYCHERLEY
(1721-1722)
LETTER I.

OBSERVATIONS on the Paradise Lost *of* Milton

To Dr. S——

SIR,

I was no sooner determin'd within my self to make some Observations on the *Paradise Lost* of *Milton,* than I resolv'd to direct them to you, because you know the Truth of some Facts which I shall be oblig'd to relate, and because I have observ'd in you a better Taste of the greater Poetry, than in most of those with whom I have lately convers'd; which having premis'd, I shall without more Preamble enter upon the Subject of which I design to treat.

I believe, Sir, that I have told you more than once, that I, who have all my Life-time had the highest Esteem for the great Genius's of the Ancients, and especially for *Homer* and *Virgil*, and who admire them now more than ever, have yet for these last Thirty Years admir'd *Milton* above them all for one thing, and that is for having carried away the Prize of Sublimity from both Ancients and Moderns: And in most of the Treatises which I have publish'd for Thirty Years, even in those in which I have been unhappily engag'd to detect and to blame the Errors of some of my Contemporaries, I have not been able to forbear pointing at several of the matchless Beauties of *Milton*. In the *Remarks on Prince* Arthur, I cited at large the sublime Description of *Satan* in the first Book of that Poem; and the Speech of that fallen Arch-Angel in the fourth, which begins with that noble Apostrophe to the Sun.

In the *Advancement and Reformation of modern Poetry*, which was publish'd in 1700, I shew'd the vast Advantage which *Milton* had over *Ovid*, and ev'n *Virgil* himself, in his Description of Chaos and the Creation.

In the *Grounds of Criticism in Poetry*, which Book was publish'd in 1704, you know very well, Sir, that I cited at large the Description of the Descent of *Raphael* in the fifth Book, and the glorious Hymn to the Creator in the same Book, and likewise the divine Colloquy between God and *Adam* in the eighth Book.

Some Persons, who long since the Publication of the foremention'd Treatises began to write Notes on the *Paradise Lost*, have made particular mention of the same Beauties which I had mark'd out before, without making any mention of me. Tho' you know very well, Sir, that I can bring unquestionable Proof that those Persons had read the foremention'd Treatises, and read them with Applause; but I should not be in the least concern'd at the treating me so unfairly and ungenerously, if they had done Justice to *Milton*, thro' the Course of their

Criticisms, of which they have grossly fail'd in the following Respects.

I. They have not allow'd that *Milton* in the Sublimity of his Thoughts surpass'd both Ancients and Moderns.

II. In their Observations which they have made on the *Paradise Lost,* they have insisted too much upon things in which *Milton* has Equals, instead of dwelling intirely on that Sublimity which is his distinguishing and Characteristick Quality, and which sets him above Mankind.

III. In citing Passages from him which are truly sublime, they have often fail'd of setting his Sublimity in a true Light, and of shewing it to all its Advantage.

IV. In those Passages whose Sublimity they have set in a true Light, they have not observ'd, to the Honour of *Milton,* and our Country, that the Thoughts and Images are Original, and the genuine Offspring of *Milton's* transcendent Genius.

V. They have not shewn how *Milton's* Sublimity is distinguish'd from that of all other Poets in this Respect, that where he has excell'd all other Poets in what he has exprest, he has left ten times more to be understood than what he has exprest, which is the surest and noblest Mark, and the most transporting Effect of Sublimity.

To shew that they who have writ Observations on the *Paradise Lost,* have not done Justice to *Milton,* with regard to the five foremention'd Articles, is the Design and Subject of the Letters I intend to send you, which shall rather be frequent than long, my Design being to amuse and entertain you, and not to fatigue and tire you.

* * *

ALEXANDER POPE

POSTSCRIPT TO THE ODYSSEY (1723)

* * *

THE imitators of Milton, like most other imitators, are not copies but caricatures of their original; they are a hundred times more obsolete and cramp than he, and equally so in all places: whereas it should have been observed of Milton, that he is not lavish of his exotic words and phrases every where alike, but employs them much more where the subject is marvellous, vast, and strange, as in the scenes of Heaven, Hell, Chaos, &c., than where it is turned to the natural or agreeable, as in the pictures of paradise, the loves of our first parents, the entertainments of angels, and the like. In general, this unusual style better serves to awaken our ideas in the descriptions and in the imaging and picturesque parts, than it agrees with the lower sort of narrations, the character of which is simplicity and purity. Milton has several of the latter, where we find not an antiquated, affected, or uncouth word, for some hundred lines together; as in his fifth book, the latter part of the eighth, the former of the tenth and eleventh books, and in the narration of Michael in the twelfth. I wonder indeed that he, who ventured (contrary to the practice of all other Epic Poets) to imitate Homer's lownesses in the narrative, should not also have copied his plainness and perspicuity in the dramatic parts: since in his speeches (where clearness above all is necessary) there is frequently such transposition and forced construction, that the very sense is not to be discovered without a second or third reading: and in this certainly he ought to be no example.

* * *

THOMAS WARTON

ᕭᕮᕽᕮᕽ

PREFACE TO MILTON'S POEMS
UPON SEVERAL OCCASIONS (1785)

———————

*   *   *

Our author is said to be the first Englishman, who after the restoration of letters wrote Latin verses with classic elegance. But we must at least except some of the hendecasyllables and epigrams of Leland, one of our first literary reformers, from this hasty determination.

In the Elegies, Ovid was professedly Milton's model for language and versification. They are not, however, a perpetual and uniform tissue of Ovidian phraseology. With Ovid in view, he has an original manner and character of his own, which exhibit a remarkable perspicuity of contexture, a native facility and fluency. Nor does his observation of Roman models oppress or destroy our great poet's inherent powers of invention and sentiment. I value these pieces as much for their fancy and genius, as for their style and expression.

That Ovid among the Latin poets was Milton's favourite, appears not only from his elegiac but his hexametric poetry. The versification of our author's hexameters has yet a different structure from that of the Metamorphoses: Milton's is more clear, intelligible, and flowing; less desultory, less familiar, and less embarrassed with a frequent recurrence of periods. Ovid is at once rapid and abrupt. He wants dignity: he has too much conversation in his manner of telling a story. Prolixity of paragraph, and length of sentence, are peculiar to Milton. This is seen, not only in some of his exordial invocations in the *Para-*

dise Lost, and in many of the religious addresses of a like cast in the prose-works, but in his long verse. It is to be wished that in his Latin compositions of all sorts, he had been more attentive to the simplicity of Lucretius, Virgil, and Tibullus. . . .

Milton's Latin poems may be justly considered as legitimate classical compositions. . . . Milton was a more perfect scholar than Cowley, and his mind was more deeply tinctured with the excellencies of antient literature. He was a more just thinker, and therefore a more just writer. In a word, he had more taste, and more poetry, and consequently more propriety. If a fondness for the Italian writers has sometimes infected his English poetry with false ornaments, his Latin verses, both in diction and sentiment, are at least free from those depravations.

Some of Milton's Latin poems were written in his first year at Cambridge, when he was only seventeen: they must be allowed to be very correct and manly performances for a youth of that age. And considered in that view, they discover an extraordinary copiousness and command of ancient fable and history. I cannot but add, that Gray resembles Milton in many instances. Among others, in their youth they were both strongly attached to the cultivation of Latin poetry.

*　　*　　*

WILLIAM BLAKE

THE MARRIAGE OF HEAVEN
AND HELL (1793)

* * *

Those who restrain desire, do so because theirs is weak enough to be restrained; and the restrainer or reason usurps its place & governs the unwilling.

And being restrain'd, it by degrees becomes passive, till it is only the shadow of desire.

The history of this is written in *Paradise Lost,* & the Governor or Reason is call'd Messiah.

And the original Archangel, or possessor of the command of the heavenly host, is call'd the Devil or Satan, and his children are call'd Sin & Death.

But in the Book of Job, Milton's Messiah is call'd Satan.

For this history has been adopted by both parties.

It indeed appear'd to Reason as if Desire was cast out; but the Devil's account is, that the Messiah fell, & formed a heaven of what he stole from the Abyss.

This is shewn in the Gospel, where he prays to the Father to send the comforter, or Desire, that Reason may have Ideas to build on; the Jehovah of the Bible being no other than he who dwells in flaming fire.

Know that after Christ's death, he became Jehovah.

But in Milton, the Father is Destiny, the Son a Ratio of the five senses, & the Holy-ghost Vacuum!

Note: The reason Milton wrote in fetters when he wrote of Angels & God, and at liberty when of Devils & Hell, is because he was a true Poet and of the Devil's party without knowing it.

* * *

WILLIAM WORDSWORTH

LONDON, 1802

Milton! thou shouldst be living at this hour:
England hath need of thee: she is a fen
Of stagnant waters: altar, sword, and pen,
Fireside, the heroic wealth of hall and bower,
Have forfeited their ancient English dower
Of inward happiness. We are selfish men;
Oh! raise us up, return to us again;
And give us manners, virtue, freedom, power.
Thy soul was like a Star, and dwelt apart;
Thou hadst a voice whose sound was like the sea:
Pure as the naked heavens, majestic, free,
So didst thou travel on life's common way,
In cheerful godliness; and yet thy heart
The lowliest duties on herself did lay.

JOHN KEATS

LETTERS (1818-1819)

* * *

You say "I fear there is little chance of any thing else in this life." you seem by that to have been going through with a more painful and acute zest the same labyrinth that I have—I have come to the same conclusion thus far. My Branchings out therefrom have been numerous: one of them is the consideration of Wordsworth's genius and as a help, in the manner of gold being the meridian Line of worldly wealth,—how he differs from Milton.—And here I have nothing but surmises, from an uncertainty whether Miltons apparently less anxiety for Humanity proceeds from his seeing further or no than Wordsworth: And whether Wordsworth has in truth epic passion, and martyrs himself to the human heart, the main region of his song. . . . We feel the "burden of the Mystery," To this Point was Wordsworth come, as far as I can conceive when he wrote 'Tintern Abbey' and it seems to me that his Genius is explorative of those dark Passages. Now if we live, and go on thinking, we too shall explore them—he is a Genius and superior [to] us, in so far as he can, more than we, make discoveries, and shed a light in them—Here I must think Wordsworth is deeper than Milton—though I think it has depended more upon the general and gregarious advance of intellect, than individual greatness of Mind—From the *Paradise Lost* and the other Works of Milton, I hope it is not too presuming, even between ourselves to say, that his Philosophy, human and divine, may be tolerably understood by one not much advanced in years, In his time englishmen were just emancipated from a great superstition—and Men had got hold of certain points and resting places in reasoning which were too newly born to be doubted, and too much opposed by the Mass of Europe not to be thought etherial and authentically divine—who could gainsay his ideas on virtue, vice, and Chastity in Comus, just at the time of the dismissal of Cod-pieces and a hundred other disgraces? who would not rest satisfied with his hintings at good and evil in the *Paradise Lost,* when just free from the inquisition and burning in Smithfield? The Reformation produced such immediate and great benefits, that Protestantism was considered under the immediate eye of heaven, and its own remaining Dogmas and superstitions, then, as it were, regenerated, constituted those resting places and seeming sure points of Reasoning—from that I have mentioned, Milton, whatever he may have thought in the sequel, appears to have been content with these by his writings—He did not think into the human heart, as Wordsworth has done—Yet Milton as a Philosopher, had sure as great powers as Wordsworth—What is then to be inferr'd? O many things—It proves there is really a grand march of intellect—, It proves that a mighty providence subdues the mightiest Minds to the service of the time being, whether it be in human Knowledge or Religion. [May 3, 1818]

*   *   *

I am convinced more and more every day that (excepting the human friend Philosopher) a fine writer is the most genuine Being in the World. Shakspeare and the paradise Lost every day become greater wonders to me. [August 14, 1819]

*   *   *

I always somehow associate Chatterton with autumn. He is the purest writer in the English Language. He has no French idiom, or particles like Chaucer—'tis genuine English Idiom in English Words. I have given up Hyperion—there were too many Miltonic inversions in it—Miltonic verse can not be written but in an artful or rather artist's humour. I wish to give myself up to other sensations. [September 21, 1819]

*　　*　　*

I shall never become attach'd to a foreign idiom so as to put it into my writings. The Paradise lost though so fine in itself is a curruption of our language—it should be kept as it is unique—a curiosity—a beautiful and grand Curiosity. The most remarkable Production of the world. A northern dialect accommodating itself to greek and latin inversions and intonations. The purest english I think—or what ought to be the purest—is Chatterton's. The Language had existed long enough to be entirely uncorrupted of Chaucer's gallicisms, and still the old words are used. Chatterton's language is entirely northern. I prefer the native music of it to Milton's cut by feet. I have but lately stood on my guard against Milton. Life to him would be death to me. Miltonic verse cannot be written but it [*for* in] the verse of art—I wish to devote myself to another sensation. [September 21, 1819]

*　　*　　*

PERCY BYSSHE SHELLEY

A DEFENCE OF POETRY (1821)

* * *

MILTON's poem contains within itself a philosophical refutation of that system of which, by a strange and natural antithesis, it has been a chief popular support. Nothing can exceed the energy and magnificence of the character of Satan as expressed in *Paradise Lost.* It is a mistake to suppose that he could ever have been intended for the popular personification of evil. Implacable hate, patient cunning, and a sleepless refinement of device to inflict the extremest anguish on an enemy, these things are evil; and, although venial in a slave, are not to be forgiven in a tyrant; although redeemed by much that ennobles his defeat in one subdued, are marked by all that dishonours his conquest in the victor. Milton's Devil as a moral being is as far superior to his God, as one who perseveres in some purpose which he has conceived to be excellent in spite of adversity and torture, is to one who in the cold security of undoubted triumph inflicts the most horrible revenge upon his enemy, not from any mistaken notion of inducing him to repent of a perseverance in enmity, but with the alleged design of exasperating him to deserve new torments. Milton has so far violated the popular creed (if this shall be judged to be a violation) as to have alleged no superiority of moral virtue to his god over his devil. And this bold neglect of a direct moral purpose is the most decisive proof of the supremacy of Milton's genius. He mingled as it were the elements of human nature as colours upon a single pallet, and arranged them in the composition of his great picture according to the laws of epic truth, that is, according to the laws of that principle by which a series of actions of the external universe and of intelligent and ethical beings is calculated to excite the sympathy of succeeding generations of mankind. The *Divina Commedia* and *Paradise Lost* have conferred upon modern mythology a systematic form; and when change and time shall have added one more superstition to the mass of those which have arisen and decayed upon the earth, commentators will be learnedly employed in elucidating the religion of ancestral Europe, only not utterly forgotten because it will have been stamped with the eternity of genius.

*   *   *

THOMAS BABINGTON MACAULAY

ESSAY ON MILTON (1825)

---

*   *   *

THE only poem of modern times which can be compared with the *Paradise Lost* is the *Divine Comedy*. The subject of Milton, in some points, resembled that of Dante; but he has treated it in a widely different manner. We cannot, we think, better illustrate our opinion respecting our own great poet, than by contrasting him with the father of Tuscan literature.

The poetry of Milton differs from that of Dante, as the hieroglyphics of Egypt differed from the picture-writing of Mexico. The images which Dante employs speak for themselves; they stand simply for what they are. Those of Milton have a signification which is often discernible only to the initiated. Their value depends less on what they directly represent than on what they remotely suggest. However strange, however grotesque, may be the appearance which Dante undertakes to describe, he never shrinks from describing it. He gives us the shape, the colour, the sound, the smell, the taste; he counts the numbers; he measures the size. His similes are the illustrations of a traveller. Unlike those of other poets, and especially of Milton, they are introduced in a plain, business-like manner; not for the sake of any beauty in the objects from which they are drawn; not for the sake of any ornament which they may impart to the poem; but simply in order to make the meaning of the writer as clear to the reader as it is to himself. The ruins of the precipice which led from the sixth to the seventh circle of hell were like those of the rock which fell into the Adige on the south of

Trent. The cataract of Phlegethon was like that of Aqua Cheta at the monastery of St. Benedict. The place where the heretics were confined in burning tombs resembled the vast cemetery of Arles.

Now let us compare with the exact details of Dante the dim intimations of Milton. We will cite a few examples. The English poet has never thought of taking the measure of Satan. He gives us merely a vague idea of vast bulk. In one passage the fiend lies stretched out huge in length, floating many a rood, equal in size to the earth-born enemies of Jove, or to the sea-monster which the mariner mistakes for an island. When he addresses himself to battle against the guardian angels, he stands like Teneriffe or Atlas; his stature reaches the sky. Contrast with these descriptions the lines in which Dante has described the gigantic spectre of Nimrod. "His face seemed to me as long and as broad as the ball of St. Peter's at Rome; and his other limbs were in proportion; so that the bank, which concealed him from the waist downwards, nevertheless showed so much of him that three tall Germans would in vain have attempted to reach his hair." We are sensible that we do no justice to the admirable style of the Florentine poet. But Mr. Cary's translation is not at hand; and our version, however rude, is sufficient to illustrate our meaning.

Once more, compare the lazar-house in the eleventh book of the *Paradise Lost* with the last ward of Malebolge in Dante. Milton avoids the loathsome details, and takes refuge in indistinct but solemn and tremendous imagery, Despair hurrying from couch to couch to mock the wretches with his attendance, Death shaking his dart over them, but, in spite of supplications, delaying to strike. What says Dante? "There was such a moan there as there would be if all the sick who, between July and September, are in the hospitals of Valdichiana, and of the Tuscan swamps, and of Sardinia, were in one pit together; and such a stench was issuing forth as is wont to issue from decayed limbs."

We will not take upon ourselves the invidious office of settling precedency between two such writers. Each in his own department is incomparable; and each, we may remark, has wisely, or fortunately, taken a subject adapted to exhibit his peculiar talent to the greatest advantage. The *Divine Comedy* is a personal narrative. Dante is the eye-witness and ear-witness of that which he relates. He is the very man who has heard the tormented spirits crying out for the second death, who has read the dusky characters on the portal within which there is no hope, who has hidden his face from the terrors of the Gorgon, who has fled from the hooks and the seething pitch of Barbaric-cia and Draghignazzo. His own hands have grasped the shaggy sides of Lucifer. His own feet have climbed the mountain of expiation. His own brow has been marked by the purifying angel. The reader would throw aside such a tale in incredulous disgust, unless it were told with the strongest air of veracity, with a sobriety even in its horrors, with the greatest precision and multiplicity in its details. . . .

Of all the poets who have introduced into their works the agency of supernatural beings, Milton has succeeded best. Here Dante decidedly yields to him: and as this is a point on which many rash and ill-considered judgements have been pronounced, we feel inclined to dwell on it a little longer. The most fatal error which a poet can possibly commit in the management of his machinery, is that of attempting to philosophize too much. Milton has been often censured for ascribing to spirits many functions of which spirits must be incapable. But these objections, though sanctioned by eminent names, originate, we venture to say, in profound ignorance of the art of poetry. . . .

Poetry which relates to the beings of another world ought to be at once mysterious and picturesque. That of Milton is so. That of Dante is picturesque indeed beyond any that ever was written. Its effect approaches to that produced by the pencil or the chisel. But it is picturesque to the exclusion of all mystery. This is a fault on the right side, a fault inseparable from the plan of Dante's poem, which, as we have already observed, rendered the utmost accuracy of description necessary. Still it is a fault. The supernatural agents excite an interest; but it is not the interest which is proper to supernatural agents. We feel that we could talk to the ghosts and demons, without any emotion of unearthly awe. We could, like Don Juan, ask them to supper, and eat heartily in their company. Dante's angels are good men with wings. His devils are spiteful ugly executioners. His dead men are merely living men in strange situations. . . .

The spirits of Milton are unlike those of almost all other writers. His fiends, in particular, are wonderful creations. They are not metaphysical abstractions. They are not wicked men. They are not ugly beasts. They have no horns, no tails, none of the fee-faw-fum of Tasso and Klopstock. They have just enough in common with human nature to be intelligible to human beings. Their characters are, like their forms, marked by a certain dim resemblance to those of men, but exaggerated to gigantic dimensions, and veiled in mysterious gloom. . . .

We would add that the poetry of these great men has in a considerable degree taken its character from their moral qualities. They are not egotists. They rarely obtrude their idiosyncrasies on their readers. They have nothing in common with those modern beggars for fame, who extort a pittance from the compassion of the inexperienced by exposing the nakedness and sores of their minds. Yet it would be difficult to name two writers whose works have been more completely, though undesignedly, coloured by their personal feelings. The character of Milton was peculiarly distinguished by loftiness of spirit; that of Dante by intensity of feeling.

*　　　*　　　*

RALPH WALDO EMERSON

MILTON (1838)

---

*   *   *

W<small>E HAVE</small> lost all interest in Milton as the redoubted dis-
putant of a sect; but by his own innate worth this man has
steadily risen in the world's reverence, and occupies a more
imposing place in the mind of men at this hour than ever
before. . . .

It is the prerogative of this great man to stand at this hour
foremost of all men in literary history, and so (shall we not
say?) of all men, in the power *to inspire*. Virtue goes out of him
into others. Leaving out of view the pretensions of our contemporaries (always an incalculable influence), we think no
man can be named whose mind still acts on the cultivated intellect of England and America with an energy comparable to that
of Milton. As a poet, Shakspeare undoubtedly transcends, and
far surpasses him in his popularity with foreign nations; but
Shakspeare is a voice merely; who and what he was that sang,
that sings, we know not. Milton stands erect, commanding, still
visible as a man among men, and reads the laws of the moral
sentiment to the new-born race. There is something pleasing
in the affection with which we can regard a man who died a
hundred and sixty years ago in the other hemisphere, who, in
respect to personal relations, is to us as the wind, yet by an
influence purely spiritual makes us jealous for his fame as for
that of a near friend. He is identified in the mind with all select
and holy images, with the supreme interests of the human race.
If hereby we attain any more precision, we proceed to say that

we think no man in these later ages, and few men ever, possessed so great a conception of the manly character. Better than any other he has discharged the office of every great man, namely, to raise the idea of Man in the minds of his contemporaries and of posterity,—to draw after Nature a life of man, exhibiting such a composition of grace, of strength and of virtue, as poet had not described nor hero lived. Human nature in these ages is indebted to him for its best portrait. Many philosophers in England, France and Germany have formally dedicated their study to this problem; and we think it impossible to recall one in those countries who communicates the same vibration of hope, of self-reverence, of piety, of delight in beauty, which the name of Milton awakens. . . .

The idea of a purer existence than any he saw around him, to be realized in the life and conversation of men, inspired every act and every writing of John Milton. . . .

As basis or fountain of his rare physical and intellectual accomplishments, the man Milton was just and devout. He is rightly dear to mankind, because in him, among so many perverse and partial men of genius,—in him humanity rights itself; the old eternal goodness finds a home in his breast, and for once shows itself beautiful. His gifts are subordinated to his moral sentiments; and his virtues are so graceful that they seem rather talents than labors. Among so many contrivances as the world has seen to make holiness ugly, in Milton at least it was so pure a flame that the foremost impression his character makes is that of elegance. The victories of the conscience in him are gained by the commanding charm which all the severe and restrictive virtues have for him. . . .

Native honor never forsook him. It is the spirit of *Comus*, the loftiest song in the praise of chastity that is in any language. It always sparkles in his eyes. It breathed itself over his decent form. It refined his amusements, which consisted in gardening, in exercise with the sword and in playing on the organ. It engaged his interest in chivalry, in courtesy, in whatsoever savored of generosity and nobleness. This magnanimity shines in all his life. . . .

To this antique heroism, Milton added the genius of the Christian sanctity. Few men could be cited who have so well understood what is peculiar in the Christian ethics, and the precise aid it has brought to men, in being an emphatic affirmation of the omnipotence of spiritual laws, and, by way of marking the contrast to vulgar opinions, laying its chief stress on humility. The indifferency of a wise mind to what is called high and low, and the fact that true greatness is a perfect humility, are revelations of Christianity which Milton well understood. They give an inexhaustible truth to all his compositions. His firm grasp of this truth is his weapon against the prelates. . . .

His private opinions and private conscience always distinguish him. That which drew him to the party was his love of liberty, ideal liberty; this therefore he could not sacrifice to any party. . . . Truly he was an apostle of freedom; of freedom in the house, in the state, in the church; freedom of speech, freedom of the press; yet in his own mind discriminated from savage license, because that which he desired was the liberty of the wise man, containing itself in the limits of virtue. . . . The tracts he wrote on these topics are, for the most part, as fresh and pertinent to-day as they were then. The events which produced them, the practical issues to which they tend, are mere occasions for this philanthropist to blow his trumpet for human rights. They are all varied applications of one principle, the liberty of the wise man. He sought absolute truth, not accommodating truth. His opinions on all subjects are formed for man as he ought to be, for a nation of Miltons. . . .

Was there not a fitness in the undertaking of such a person to write a poem on the subject of Adam, the first man? By his sympathy with all Nature; by the proportion of his powers; by great knowledge, and by religion, he would reascend to the height from which our nature is supposed to have descended.

From a just knowledge of what man should be, he described what he was. . . .

The perception we have attributed to Milton, of a purer ideal of humanity, modifies his poetic genius. The man is paramount to the poet. His fancy is never transcendent, extravagant; but as Bacon's imagination was said to be "the noblest that ever contented itself to minister to the understanding," so Milton's ministers to the character. Milton's sublimest song, bursting into heaven with its peals of melodious thunder, is the voice of Milton still. Indeed, throughout his poems, one may see, under a thin veil, the opinions, the feelings, even the incidents of the poet's life, still reappearing. . . . It was plainly needful that his poetry should be a version of his own life, in order to give weight and solemnity to his thoughts; by which they might penetrate and possess the imagination and the will of mankind. . . . His own conviction it is which gives such authority to his strain. Its reality is its force. If out of the heart it came, to the heart it must go. . . .

Are not all men fortified by the remembrance of the bravery, the purity, the temperance, the toil, the independence and the angelic devotion of this man, who, in a revolutionary age, taking counsel only of himself, endeavored, in his writings and in his life, to carry out the life of man to new heights of spiritual grace and dignity, without any abatement of its strength?

*   *   *

WALTER SAVAGE LANDOR

 ᗰᗰᗰᗰ

SOUTHEY AND LANDOR (1846)

---

*   *   *

Surely it is a silly and stupid business to talk mainly about the moral of a poem, unless it professedly be a fable. A good epic, a good tragedy, a good comedy, will inculcate several. . . . Why should the machinery of the longest poem be drawn out to establish an obvious truth, which a single verse would exhibit more plainly, and impress more memorably? Both in epic and dramatic poetry it is action, and not moral, that is first demanded. The feelings and exploits of the principal agent should excite the principal interest. The two greatest of human compositions are here defective: I mean the *Iliad* and *Paradise Lost.* . . . In the *Paradise Lost* no principal character seems to have been intended. There is neither truth nor wit however in saying that Satan is hero of the piece, unless, as is usually the case in human life, he is the greatest hero who gives the widest sway to the worst passions. It is Adam who acts and suffers most, and on whom the consequences have most influence. This constitutes him the main character; although Eve is the more interesting, Satan is the more energetic, and on whom the greater force of poetry is displayed. The Creator and his angels are quite secondary. . . .

> Yielded with coy submission, modest pride,
> And sweet, reluctant, amorous, delay.

I would rather have written these two lines than all the poetry that has been written since Milton's time in all the regions of the earth. We shall see again things equal in their way to the best of them: but here the sweetest of images and sentiments is seized and carried far away from all pursuers. . . .

It appears then on record that the first overt crime of the refractory angels was *punning*: they fell rapidly after that. . . .

It is impossible not to apply to Milton himself the words he has attributed to Eve:

> From thee
> How shall I part? and whither wander down
> Into a lower world?

My ear, I confess it, is dissatisfied with everything, for days and weeks, after the harmony of *Paradise Lost*. Leaving this magnificent temple, I am hardly to be pacified by the fairy-built chambers, the rich cupboards of embossed plate, and the omnigenous images of Shakespeare. . . .

After I have been reading the *Paradise Lost,* I can take up no other poet with satisfaction. I seem to have left the music of Handel for the music of the streets, or at best for drums and fifes. Although in Shakespeare there are occasional bursts of harmony no less sublime, yet, if there were many such in continuation, it would be hurtful, not only in comedy, but also in tragedy. . . . In our English heroic verse, such as Milton has composed it, there is a much greater variety of feet, of movement, of musical notes and bars, than in the Greek heroic; and the final sounds are incomparably more diversified. My predilection in youth was on the side of Homer; for I had read the *Iliad* twice, and the *Odyssea* once, before the *Paradise Lost.* Averse as I am to everything relating to theology, and especially to the view of it thrown open by this poem, I recur to it incessantly as the noblest specimen in the world of eloquence, harmony, and genius.

* * *

ALFRED LORD TENNYSON

MILTON (ALCAICS) (1863)

O MIGHTY-MOUTH'D inventor of harmonies,
O skill'd to sing of Time or Eternity,
  God-gifted organ-voice of England,
    Milton, a name to resound for ages;
Whose Titan angels, Gabriel, Abdiel,
Starr'd from Jehovah's gorgeous armories,
  Tower, as the deep-domed empyrean
    Rings to the roar of an angel onset!
Me rather all that bowery loneliness,
The brooks of Eden mazily murmuring,
  And bloom profuse and cedar arches
    Charm, as a wanderer out in ocean,
Where some refulgent sunset of India
Streams o'er a rich ambrosial ocean isle,
  And crimson-hued the stately palm-woods
    Whisper in odorous heights of even.

GERARD MANLEY HOPKINS

LETTERS (1877-1879)*

ALL English verse, except Milton's, almost, offends me as "licentious." Remember this. . . .

The choruses in *Samson Agonistes* are intermediate between counterpointed and sprung rhythm. In reality they are sprung, but Milton keeps up a fiction of counterpointing the heard rhythm (which is the same as the mounted rhythm) upon a standard rhythm which is never heard but only counted and therefore really does not exist. The want of a metrical notation and the fear of being thought to write mere rhythmic or (who knows what the critics might not have said?) even unrhythmic prose drove him to this. Such rhythm as French and Welsh poetry has is sprung, counterpointed upon a counted rhythm, but it differs from Milton's in being little calculated, not more perhaps than prose consciously written rhythmically, like orations for instance; it is in fact the *native rhythm* of the words used bodily imported into verse; whereas Milton's mounted rhythm is a real poetical rhythm, having its own laws and recurrence, but further embarassed by having to count. [August 21, 1877 to Bridges]

*   *   *

I quite agree with what you write about Milton. His verse as one reads it seems something necessary and eternal (so to me does Purcell's music). . . . Milton's art is incomparable, not only in English literature but, I shd. think, almost in any;

* From *The Letters of Gerard Manley Hopkins to Robert Bridges*, C. C. Abbott, ed., London, Oxford University Press, 1935, and *The Correspondence of Gerard Manley Hopkins and Richard Watson Dixon*, C. C. Abbott, ed., London, Oxford University Press, 1935. Reprinted by permission of the Oxford University Press.

equal, if not more than equal, to the finest of Greek or Roman. And considering that this is shewn especially in his verse, his rhythm and metrical system, it is amazing that so great a writer as Newman should have fallen into the blunder of comparing the first chorus of the *Agonistes* with the opening of *Thalaba* as instancing the gain in smoothness and correctness of versification made since Milton's time—Milton having been not only ahead of his own time as well as all aftertimes in verse-structure but these particular choruses being his own highwater mark. It is as if you were to compare the Panathenaic frieze and a teaboard and decide in the teaboard's favour.

I have paid a good deal of attention to Milton's versification and collected his later rhythms: I did it when I had to lecture on rhetoric some years since. I found his most advanced effects in the *Paradise Regained* and, lyrically, in the *Agonistes*. I have often thought of writing on them, indeed on rhythm in general; I think the subject is little understood. . . .

I should add that Milton is the great standard in the use of counterpoint. In *Paradise Lost* and *Regained,* in the last more freely, it being an advance in his art, he employs counterpoint more or less everywhere, markedly now and then; but the choruses of *Samson Agonistes* are in my judgment counterpointed throughout; that is, each line (or nearly so) has two different coexisting scansions. But when you reach that point the secondary or "mounted rhythm," which is necessarily a sprung rhythm, overpowers the original or conventional one and then this becomes superfluous and may be got rid of; by taking that last step you reach simple sprung rhythm. Milton must have known this but had reasons for not taking it. [October 5, 1878 to Dixon]

*   *   *

No doubt my poetry errs on the side of oddness. I hope in time to have a more balanced and Miltonic style. [February 15, 1879 to Bridges]

*   *   *

MATTHEW ARNOLD

MILTON (1888)

* * *

I F TO our English race an inadequate sense for perfection of work is a real danger, if the discipline of respect for a high and flawless excellence is peculiarly needed by us, Milton is of all our gifted men the best lesson, the most salutary influence. In the sure and flawless perfection of his rhythm and diction he is as admirable as Virgil or Dante, and in this respect he is unique amongst us. No one else in English literature and art possesses the like distinction.

Thomson, Cowper, Wordsworth, all of them good poets who have studied Milton, followed Milton, adopted his form, fail in their diction and rhythm if we try them by that high standard of excellence maintained by Milton constantly. From style really high and pure Milton never departs; their departures from it are frequent.

Shakespeare is divinely strong, rich, and attractive. But sureness of perfect style Shakespeare himself does not possess. I have heard a politician express wonder at the treasures of political wisdom in a certain celebrated scene of *Troilus and Cressida;* for my part I am at least equally moved to wonder at the fantastic and false diction in which Shakespeare has in that scene clothed them. Milton, from one end of *Paradise Lost* to the other, is in his diction and rhythm constantly a great artist in the great style. Whatever may be said as to the subject of his poem, as to the conditions under which he received his subject and treated it, that praise, at any rate, is assured to him.

For the rest, justice is not at present done, in my opinion, to Milton's management of the inevitable matter of a Puritan epic, a matter full of difficulties, for a poet. Justice is not done to the *architectonics,* as Goethe would have called them, of *Paradise Lost;* in these, too, the power of Milton's art is remarkable. But this may be a proposition which requires discussion and development for establishing it, and they are impossible on an occasion like the present.

That Milton, of all our English race, is by his diction and rhythm the one artist of the highest rank in the great style whom we have; this I take as requiring no discussion, this I take as certain.

The mighty power of poetry and art is generally admitted. But where the soul of this power, of this power at its best, chiefly resides, very many of us fail to see. It resides chiefly in the refining and elevation wrought in us by the high and rare excellence of the great style. We may feel the effect without being able to give ourselves clear account of its cause, but the thing is so. Now, no race needs the influences mentioned, the influences of refining and elevation, more than ours; and in poetry and art our grand source for them is Milton.

To what does he owe this supreme distinction? To nature first and foremost, to that bent of nature for inequality which to the worshippers of the average man is so unacceptable; to a gift, a divine favour. "The older one grows," says Goethe, "the more one prizes natural gifts, because by no possibility can they be procured and stuck on." Nature formed Milton to be a great poet. But what other poet has shown so sincere a sense of the grandeur of his vocation, and a moral effort so constant and sublime to make and keep himself worthy of it? The Milton of religious and political controversy, and perhaps of domestic life also, is not seldom disfigured by want of amenity, by acerbity. The Milton of poetry, on the other hand, is one of those great men "who are modest"—to quote a fine remark of Leopardi, that gifted and stricken young Italian, who in his sense for poetic style is worthy to be named with Dante and Milton—

"who are modest, because they continually compare themselves, not with other men, but with that idea of the perfect
which they have before their mind." The Milton of poetry is
the man, in his own magnificent phrase, of "devout prayer to
that Eternal Spirit that can enrich with all utterance and
knowledge, and sends out his Seraphim with the hallowed fire
of his altar, to touch and purify the lips of whom he pleases."
And finally, the Milton of poetry is, in his own words again, the
man of "industrious and select reading." Continually he lived
in companionship with high and rare excellence, with the
great Hebrew poets and prophets, with the great poets of Greece
and Rome. The Hebrew compositions were not in verse, and
can be not inadequately represented by the grand, measured
prose of our English Bible. The verse of the poets of Greece
and Rome no translation can adequately reproduce. Prose cannot have the power of verse; verse-translation may give whatever of charm is in the soul and talent of the translator himself,
but never the specific charm of the verse and poet translated.
In our race are thousands of readers, presently there will be
millions, who know not a word of Greek and Latin, and will
never learn those languages. If this host of readers are ever to
gain any sense of the power and charm of the great poets of
antiquity, their way to gain it is not through translations of the
ancients, but through the original poetry of Milton, who has
the like power and charm, because he has the like great style.

Through Milton they may gain it, for, in conclusion, Milton
is English; this master in the great style of the ancients is English. Virgil, whom Milton loved and honoured, has at the end
of the *Aeneid* a noble passage, where Juno, seeing the defeat of
Turnus and the Italians imminent, the victory of the Trojan
invaders assured, entreats Jupiter that Italy may nevertheless
survive and be herself still, may retain her own mind, manners, and language, and not adopt those of the conqueror.

Sit Latium, sint Albani per secula reges!

Jupiter grants the prayer; he promises perpetuity and the future to Italy—Italy reinforced by whatever virtue the Trojan

race has, but Italy, not Troy. This we may take as a sort of parable suiting ourselves. All the Anglo-Saxon contagion, all the flood of Anglo-Saxon commonness, beats vainly against the great style but cannot shake it, and has to accept its triumph. But it triumphs in Milton, in one of our own race, tongue, faith, and morals. Milton has made the great style no longer an exotic here; he has made it an inmate amongst us, a leaven, and a power. Nevertheless he, and his hearers on both sides of the Atlantic, are English, and will remain English—

Sermonem Ausonii patrium moresque tenebunt.

The English race overspreads the world, and at the same time the ideal of an excellence the most high and the most rare abides a possession with it for ever.